CITIZENS WITHOUT FRONTIERS

CITIZENS WITHOUT FRONTIERS

ENGIN F. ISIN

B L O O M S B U R Y

NEW YORK · LONDON · NEW DELHI · SYDNEY

Bloomsbury Academic
An imprint of Bloomsbury Publishing Plc

175 Fifth Avenue	50 Bedford Square
New York	London
NY 10010	WC1B 3DP
USA	UK

www.bloomsbury.com

First published 2012

Library of Congress Cataloging-in-Publication Data
Isin, Engin F. (EnginFahri), 1959-
Citizens without frontiers / Engin F. Isin.
p. cm.
Includes bibliographical references and index.
ISBN 978-1-4411-8583-9 (pbk. : alk. paper) – ISBN 978-1-4411-1605-5
(hardcover : alk. paper)   1. World citizenship.   2. Citizenship–Philosophy.
3. Globalization.   I. Title.
JZ1320.4.I85 2012
323.6–dc23
2012020484

ISBN: HB: 978-1-4411-1605-5
PB: 978-1-4411-8583-9

Typeset by Newgen Imaging Systems Pvt Ltd, Chennai, India
Printed in the United States of America

For Evelyn

To JS/07 M 378

This Marble Monument Is Erected by the State
He was found by the Bureau of Statistics to be
One against whom there was no official complaint,
And all the reports on his conduct agree
That, in the modern sense of an old-fashioned word,
    he was a saint,
For in everything he did he served the Greater Community.
Except for the War till the day he retired
He worked in a factory and never got fired,
But satisfied his employers, Fudge Motors Inc.
Yet he wasn't a scab or odd in his views,
For his Union reports that he paid his dues,
(Our report on his Union shows it was sound)
And our Social Psychology workers found
That he was popular with his mates and liked a drink.
The Press are convinced that he bought a paper every day
And that his reactions to advertisements were normal in
    every way.
Policies taken out in his name prove that he was fully insured,
And his Health-card shows he was once in hospital but
    left it cured.
Both Producers Research and High-Grade Living declare
He was fully sensible to the advantages of the Instalment Plan
And had everything necessary to the Modern Man,
A phonograph, a radio, a car and a frigidaire.
Our researchers into Public Opinion are content
That he held the proper opinions for the time of year;
When there was peace, he was for peace: when there
    was war, he went.
He was married and added five children to the population,
Which our Eugenist says was the right number for a parent of
    his generation.
And our teachers report that he never interfered with
    their education.
Was he free? Was he happy? The question is absurd:
Had anything been wrong, we should certainly have heard.

—W. H. Auden, 'The Unknown Citizen' (1939)

CONTENTS

PREFACE

In the last 40 years, there has been an enormous focus on people who move between countries for work, travel, and I should add, escape. Whether treated as legal or illegal, these mobilities for business, education, tourism, refuge or migration involve the relocation and sometimes permanent resettlement of people. The proliferation of regimes and apparatuses to control and regulate such mobilities has been widely discussed. Less well documented is another development that has required little or no relocation. The growth of humanitarian politics, international volunteerism and transnational activism has changed politics on a global scale. These have enabled or mobilized people to act across frontiers without necessarily making claims to mobility or resettlement. Of these, perhaps the most remarkable has been what came to be known as 'without frontiers' signifying the provision of professional expertise and services without remuneration. Although the most prominent of these has been *Médecins Sans Frontières* (MSF), there have been others such as Reporters Without Borders and Lawyers Without Borders. Moreover, although it has not been identified as such, we could add 'celebrities without frontiers', as we have seen the emergence of high-profile entertainment figures involved in cross-border politics, such as Madonna, Bob Geldof, Sean Penn, Bono, Angelina Jolie and many others. Despite significant differences, their shared premise is fame converted into professional status. It is very difficult to sift through these complex terrains of politics that enable people to act across frontiers and articulate what 'citizens without frontiers' might mean. There are many activities that do not fall under the existing categories of activism and yet possibly indicate something just as significant about our present age. To begin with, 'citizens without frontiers' is a paradox. By definition, citizens are members of nation-states and they do not have the capacity to act under that name outside the nation-state of which they are members. Citizenship, in other words, does not cross frontiers. Yet, for all the reasons I already mentioned, citizens of nation-states are either implicated or deliberately involved in all those things that cross nation-state frontiers. But if citizens are to act across frontiers, they always have to leave their citizenship at home and act under the disguise of professional expertise, privilege and accreditation. To put it another way, for those who have accumulated cultural and symbolic capital associated with their professional fields, moving across frontiers is much less of an issue and is broadly accepted if not encouraged. What happens if citizens act without disguise? What if citizens act across frontiers 'as citizens'? This happens a lot more than we realize but we have yet to recognize and name it. Having failed to recognize and name it, we criminalize and punish it. I aim to identify such acts, develop a vocabulary appropriate for recognizing and investigating them, and, hopefully, contribute to our understanding of this emerging politics without disguise; or the politics of those whose acts traverse frontiers.

I have accumulated considerable debt to colleagues and institutions for which I am grateful and without which this book would not be possible. For the invitation to deliver a keynote at Royal Geographical Society with the Institute of British Geographers (RGS–IBG) Annual International Conference in 2003 to Luke Desforges, Rhys Jones and Mike Woods. (Until recently, I had forgotten that it was entitled 'citizens without frontiers'.) For inviting me to write it as a book to Marie-Claire Antoine at Bloomsbury and her subsequent guidance and counsel. For participating in the 17 June 2011 (London) workshop to Linda Bosniak, Enrica Rigo, Vicki Squire; for participating in the 8 July 2011 (London) workshop to Claudia Aradau, Stuart Elden, Sandro Mezzadra, Zaki Nahaboo and Jackie Stevens; for participating in the 7 September 2011 (Toronto) workshop to Mariana Valverde, Audrey Macklin, Kim Rygiel and Peter Nyers; for participating in the 28 October 2011 (London) workshop to Alessandra Marino, Deena Dajani, Zaki Nahaboo, Lisa Pilgram, Dana Rubin, Aya Ikegame, Leticia Sabsay and Jack Harrington; and, for participating in the 8 December 2011 (Milton Keynes) workshop to John Allen, John Clarke, Jef Huysmans, Raia Prokhovnik and Michael Saward. I am also grateful to Jef Huysmans and the Centre for Citizenship, Identities and Governance (CCIG) in the Faculty of Social Sciences at the Open University for providing wonderful intellectual support and for funding these workshops. Cynthia Weber kindly read and made sense of senseless fragments and provided critical comments. Zaki Nahaboo provided brilliant research assistance on the acts including drafting many original narratives and feedback on these acts. Kim Rygiel, Anne McNevin and Rada Iveković asked penetrating and stimulating questions during two interviews. I am grateful to Lisa Pilgram and Anne Paynter for their brilliant attitude and fortitude in keeping things moving and creating spaces for me to write. For providing a brilliantly close and attentive copy-editing, I thank Jack Harrington. For engaging with 'theorizing acts' during *Enacting European Citizenship* project, I am grateful to Anaïs Faure Atger, Ayşe Çağlar, Bahar Rumelili, Bora Isyar, Claudia Aradau, Didier Bigo, Elspeth Guild, Fuat Keyman, Ivars Indāns, Jef Huysmans, Joe Painter, Kristīne Krūma, Michael Saward, Paula Macioti, Prem Kumar Rajaram, Rutvica Andrijasevic, Sandra Mantu, Sebastian Mehling, Sergio Carrera, Vicki Squire and Zsuzsanna Arendas. I owe a debt of gratitude to Michael Saward for being an inspiring co-investigator and co-editor during

Enacting European Citizenship project and book. His attentive and constructive engagement with questions that our collaborative research raised influenced the ideas expressed in this book significantly. I am most grateful to Alessandra Marino, Iker Barbero, Deena Dajani, Lisa Pilgram, Helen Arfvidsson, Stephan Scheel and Paola Macioti for engaging their research with 'acts of citizenship'. The book was made possible by European Research Council (ERC) for funding *Enacting European Citizenship* (2008–10) and *Citizenship after Orientalism* (2010–14) projects for which I am thankful. Words fail me to express my gratitude to Evelyn Ruppert to whom this book is dedicated.

CHAPTER ONE

Of Those Whose Acts Traverse Frontiers

Of all those movements with the name 'without frontiers' we have witnessed since the 1970s, *Médecins Sans Frontières* (MSF) is perhaps the most recognizable. What does that name signify? It is translated from French as 'doctors without borders'. But the French word 'frontières' does not mean simply borders or at least, if it does, only marginally so. Rather, it also indicates front lines, extremities or edges of something. Used figuratively, it implies limits (e.g. frontiers of science) and, by extension, it is used to indicate the unknown (e.g. the final frontier). Used literally, it indicates the outer borders of a settlement or, more importantly, defending or protecting them. So translating 'frontières' as 'borders' loses its nuance and translating 'sans frontières' as 'without borders' loses its performative force. As regards MSF what limits are we talking about then? Is it simply that its practitioners – in this case doctors – declare their loyalty beyond the frontiers of the jurisdiction that accredited and licensed them? MSF was founded in 1971 in Paris as an international aid group and evolved into an organization whose mission ranged 'from emergency medical assistance and healthcare training to humanitarian assistance'.[1] It is run by medical professionals but can also be joined by professionals in other fields. That sounds very much like a standard international non-profit organization.[2] So why is the name 'without frontiers' used then? At first glance, the limits that these professionals declare themselves 'without' appear to be those laws and norms that govern their profession. Today, every profession, unlike the thirteenth- and fourteenth-century guilds, is governed by rules that are typically made or enforced by the authority of the state. The modern medical profession recognizes that authority. Does it mean that doctors are against the state and want to operate regardless of its authority?[3] Does it mean that doctors want to belong to another authority that is beyond the state?

What does 'without frontiers' signify?

Although there may be practitioners who harbour such ideals, MSF, to my knowledge, never rejected the authority of the state as such – at least not at the outset.[4] Moreover, the limits that MSF declares itself 'without' are more than an aspiration to practise medicine without rules especially not those made by the state. Clearly, we need to look deeper into the logics of the movement to make sense of that name 'without frontiers'. These logics become apparent in its practices and ethos of not only serving patients, the ill, the victims, and the wounded, but also in creating autonomy and authority to function beyond the limits of the state. How does MSF define those limits? It turns out that those are both the political and practical limits of the state as such. I would like to propose that MSF is, above all, a movement 'traversing frontiers'. I will certainly elaborate on this phrase but it indicates that rather than merely interrogating the rules that govern the medical profession, it actually extends its reach beyond limits that are imposed on its practitioners by the state.

This traversing is significant. Perhaps implicit in it is the fact that national, corporate and religious powers are not only the causes of wars, deprivation, oppression, violence and other forms of domination but they also actively block assistance to those who are adversely affected by such violence. The declaration 'without' acknowledges that doctors must act against frontiers, reaching beyond the limits imposed on them by states, corporations and religious authorities. Also implicit in its traversing is the recognition and revelation that there are vast inequalities in the world that divide those who have access to proper care and those who do not. Thus, for those who have the privileges and accreditation, traversal becomes an obligation as the foundation of their autonomy.

To avoid misunderstanding, the suggestion here is not to overlook how, over the last 40 years, MSF has changed and grown more complex, especially with its development in several other countries.[5] I will come back to this. But I want to isolate the logics of this movement in order to understand the broader appeal of the name 'without frontiers'. As I mentioned, over the last 40 years, we have seen academics, accountants, architects, engineers, lawyers, reporters, teachers and other professionals organizing or identifying themselves with that name.[6] That is why we have perhaps become accustomed to the name 'without frontiers'. Taken together, 'without frontiers' signifies a number of crucial issues. These movements are radically different from business, professional and diplomatic travellers. First, travelling business people, professionals and diplomats are protected in the practice of their profession. Particularly in the last 20 years under the banner 'globalization', the movements of such people have become much easier, smoother and more straightforward. For them, travel and work are increasingly asserted, claimed and obtained as of right. Second, corporations, organizations and governments remunerate professional services and they engage in exchange and transactions. By contrast, movements without frontiers are neither commercial nor protected. In fact, state, corporate and religious authorities often do not endorse or support their movements and attempt to inhibit their activities. It is in this sense that I think the founding aspect of these movements is traversing frontiers.

It is about time I explain that phrase 'traversing frontiers'. There are four distinct but related senses of the word 'traverse'.[7] It first refers to the act to 'traverse' in a physical sense. The actions involve passing through a gate, or crossing a river, bridge or other place forming a boundary. The actions of 'traverse' also involve passing over, or going through (a region, etc.) as well as passage or crossing from side to side and from end to end, or in any course. In this first sense, its usage closely resembles to that of 'across'. However, its second meaning involves non-physical acts such as opposition or thwarting: something that crosses, thwarts or obstructs; or something that can form opposition, an obstacle or an impediment; things that constitute a trouble, vexation, a mishap, misfortune, adversity can all be called traverses. In fact, in law, it can mean denying an alleged misdeed by the other side. These two meanings (physical and non-physical) coming together and indicating not simply a crossing but with obstruction (or obstructed) or thwarting (or thwarted) is one reason why I want to use traversing frontiers rather than crossing to capture these frictions. Moreover, in its third sense, 'traverse' denotes the way across, path, track or course. So traverse is not only action but also that which it produces: a path, track or trace. In this sense, it denotes the remains and traces of acts of traversing frontiers as courses and paths that we can recognize, and follow. Finally, and in a concrete sense, 'traverse' denotes something that is placed or extends across, a kind of bridge or connection. With these two added senses, 'traverse' not only denotes acts of crossing against but also leaving remains or traces and building bridges. Clearly, taken together, these four senses signify 'without frontiers' much more strongly than merely crossing, across or even without or beyond frontiers.

To understand all these movements 'without frontiers' is a difficult task. At the outset, it would be wrong to give only a positive image of academics, accountants, architects, engineers, lawyers, reporters and teachers claiming to act without frontiers. These movements raise various troubling questions about the dominant humanitarian or human rights politics. To mark its fortieth anniversary, for example, MSF itself recently discussed the difficult compromises that it makes to negotiate its activities.[8] Marie Noelle Rodrigue, operations director of MSF in Paris, accepted '. . . the price it is necessary for an organization to pay so that you are helping the victims' and recognized that 'often that means making a compromise to a degree where you are helping the authorities'.[9] Clearly, although such movements, or at least some of them, have been increasingly subsumed under human rights politics, it is important to recognize that movements 'without frontiers' cannot be seen only as human rights politics or as transnational (or global) activism that is mobilized through human rights. Admittedly, they are implicated in human rights regimes and their compromises, but they also operate with quite distinct principles, and we ought not to see these movements as identical or equivalent to what has come to be known as 'global activism' or 'international volunteerism'.[10] To be sure, movements without frontiers share a non-commercial and non-profit ethos with activism and volunteerism. They can even be considered as a species of global activism and perhaps share some elements with international volunteerism. Yet, these movements indicate a new kind of politics for which we do not yet have a name; or perhaps we have not yet taken seriously the name they have given themselves.

Professions, citizens, activists

Going back to MSF – its ethos, concerns and limits or, more precisely, its logics – it is well worth critical consideration.[11] The claims that the movement does not differentiate creed, religion, politics or race when providing medical assistance, that it exercises 'universal medical ethics' and that it maintains independence from established political, economic or religious authorities all indicate an aspect of traversing frontiers. MSF clearly distinguishes between those norms that it accepts as given and those that it establishes without limits. In fact, our professional lives may well consist in managing the tension or even conflict between direct, intentional, regulated and recognizable duties and indirect, unintentional, open, indeterminate and yet affective obligations that implicate our lives in the lives of others. MSF's ethos illustrates this tension or conflict. When MSF was awarded the Nobel Peace Prize in 1999, James Orbinski, its then director, stated this in his acceptance speech quite well. He named this tension or conflict as the most important thing that mobilized the movement. He said '. . . we push the political to assume its inescapable responsibility'.[12] He added 'humanitarianism is not a tool to end war or to create peace. It is a citizen's response to political failure. It is an immediate, short term act that cannot erase the long term necessity of political responsibility.'[13] The use of 'citizen' is ambiguous here. Why is it used when a professional ethos is being discussed? What is implicit in this push for the political to assume its responsibility is that rules and regulations that order our professional lives do not necessarily exhaust our responsibilities towards ourselves and others. We are answerable beyond the direct responsibilities that govern our lives so that we can modify them. It establishes a capacity to act with certain autonomy. We, of course, learn, endorse and uphold laws and norms under which we live and responsibilities that we must fulfil. We also engage ourselves with others and question our relationships and the effects of our actions or inactions on others. This engagement often implicates us in tension or conflict with laws and norms that we uphold. That much is clear. What is ambiguous is whether citizens have the same capacity as professionals to make these claims.

It is this tension (and conflict) that perhaps explains the proliferation of movements called 'without frontiers' since the 1970s. Acting as responsible professionals within the confines of the state that define those responsibilities can no longer answer our obligations to others elsewhere; nor can it answer the consequences of the actions or inactions of our governments in our name. These movements, despite their differences, operate with similar logics of answerability: that their obligations are principled, that such obligations extend beyond or across frontiers and that these obligations are not expressly authorized by established national, corporate or religious authorities.

What we have learned from (or been reminded by) these movements with the name 'without frontiers' over the last few decades is that each profession is (or ought to be) governed by obligations that are beyond the regulations of a jurisdiction under whose authority it is licensed. The fact that we began with an example from the medical profession is not an accident. It is not insignificant that the Hippocratic oath is considered a fundamental aspect of the profession of medicine. Regardless of closed concerns, it obliges its practitioners to open principles that are held to be common. The idea here is to recognize that doctors are not only responsible to enclosing regulations, norms, and laws that govern their profession, they are also answerable to their principles.[14] This may sound like what is often considered as a 'calling' or 'vocation' associated with professions. But calling or vocation indicates inward-directed orientations developed against outward-directed pressures whereas these movements question this distinction.

Citizens without frontiers

The question I want to raise is why have we not witnessed a mobilization called 'citizens without frontiers'? What exactly would such a movement involve? And here we encounter a problem. The very term 'citizens without frontiers' is paradoxical. Citizenship is a bounded concept. It is bound up with the state if not the nation that signifies its authority and limits. Unlike academics, accountants, architects, engineers, lawyers, reporters and teachers, the 'membership' of citizens is strictly considered within the frontiers of the state. In fact, the very frontiers of the state become possible by defining some people as 'its' citizens. That it is acquired by birth, residence or blood and these binding it to the authority and territory of the nation-state constitute citizenship. Without binding people into a body and bounding them with an authority, the modern state would be inconceivable. In a way, boundedness is the very condition of citizenship. Is 'citizens without frontiers' not then an empty concept?[15]

As many scholars observe, it is this boundedness of citizenship to the nation-state that has become problematic in the age of migration and globalization.[16] In the fields of migration and security studies, for example, many have noted that with the increasing movements of people across boundaries, there have been transnational, cosmopolitan and global forms of citizenship where dual and multiple nationalities are being negotiated.[17] Some have attempted to develop concepts of cosmopolitan or global citizenship. Others have called for open borders.[18] Yet, all these presuppose, I submit, a moving subject rather than an acting subject. To put it another way, the focus is the mobility rather than the ability to act across frontiers. I want to turn the tables around and call all those who traverse frontiers citizens, blurring, if not obliterating, the boundaries between migrants and citizens. To do so, I want to draw inspiration from all those movements with the name 'without frontiers' in order to use it as a foundation to articulate the concept 'citizens without frontiers'.

Can we learn from those who do not necessarily move but traverse frontiers without professional accreditation or privilege? To put it another way, is it possible to shift our focus from the moving subject to the acting subject traversing frontiers? These acts may involve work, travel or escape but to focus on issues such as dual and multiple nationalities or regulation of movements is to be distracted from the fact that these are acts.[19] What makes these acts of citizens without frontiers revealing is their traversal qualities: with specific interventions, each creates concrete series of resonances, solidarities (or enmities), alliances and intensities across space and time and effectively resists universalizing narratives and unifying interpretations.[20] The qualities of acts traversing frontiers such as those of WikiLeaks, Anonymous, the Occupy, Gaza Flotilla, The Pirate Party, Climate Camp, No One Is Illegal, Waging Peace, Open Rights, If the World Could Vote and Banksy on the Wall are too heterogeneous to confine within our known categories. These are only the most known and recognized instances. There are literally thousands if not millions more acts such as these.

Interrogating and transgressing frontiers

The movements 'without frontiers' are recent; they can only be traced back to the 1970s. There were doubtless many originary moments for these movements without frontiers and the founding of MSF was certainly an important one. I want to briefly focus on a speech Michel Foucault gave at the United Nations headquarters in Geneva in 1981 on 'confronting government'. It signals something qualitatively different in that it addresses an international public. Foucault said 'There exists an international citizenship that has its rights and its duties, and that obliges one to speak out against every abuse of power, whoever its author, whoever its victims.'[21] Then he added as if it was self-evident: 'After all, we are all members of the community of the governed, and thereby obliged to show mutual solidarity.'[22] Calling this 'international citizenship' Foucault defines its duty '. . . to always bring the testimony of people's suffering to the eyes and ears of governments, sufferings for which it's untrue that they are not responsible. The suffering of men must never be a silent residue of policy.'[23] Foucault claims that the suffering of other men, or rather witnessing thereof, 'grounds an absolute right to stand up and speak to those who hold power'.[24] Insisting that we must refuse a division of labour between those who act (governments) and those who talk (citizens), Foucault emphasizes that 'Amnesty International, *Terre des Hommes* and *Médecins du monde* are initiatives that have created this new right – that of private individuals to effectively intervene in the sphere of international policy and strategy'. What does Foucault mean by 'private individuals'? Obviously, he cannot use 'citizens' because that would mean 'nationals'. The kind of right that he is claiming as new cannot be confined to citizens as nationals. Yet, 'private individuals' is a problematic phrase for a statement of solidarity that traverses frontiers. The themes in this short and succinct statement are nonetheless quite significant. The declaration that although we might reside under different jurisdictions we share the same condition of being governed and claim that we have a right to responsibility were ambitious declarations.

Those were the 1980s. It appears that Foucault was basically concerned with 'international citizenship as witnessing': recognizing the suffering of the Other and the responsibility to act against it. Or perhaps he was expressing the answerability of citizenship as a ground for an absolute right. Both are plausible interpretations. But I want to contrast this with an episode in 1979 when Foucault briefly worked as a 'reporter without frontiers' in Iran. A couple of years before his speech that I just quoted, in a dialogue with an Iranian writer Baqir Parham, Foucault was discussing why he was visiting Iran. He insisted that he was not visiting as a 'universal intellectual' but as a 'specific intellectual' to use his skills in solidarity with those who were revolting against an oppressive regime.[25] He did not make this claim lightly as he had thought about it seriously.[26] Arguing that 'engineers, lawyers, doctors, healthcare workers and social workers, researchers in the humanities, all form a social layer in our society whose numbers, as well as whose economic and political significance, are constantly increasing', he concluded that

> the role of the intellectual is perhaps not so much, or maybe not only, to stand for the universal values of humanity. Rather, his or her responsibility is to work on specific objective fields, the very fields in

which knowledge and sciences are involved, and to analyze and critique the role of knowledge and technique in these areas in our present-day society.[27]

Let me note that here his focus is not 'private individuals' but 'specific intellectuals' acting with professional capacities.[28] Yet, there is a paradox here. Two years later, Foucault would use 'private individual' as the subject of this kind of politics traversing frontiers instead of 'intellectual' or, more accurately, 'professional'. In my view, this is not a contradiction or confusion in Foucault, but simply points to the absence of a vocabulary with which to think about the new kind of politics that 'without frontiers' movements signify.

Since the 1970s and the 1980s, discussions and debates have subsumed 'citizens without frontiers' under various disguises such as global activism, humanitarianism and even global or cosmopolitan citizenship. Much of what can be described as acts traversing frontiers has been interpreted from the perspective of human rights or civil society discourses. The struggles against the apartheid regime in South Africa, the struggles against oppression in the Soviet Union and eastern Europe, secessionist movements, the environmental movement, the solidarity movements with refugees, aliens and other 'irregular' migrants have all triggered a complex mixture of interventionist, humanitarian and human-rights based forms of politics. The most recent of these were the so-called Arab revolutions in Tunisia, Egypt, Libya and other Middle Eastern states. There are already massive literatures about each and every one of these political struggles and broad interpretations under various rubrics such as 'global social movements', 'global civil society', 'multitude' and 'global democracy'.

The problem with these interpretations is that the manifold events that are shaping the worlds which we come to inhabit are multiple, complex and heterogeneous. Grand narratives that attempt to capture them are powerless in the face of these complexities. But, more importantly, interpreting acts traversing frontiers as participating in the formation of a singular or unified global or cosmopolitan society runs the risk of bounding citizenship again. It is almost as if just before we understand the promises and possibilities of acts traversing frontiers, we want to limit them to what we already know. To my knowledge, nobody suggested that there should be a global or supranational body regulating academics, architects, doctors or engineers. We have learned (once again) in 2011 how difficult it is to regulate financiers or investors. As professions go about their business of constructing transnational fields in which they acquire the capacity and authority to act without frontiers, why should we call for cosmopolitan or global citizenship? The significance of traversing frontiers as a field in which we can act in our capacity as citizens cannot be underestimated. Nor can we underestimate the damage inflicted by politics under disguise, which occurs sometimes through so-called civil-society groups engaging in clandestine activities and even spying operations across frontiers.

My task is to interpret these heterogeneous acts in contemporary politics whose subjects constitute themselves as citizens beyond both the figurative and literal frontiers that constrain them. 'Citizens without frontiers' signifies the kind of politics and political subjects that are emerging and what happens when they enact their political subjectivity by traversing frontiers. Yet, it is not enough to think about political subjectivity traversing frontiers. It is not enough to document acts that institute subjects without frontiers. It is not enough to interpret these acts through histories (or by giving them histories) that open up ways of enacting citizenship beyond the state and nation. My aim is also to participate in creating or constructing a field in which a new figure can acquire capacities to act as a citizen.[29]

'We, the people' and 'we, the connected'

Contemporary states everywhere have control over the movements, life and death of people whom they define as their citizens, and control over the entry and exit of people whom they define as non-citizens. These two forms of control (over citizens and non-citizens) are based on, or rather draw their legitimacy from, a history of states and nations as enclosed and enclosing entities that are 'self' governed and determined. From where is this power over life and death of subjects derived? How does this power persist despite the increasing movement of people, ideas, images and products across borders that states consider as their sovereign territory? How does this narrative exist against the fantasy of the sovereign (free) citizen? How do people challenge and resist this narrative? How do these enclosed and enclosing spaces appear as spaces for freedom rather than incarceration? Rather than engaging proposed 'solutions' (cosmopolitan democracy, international order, federalism), theories (nationalism, cosmopolitanism, globalism, internationalism) or proposals (cosmopolitics, empire), my task is to investigate how those who constitute themselves as citizens without frontiers are negotiating, interrogating and exposing the paradoxes of enclosed and enclosing citizenship.

Yet, sovereignty is not the only dominant narrative of our times. The other, which is becoming dominant, is the way in which we have been 'connected' through communication media, and especially the internet-based social media. It is first necessary to understand how both these narratives presuppose each other. There is a recognizable shift in contemporary politics of citizenship from the *sovereignty* narrative to the *connectivity* narrative. But questioning nationalism and cosmopolitanism or human rights regimes is not enough. We must develop an image of citizenship based on what people do (acts) rather than making theoretical or practical and ostensibly normative proposals.[30]

It is often said that citizenship is a domain of struggle. This is no less true than any time before. Consider these examples. There are walls being erected everywhere as separation barriers and borders.[31] There are now also prominent firewalls which are, in effect, controlled cyberspace bubbles. China is censoring internet communications through such a bubble that it calls 'Golden Shield'. Saudi Arabia, a theocratic state, is attempting to control all communication devices and liberal democratic states are following suit. Turkey is instituting a new great firewall. The US government is debating birthright citizenship rights for non-citizens. It is also building a separation barrier across the Mexican border. Israel is eliminating the rights of its Arab citizens. The United Kingdom is increasing its immigration and asylum controls for non–European Union citizens. There are numerous examples that illustrate how states are deciding who (and what) can enter and exit their territory and what can and cannot be done within their territories and by whom.

These issues have been discussed extensively in migration studies, ethnic and racial studies, diaspora studies, international studies and citizenship studies. At the centre of all these debates, there have been two grand narratives. On the one hand, we increasingly hear how the sovereignty of the state is, depending on the interpretation, waxing or waning. On the other hand, we also increasingly hear how everyday lives have become connected across borders, and how this connectivity is seen to be creating either a new rootedness or a new rootlessness. These two are grand narratives because they dominate ways of seeing and experiencing ourselves and others. It is not that their domination is absolute and that there are no counter-narratives producing different accounts of ourselves and others.[32] Yet, sovereignty and connectivity increasingly function as mutually dependent narratives. That the sovereign state controls not only who can be admitted to its territory but how that citizen conducts himself or herself as its member is surely related to various movements whose subjects constitute themselves beyond and across such frontiers that the sovereign states have created. If sovereignty shapes how we approach citizenship, connectivity shows up its limits and intensifies how it is captured. Yet, connectivity is increasingly articulated in terms inherited from sovereignty. I submit that sovereignty or the 'we, the people' narrative and connectivity or the 'we, the connected' narrative depend on each other as integrating and unifying discourses. Citizens without frontiers act through or produce interstitial spaces between sovereignty and connectivity, and create political subjectivities that traverse frontiers. It is these acts that traverse frontiers and produce political subjectivities that are creative, inventive and autonomous despite limits imposed upon them. The basic sources of interpretation are the acts of those who produce such political subjectivities.

Making citizens activists

How do we understand these manifold and paradoxical acts of subjectivity, solidarity, hostility, hospitality, belonging and rights? Consider the following broad problem as the question of citizenship. For centuries, theorizing about political subjectivity began with the figure of the citizen. Whether one is for or against interpreting that line of thought that began with the ancient Greeks and Romans as 'occidental', whether one sees radical breaks between ancient Greco-Roman, 'medieval' or modern thought, whether one sees the first as an appropriation of the last, the fact is that there *is* a line of thought that has constituted itself as an inheritor, and sees itself or interprets itself as being a continuation, of 'occidental' thought. The citizen as a figure of the political has been at the centre of that thought and has constituted the perspective from which the political has been understood, activated, practised and enacted.[33] This figure of the citizen has been masculine, white, occidental and Christian and has dominated the spaces of imagination and the imaginations of space. *Yet, that figure of the citizen is also bounded.* It is not only that the citizen was enacted in the agora, forum, guildhall and the assembly but also that this always took place within and through territorialized boundaries and limits whether this is envisaged as polis, civitas, state or nation. Since the late eighteenth century, the figure of the citizen has been territorialized first within the state-form and then the nation-form. Since the late nineteenth century, but especially from the middle of the twentieth century onwards, another figure of the political has also been emerging. This figure does not yet have a name but has a history. The dispossessed, marginalized, subjugated, subaltern, nomadic, excluded, at least in intellectual and activist imaginaries, has become the figure through which the political is enacted, theorized and understood. This figure has mobilized and assembled different spaces of imagination and imaginations of space. The agora, forum, guildhall and the assembly are displaced and now the citizen conducts himself or herself, at least in intellectual and activist imaginaries, in the street, square, school, hospital, asylum, prison and camp and these have become the sites and spaces through which the political is staged and enacted. Yet, *these sites are still confined within borders.* They are not only contained within the state but also they are themselves containers of state authority. More recently, a new figure of the citizen has emerged – one who *moves* across frontiers. This is the figure of the migrant.[34]

It is this figure that I want to rename by shifting the focus from the moving subject to the acting subject. To put it differently, the figure of the migrant needs to be displaced and this is the task that lies ahead. The figure of politics does not necessarily move across but acts (interrogates and transgresses) against frontiers. This figure is the 'citizen without frontiers'. This idea evokes two imaginaries. First, it evokes an imaginary that enacts citizens as subjects against frontiers. It imagines citizens without frontiers as a politics against frontiers. This imaginary produces the figure of the frontier as a generalized form of otherness that citizens destabilize. Second, it evokes interstitial and liminal spaces in and through which strangers, outsiders and aliens are imagined, produced and enacted. This imaginary produces the figure of the frontier as a generalized form of otherness that citizens create.

Those acts that *Citizens without Frontiers* witnesses and resignifies interrogate and transgress borders that are imposed on political subjectivities. As we witness acts of citizens without frontiers as those of 'activist citizens' across continents, namely Asia, the Americas, Africa and Europe, we recognize that these acts are rarely protected let alone sanctioned by dominant practices. These acts call into question two grand narratives of our times: sovereignty, which is fading, and connectivity, which is incipient. To put it differently, we may well be in that space (or time) of in between 'no longer' and 'not yet' that provides opportunities for thinking and acting differently.

Three genres of writing

The book features three genres (chapters, notes and acts) to fulfil different functions and to perform different personas. I use conventional chapters to discuss theoretical and political issues that are embedded in and draw from various academic fields as a device to engage readers who may be familiar with some but not all of these fields. I try to push contentious issues into another genre, that of notes, although this perhaps makes these sections less engaging for specialists in the fields concerned. It may sound odd to claim that notes are a genre. Perhaps, notes are a dying genre in the age of the automated simplicity of the so-called author-date significations that are so wonderfully ambiguous that they are sometimes (perhaps often) of questionable use. However, I use notes in both the conventional sense of citation and elaboration and also for setting aside some controversies in order to achieve a relatively straightforward prose.

Yet, notes are both conventional and unconventional. Their mechanics are conventional, but it is in these notes that I describe many vexing questions that yet remain unresolved. These notes at least show that it is often not only the questions but also the ways in which they are addressed in the relevant literatures that trouble me.

Acts are the least conventional genre in the book. They interpret (witness and resignify) deeds of interrogation and transgression or deeds that should make us interrogate or transgress the limits imposed upon political subjectivities by frontiers.[35] These acts focus on events such as the information leaked about the war in Afghanistan through WikiLeaks or, to take another example, conscientious objections to a war in a country that does not recognize such an objection. It should be said at the outset that a fundamental feature of an act of citizenship is that it exercises either a right that does not exist or a right that exists but which is enacted by a political subject who does not exist in the eyes of the law. Not all these acts are acts of citizenship. These acts also illustrate other aspects of theorizing acts such as how the tension between responsibility and answerability plays out; how subjects become actors without motives and intentions and yet create purposeful scenes; how actions get interpreted as acts; how acts produce sites of contention and span scales of attention and, most significantly, how acts traverse frontiers and rupture our given habitus and practices of political subjectivity. Each act described does not cover all these issues. This is because I want to keep these acts as relatively short and quick illustrative examples. But it is also because, especially taken together, these acts go beyond my expertise and skills to provide full sociological, anthropological and political accounts. This is both their strength and weakness. If you accept them as invitations to think about how subjects become political by traversing frontiers, then you may be rewarded not least because you will have to do some thinking that I have not done. If you find this approach intriguing, there are now a number of studies that focus on acts of citizenship.[36] Clearly, the specific concern of this book is those acts that constitute subjects as citizens against frontiers – citizens without frontiers. The 20 acts that the book features do not hold together as one coherent argument. Nor are these 'case studies' that constitute a body of evidence for an argument. If you search for that one body of evidence, you will be disappointed. There are tensions, paradoxes and aporias within and across these acts. Arguably, what they essentially demonstrate is the impossibility of imposing any general theory on them. Yet, writing about acts is an act of interpretation with its own vocabulary, or analytics. It is not spontaneous or impulsive. In fact, writing about these acts in itself has exactly the same qualities that I claim that acts have. (This will make a lot more sense once you read Chapter 4.) Hopefully, these acts demonstrate the value of approaching them with a relatively robust (though still developing) vocabulary or analytics that can enable us to trace forms of responsibility and answerability that they traverse, and political subjectivities that they produce. In this sense, acts exemplify a different style of practising social and political thought, which identifies and recognizes the formation of political subjectivities across or against frontiers that would otherwise have remained within the remit of the grand narratives of sovereignty and connectivity.

Chapter 2 focuses on sovereignty as a narrative through which we understand others and ourselves as political subjects. The chapter emphasizes that trying to interpret sovereignty from within its assumptions leads to intellectual and political cul-de-sacs. To put it differently, it is impossible to answer questions such as 'what is sovereignty?' But if we ask 'what is called sovereignty?' it opens up possibilities for understanding how, why and for whom sovereignty has become a problem. By first tracing the genealogies of 'we, the people', Chapter 2 identifies people, territory and sovereignty as the crux of the question of bounded citizenship. It also considers the counter-narratives of 'we, the people' but questions whether using 'people' makes it possible to escape the limits that frontiers impose on citizenship as a bounded political subjectivity. Chapter 3, using 'topological' insights, signals the birth of a new grand narrative, 'we, the connected'. It then considers how we might imagine interstitial or traversal spaces between connectivity and sovereignty and why citizens without frontiers might also define an interstitial or traversal citizenship. As I previously mentioned, Chapter 4 presents the idea of 'enacting citizenship' – a style of theorizing that considers citizenship as political subjectivity and its performativity. This chapter is the latest of a series of essays on 'acts of citizenship' that I have been developing as a style of theorizing political subjectivity. This style engages literatures on performativity and supplements it with enactment. It outlines how interstitial citizenship can be thought of through performativity, enactment and activism, and as a political subjectivity traversing frontiers. Chapter 5 presents various elements of 'citizens without frontiers' as 'activist citizenship'. It is in this chapter that I begin to indicate that 'citizens without frontiers' traverse not only actual frontiers (borders, boundaries, zones) but also virtual (or symbolic) frontiers by acting in place of or against how they are supposed to act. I name this broader conception of citizenship 'traversing citizenship'. Chapter 6 returns to sovereignty and connectivity narratives and suggests how citizens traversing frontiers reveal possibilities of politics without frontiers and how citizens without frontiers destabilize the established narratives of politics.

ACT 1. OF TREASON: WIKILEAKS

Millions of people have done it millions of times. Turn the personal computer on, search for and select some files, and copy them to something like a CD or DVD to share them. It has been an ordinary aspect of contemporary life for some time (although CDs and DVDs are gradually disappearing into the cloud). Yet, when Bradley Manning, a United States Army soldier, performed the same routine actions, it had profound consequences. Manning was caught in an act that for some was betrayal if not treason while for others it was patriotism if not heroism.

What transformed these routine actions into an international event and thus either an act of treason or heroism was the creation of an extraordinary infrastructure, WikiLeaks, a name borrowed from another ubiquitous internet infrastructure, Wikipedia. It is best to consider WikiLeaks as a form or an infrastructure before recognizing it as an organization. As a form it claims that it enables anyone with information on any wrongdoing to broadcast it with anonymity and security. It is a whistleblowing infrastructure that enables people to act on information on a wrongdoing as they understand it. While it is doubtful whether it can guarantee such anonymity, more importantly, it depends on reasonably heavy editorial and curatorial practices. Yet, we have learned, when the value of such information exceeds its intentions both the anonymity and security of the subject that enacts 'whistleblowing' can be brought into focus by state authorities.

WikiLeaks defines itself as 'a non-profit media organization dedicated to bringing important news and information to the public'. As we shall see its self-definition turned out to be not as stable as that statement calmly wishes since it had to make numerous adjustments in its presentation. For various political and legal reasons, WikiLeaks changed its image over the years.[37] Most recently, it considers itself as providing, again in its words, 'an innovative, secure and anonymous way for independent sources around the world to leak information to our journalists'. It claims to 'publish material of ethical, political and historical significance while keeping the identity of our sources anonymous, thus providing a universal way for the revealing of suppressed and censored injustices.'[38] Can we consider WikiLeaks as an organization for 'journalists without frontiers' with a political intent? It expressly positions itself against oppression and injustice. But, as ever, we are more concerned with deeds than self-descriptions. So let us take a closer look at a couple.

The main controversies that brought WikiLeaks into the open were the disclosing of the Afghan War diary, Iraq War logs and later the United States diplomatic cables.[39] Many of these documents were either classified as confidential or secret. Since early 2010 its campaign has amassed significant legal and media attention. One particular incident brought the organization under the radar of the US government. Bradley Manning, employed as an intelligence analyst, breached his professional role by operating as an activist for WikiLeaks. Manning gave to WikiLeaks videos of American helicopters shooting at people in Baghdad (with Reuters journalists being killed) and field reports on the wars in Afghanistan and Iraq.[40] What received most attention were the diplomatic cables, of which

Bradley Manning was the source for over 150,000.[41] The case is not simply that of his violating a military code or national security laws, but it also involves the act of breaking ordinary law.

Some commentators declare that WikiLeaks has been a 'game changer' and that 'it changed everything'.[42] Beyond the giddy excitement of such rhetoric, it is difficult to deny that the consequences of WikiLeaks as an act of disclosure are far-reaching and yet impossible to fully comprehend – at least as yet.[43] Governing authorities are always involved, on the one hand, in amassing massive volumes of data about subjects and citizens and, on the other, in making these data as secret or as safe as possible for state security. The open secret also known as state espionage (leaving aside industrial and corporate espionage) simply assumes this principle. What renders WikiLeaks a 'game changer' is probably its ability to broadcast information to vast numbers of people beyond the immediate control of government and controlled media. It is also probably its ability to act as a conduit to turn such acts of disclosure into a possible and imaginable, if not desirable, repertoire. Combined together, it becomes a potent infrastructure for enactment of disclosure of any body of secret information not just that of governments. That is why there is considerable concern shown about WikiLeaks by banks and other corporations.

WikiLeaks was officially launched in December 2006. Unlike conventional media outlets, it exploits the anonymity and deterritorialization that cyberspace provides and it purports to live by a legally unbounded journalistic philosophy for public and legal interest. Through sophisticated encrypted dropbox technology, 'citizen journalists' as whistleblowers can submit information anonymously which is then filtered, assessed for authenticity and potential impact and then distributed to media outlets.[44] This has enabled a variety of people, who would otherwise be unable, to share internationally significant and confidential diplomatic and military information with publics. Although one may debate the motivations of the 'core' editorial team, the WikiLeaks conduit takes the concept of free press quite literally. If it were to have an overarching mission it is greater accountability of government and private institutions. By disregarding national and industrial secrecy laws, which restrain news reporting, it takes the United Nations Declaration of Human Rights article 19 as an organizing principle. WikiLeaks interprets this as the freedom to hold, express and disseminate information 'through any media regardless of frontiers'.[45] The sources and advisory board of WikiLeaks attempt to rebalance access to information asymmetry, which exists in the international community at both an interstate (e.g. closed discussions between embassies about third parties) and a public interest level (confidential documents which fail to reach conventional media outlets or gag orders which prevent stories being run).

With its operations and reach traversing frontiers as well as the possibilities of protest and freedom of expression afforded by national or professional roles, it allows a bypassing of established pathways and status requirements for holding governments and other institutions to account. This occurs in the informal setting of media pressure, the bolstering of existing contentious politics and sometimes-direct impact on decision-making. An example of this is the fuelling of protest in the January 2011 Tunisian riots where it was speculated that WikiLeaks activists leaked remarks made by the US Embassy about the opulence of President Bin Ali and his family sparking further anger against the president.[46] Breaching industrial legal boundaries is also a prevalent feature. Almost straight from a Hollywood blockbuster, we find the story of a Swiss banker threatening to expose tax evasion leading to his arrest for breaking secrecy laws.[47] Acting without frontiers is also reflected in the very structure of the organization, with its numerous servers and domain names able to operate once one has been threatened with closure, as was the case when in June 2011 its main provider ceased hosting its operations.[48]

What makes WikiLeaks a potent infrastructure is that it enables subjects behind computer screens to enact themselves as activist citizens and as citizens without frontiers. This potency is not without its paradoxes. While a technologically savvy 'core' receives, filters and releases information, a growing base of people supports WikiLeaks to the point of active involvement, which itself is made possible through the 'core' providing the means.[49] This gives a powerful performative force for breaking established repertoires or scripts of dissent. If the prescribed medium of expressing dissent, for example, official channels of communication with authorities, is itself compromised or part of a system which reflects upholding the information asymmetry of citizen and government, then these acts allow for voices to be heard which would otherwise be drowned out by bureaucracy or public indifference. Yet, a tension between the 'core' and the 'base' become palpable as its anonymous base is cut off from means of filtering and presenting the information that they have provided or procured. This paradox exposes a claim made by WikiLeaks founder Julian Assange that WikiLeaks provides information by the people and for the people who are too cozy for comfort.[50] It must be admitted that WikiLeaks, for all its flaws, provided an infrastructure, a repertoire, if you like, for creative, inventive and autonomous acts of disclosure that raised significant questions about open and closed secrets in governing modern states. It laid bare what we already know, that state authorities can act across borders with impunity while for citizens this remains dangerous. WikiLeaks has shown this poignantly and, with or without it, the politics of access to information, transparency of government action and accountability of states to their citizens will remain as vital issues as ever in the age of electronic dissemination and communication.

ACT 2. OF RAGE: RACHEL CORRIE

On 30 May 2010, a flotilla of ships set sail for Gaza for the claimed purposes of delivering building materials, medical supplies and school equipment. It was, however, effectively breaking the Israeli government's blockade of the territory.[51] It was an assembly of some 600 activists from more than 30 countries, including politicians, novelists and doctors, speaking and acting beyond organizations or nations but in solidarity with the plight of the Palestinian people. Three groups staged this act: the Free Gaza Movement, the Foundation for Human Rights and Freedoms and Humanitarian Relief (IHH, İnsan Hak ve Hürriyetleri ve İnsani Yardım Vakfı in Turkish) and Ship to Gaza. After departing from Greece, Turkey and Ireland six ships regrouped in Cyprus. Their journey to Gaza was interdicted when the vessels were stopped 60 km from the Gaza coast, beyond the limits of the maritime blockade in international waters.[52] On 31 May, Israel Defence Forces (IDF) naval commandos boarded the IHH-owned ship, *Mavi Marmara*. Arguably, both parties transgressed existing state borders. The IDF broke the state jurisdiction of military operations and the activists sought to challenge the legality of the blockade. A small area of international maritime space became a site of struggle over rights, territories and authority. What happened next has been subject to international debate as activists and soldiers violently clashed, with blame attributed for the violence to both sides.[53] The consequence of the raid was the death of nine activists.[54]

Two ships were absent from the initially proposed eight strong Gaza flotillas, as they suffered technical difficulties: the *Challenger 2* and the *Rachel Corrie*. *Challenger 2* aborted but the *Rachel Corrie* continued its mission of delivering humanitarian aid despite hearing what transpired on 31 May.[55] The *Rachel Corrie* never reached its destination and was intercepted by the IDF on 5 June and rerouted to port Ashdod without bloodshed. Binyamin Netanyahu used the contrast between the incident with the *Mavi Marmara* and the *Rachel Corrie* to illustrate the lack of respect he had for the former who 'were violent extremist supporters of terrorists'.[56]

The *Rachel Corrie* was a Cambodian-flagged, Irish-owned aid vessel funded by Perdana Global Peace Organization, a Malaysian non-governmental organization. It was named after an activist for the International Solidarity Movement: Rachel Corrie, an American college student present in Gaza as an activist in support of the Palestinian people. In March 2003, Rachel Corrie died after being run over by an Israeli bulldozer while protesting against the destruction of Palestinian homes.[57] It can be said that Corrie's act of solidarity was a precursor to the formation of the flotilla that included a ship carrying her name. Corrie's act signified a solidarity with not a 'collection of deprived refugees', as Edward Said suggests, but with 'the gravity and the density of the living history of the Palestinian people'.[58] This kind of solidarity, Said continued, was not confined to a few 'intrepid souls here and there, but is recognized the world over'.[59] As we shall see in Chapter 4, this recognition 'world over' was also an invitation to action, a repertoire under which to act against frontiers.

There is a double act that carries the same name: 'Rachel Corrie'. How political subjectivity traverses frontiers and creates solidarities is illustrated by both Rachel Corrie and the *Rachel Corrie* as acts of resistance to borders, whether the illegality of Palestinian housing or the illegality of passing the Gaza blockade. The force of the Gaza Flotilla is its naked presence that defies where an act can be staged and how it can have an impact upon and shape international opinion. What is particularly symbolic about Rachel Corrie is not primarily the act of standing in the path of a bulldozer but how she broke from her own milieu to engage in frontline activism in a war zone. This is perhaps why Foucault thought that revolt was never useless as it expressed an irreducible quality.[60] For him

the impulse by which a single individual, a group, a minority, or an entire people says, 'I will no longer obey,' and throws the risk of their life in the face of an authority they consider unjust seems to me to be something irreducible. Because no authority is capable of making it utterly impossible.[61]

The sheer force of revolt is that

one does not dictate to those who risk their lives facing a power. Is one right to revolt, or not? Let us leave the question open. People do revolt; that is a fact. And that is how subjectivity (not that of great men, but that of anyone) is brought into history, breathing life into it.[62]

Yet, what Foucault does not emphasize here are the grounds on which it becomes possible to act. Those grounds always come into being with considerable collective preparation, practice and training. The event that an act produces might be a rupture but, as we shall see in Chapter 4, producing it requires inventing repertoires and making grounds.

Rachel Corrie came from a fairly affluent family in small-town Olympia, an hour from Seattle. The family had no particular attachment to the Palestinian cause. Her mother was a teacher, and her father an insurance executive.[63] The shock of moving from relative calm to conflict is captured in the play *My Name is Rachel Corrie*, which we can consider as the third act carrying the same name. It depicts a journey from comfortable middle-class America to the desperate and deadly situation of Rafah as one of breaking with an 'average' liberal college life to jump the barricades. It seeks to capture the feelings of anxiety, fear and anger as she embarks upon something unprecedented in her life so far. Yet what inspired her has been reduced to a narrative of her life in the media, the various psychological and social forces which contribute to her journey.[64] However, what escapes this is the act of breaking scripted forms of activity to enter a space of hopefulness brought on by hopelessness. Rachel's subjectivity is brought into history in solidarity with those whom she did not consider deprived but subjected to injustice. Rachel's act traversing frontiers exceeds the ethos by which she is meant to live, a narrative scripted by national citizenship or nationality. Her act becomes a rupture that carries that ethos to the *Rachel Corrie*.

ACT 3. OF DISOBEDIENCE: CONSCIENTIOUS OR CIVIL?

On 6 June 2010, Sezai Ozan Zeybek declared: This war ought to end.[65] His declaration did not refer to a particular war (though he seems to have had Turkey's unmentionable war against the Kurds in mind) but war itself. This would not constitute an act in any state that recognizes conscientious objection as a human right. Yet Turkey is one of the two remaining states in the world that does not recognize it.[66] That renders Ozan's declaration an act, a rupture. It is also a crime. Zeybek says 'I write this declaration to estrange the Turkish public from military service.' Although described under the rights discourse known as 'conscientious objection', this act is not merely an objection to war on ethical grounds. It is a political act, but what does it mean to estrange a public? Can an act have performative force to estrange a public? The audacity of the act is that it can. Or at least it can assert that it can. Zeybek admits that this is not an easy task

> because the idea that every Turkish man is born a soldier has been engraved into our minds in our childhoods. In this country, even children's games are infected with weapons, enemies, death and guilt . . . We are all taught that military service is a sacred duty.

Zeybek shows a childhood picture in which he wears a military uniform. Then perhaps speaking to the sovereign he says 'I do not want to be a soldier. You made me wear a uniform when I was five, but now I am 32 and I refuse to wear it again.' Zeybek also refuses to perform 'minor' duties that the Turkish military invented to make the service bearable for middle and upper-middle classes. He says

> I don't consider making music for the officers, serving their dinner, tutoring their kids without payment, running their errands, typing their letters, polishing the commander's boots, being hustled and bustled all the time as any kind of national duty. On the contrary, I recognize compulsory military service as a resource of slave-labour, as another pillar of injustice.

Nor does he want to escape or flee military service. Instead, he declares his objection to it although it is illegal to do so.

This act of declaration is signed by Ozan Sezai Zeybek. But by providing an analysis of war and the function of military, and drawing attention to the relations between them and their genuinely political economy, Zeybek wants to fulfil his aim of estranging the Turkish public from military service. The declaration is a critique of what he is asked to join as a young man. Although it is singularly signed, the declaration is also collective. According to a compilation, the first known declaration was in 1989.[67] Since then grounds for objecting to military service have been created by the organizing, networking and resisting activities of generations of men and women. Reading some 200 declarations is to participate in each and every objection and yet it is also to witness a collective repertoire that has been created with performative force under which young men and women could and can act. These declarations of creativity, inventiveness and autonomy are signed both individually and collectively.

Can the refusal to serve in the military be an act of citizenship? What does the act of a young man declaring himself as a conscientious objector signify when the state in which he holds his citizenship does not recognize such an act?[68] These questions arise from the effective individual and collective declarations of conscientious objection that these Turkish men and women have enacted.[69] There is clearly a tension between citizenship as nationality and the refusal to perform military as national service. Arguably, military service and the warrior ethic are among the building blocks of citizenship not only in modern times but also since its ancient Greek and Roman origins. But it is in modern times that the state, the military as national service and nationality are implicated in each other, and by institutionalizing war and violence they contribute to the 'we, the people' narrative. It is perhaps because of this tension that it has been difficult to articulate claims to conscientious objection as a right of citizenship. Instead, it has been formulated as a human right and that is why Amnesty International has been at the forefront of struggles for recognition of the refusal to serve in the military.[70] Although these relations are too involved to discuss further here, conscientious objection being articulated as a human right rather than citizenship right (e.g. as civil disobedience) highlights the need to rethink the state as the container of politics within its borders. It is precisely because conscientious objection traverses frontiers that it becomes an act of citizens without frontiers.

Notes

1 See C. Magone et al., eds, *Humanitarian Negotiations Revealed: The MSF Experience* (London: C. Hurst & Co Publishers, 2011).

2 S. Robins, 'Mobilizing and Mediating Global Medicine and Health Citizenship: The Politics of Aids Knowledge Production in Rural South Africa,' in *Globalizing Citizens: New Dynamics of Inclusion and Exclusion*, ed. J. Gaventa and R. Tandon (London: Zed Books, 2010), 63. Robins shows that agents such as MSF play ambitious roles in cultivating citizenship. While, on the one hand, they may be seen as agents of globalization, they also activate new political subjectivities by creating collaborative demands on the state based on needs identified by situated activists. Robins notes that when French doctors and journalists, in response to the perceived inadequacies of humanitarian aid, founded MSF in 1971 during the Biafran war in Nigeria, it was conceived as essentially a French organization. But since then it has become a much more complex movement traversing more than 83 countries for advocacy and aid. MSF has become a much more complex movement than an aid NGO as it increasingly articulates activist aims such as witnessing and shaming.

3 We cannot discuss how the professions have become dominant social groups throughout the postmodern era (since the 1980s). See E. F. Isin, *Being Political: Genealogies of Citizenship* (Minneapolis: University of Minnesota Press, 2002). Its last chapter discusses at some length the connections between cities, citizenship and the professions. As a field, 'sociology of professions' provides valuable insights on their emergence and development. E. A. Krause, *Death of the Guilds: Professions, States and the Advance of Capitalism, 1930 to the Present* (New Haven: Yale University Press, 1999); K. M. Macdonald, *The Sociology of the Professions* (London: Sage, 1995).

4 On the contrary, as Simeant illustrates, *Médecins Sans Frontières* effectively organizes itself through states. See J. Simeant, 'What Is Going Global? The Internationalization of French Ngos "without Borders",' *Review of International Political Economy* 12, 5 (2005).

5 Magone et al., eds, *Humanitarian Negotiations Revealed: The MSF Experience* provides an instructive glimpse into the changing character of the movement since its founding in 1971, and its international expansion.

6 Although I am less interested in 'professions without frontiers', I am still surprised that a book-length study does not exist. I would have thought by now that a sociologist or an anthropologist would have provided an overview of globalizing professions and their consequences. In the vast literature on social movements that has sprung up over the last few decades, as far as I know, 'professions without frontiers' has never been studied in politics or sociology. Finally, it is surprising that in the burgeoning literature on 'transnational activism' or 'global activism', the movements of what I call 'professions without frontiers', as far I know, hardly ever gets any mention. See C. Sampford, 'Professions without Borders: Global Ethics and the International Rule of Law,' in *Public Lecture* (Brisbane: Queensland University of Technology, 2009).

7   Oxford English Dictionary, traverse, n. second edition, 1989; online version
    December 2011. http://www.oed.com accessed 2 January 2012. Earlier version
    first published in New English Dictionary, 1914.

8   Magone et al., eds, *Humanitarian Negotiations Revealed: The MSF
    Experience*.

9   P. Beaumont. 2011. Médecins Sans Frontières Book Reveals Aid Agencies' Ugly
    Compromises. *The Guardian*, 20 November 2011 [cited 21 November 2011].

10 See J. Birdwell, *Service International* (London: Demos, 2011); R. Reitan,
    Global Activism (London: Routledge, 2007); S. G. Tarrow, *The New
    Transnational Activism* (Cambridge: Cambridge University Press, 2005).

11 MSF. 2011. Charter. Médecins Sans Frontières (MSF) 2011 [cited Tuesday, 8
    March 2011]. Source: http://goo.gl/15wAY.

12 J. Orbinski. 1999. Oslo Nobel Lecture: Médecins Sans Frontières, 10
    December 1999 [cited 3 June 2011]. Source: http://goo.gl/9XzR6.

13 Ibid.

14 See G. M. Nielsen, *The Norms of Answerability: Social Theory between
    Bakhtin and Habermas* (Albany, NY: State University of New York Press,
    2002).

15 That said, I had expected to find a monograph-length study on these
    movements in general. They are either subsumed under 'global activism' or
    international NGO literatures while they are distinct from both. The only
    exception is R. Debray, *Éloge Des Frontières* (Paris: Gallimard, 2010). Debray
    criticizes 'sans-frontiérisme' for desiring a borderless world. But he thinks
    that to desire such a world is not only an illusion but also a disastrous licence
    for those who are powerful to move without impunity from financiers to
    Mafia. It is a mistake to equate 'sans-frontiérisme' and 'globalism'. Much of
    what Debray attributes to sans-frontiérisme should more properly be seen as
    the tenets of globalism while the sans-frontiérisme itself actually enters into
    negotiations of the kind that Debray desires. So the dichotomy that Debray
    sets up between a borderless world and a world with borders is not a helpful
    one, as the pertinent question is how borders function, who and what they
    filter and who and what they block.

16 See G. Delanty, *Citizenship in a Global Age: Society, Culture, Politics*
    (Philadelphia, PA: Open University Press, 2000); K. Rygiel, *Globalizing
    Citizenship* (Vancouver: UBC Press, 2010); H. Schattle, *The Practices of
    Global Citizenship* (Lanham, MD: Rowman & Littlefield Publishers, 2007).

17 S. Castles and A. Davidson, *Citizenship and Migration: Globalization and the
    Politics of Belonging* (New York: Routledge, 2000); S. Castles and M. J. Miller,
    *The Age of Migration: International Population Movements in the Modern
    World* (New York: Guilford, 1993).

18 J. H. Carens, *Immigrants and the Right to Stay* (Cambridge, MA: MIT Press,
    2010); J. H. Carens, 'Aliens and Citizens: The Case for Open Borders,' *Review
    of Politics* 49 (1987).

19 A. Ong, *Flexible Citizenship: The Cultural Logics of Transnationality*
    (Durham, NC: Duke University Press, 1999); M. P. Smith and Bakker,
    Citizenship across Borders: The Political Transnationalism of El Migrante
    (Ithaca, NY: Cornell University Press, 2008).

20 See M. E. Keck and K. Sikkink, *Activists Beyond Borders: Advocacy Networks in International Politics* (Ithaca, NY: Cornell University Press, 1998); L. Reydams, ed., *Global Activism Reader* (London: Continuum, 2011).
21 M. Foucault, 'Confronting Governments: Human Rights,' in *Power*, ed. J. D. Faubion, *Essential Works of Foucault, 1954–1984* (New York: New Press, 2000), 474. The speech was later published as a statement in *Liberation*.
22 Ibid.
23 Ibid., 474–5.
24 Ibid.
25 J. Afary and K. Anderson, *Foucault and the Iranian Revolution: Gender and the Seductions of Islamism* (Chicago, IL: University of Chicago Press, 2005), 183–9.
26 Also see the conversation between Gilles Deleuze and Michel Foucault in M. Foucault, *Language Counter-Memory Practice* (Ithaca, NY: Cornell University Press, 1977).
27 Afary and Anderson, *Foucault and the Iranian Revolution: Gender and the Seductions of Islamism*, 184.
28 Of course, there is much more that can be said about Foucault's act of writing on Iran. It is not as straightforward as I presented and it is debatable whether Foucault was successful in creating new publics or even freeing himself from the questions of subjectivity to which he was drawn through his studies in Greco-Roman and early Christian practices of the self. M. Foucault, *The Care of the Self*, vol. 3, *History of Sexuality* (New York: Pantheon, 1986); M. Foucault, *The Use of Pleasure*, trans. R. Hurley, vol. 2, *History of Sexuality* (New York: Pantheon, 1985). Yet, there is something remarkably refreshing and inspiring in Foucault's approach to Iran compared to what we have witnessed during the so-called Arab Spring in 2011 when some intellectuals were very quick to interpret the Egyptian and Tunisian uprisings as 'universal' revolutions and so on. Foucault was so insistent not to name the Iranian uprisings as a 'revolution' precisely because of their historic traces and images.
29 See E. F. Isin, 'Citizenship in Flux: The Figure of the Activist Citizen,' *Subjectivity*, 29 (2009).
30 The politics of making this choice is itself too involved to dwell on and elaborate here. It will have to wait for another occasion.
31 The prominent examples are the US–Mexico border and the Israeli wall. See W. Brown, *Walled States, Waning Sovereignty* (New York: Zone, 2010).
32 See for examples and discussion M. G. W. Bamberg and M. Andrews, *Considering Counter-Narratives: Narrating, Resisting, Making Sense* (Amsterdam: John Benjamins Pub. Co, 2004). Bamberg and Andrews provide this description of what they call 'master' narratives: 'One of the key functions of master narratives is that they offer people a way of identifying what is assumed to be a normative experience. In this way, such storylines serve as a blueprint for all stories; they become the vehicle through which we comprehend not only the stories of others, but crucially of ourselves as well. For ultimately, the power of master narratives derives from their internalization. Wittingly or unwittingly, we become the stories we know, and the master narrative is reproduced. But of course it is not so simple. When, for whatever reason, our own experiences do not match the master

narratives with which we are familiar, or we come to question the foundations of those dominant tales, we are confronted with a challenge. How can we make sense of ourselves, and our lives, if the shape of our life story looks deviant compared to the regular lines of the dominant stories? The challenge then becomes one of finding meaning outside of the emplotments which are ordinarily available. We become aware of new possibilities.' Ibid., 1. We will see many examples of both the 'we, the people' and the 'we, the connected' grand narratives that fit this description very well.

33 This is the central argument of Isin, *Being Political: Genealogies of Citizenship*.

34 A. Sayad, *The Suffering of the Immigrant* (Cambridge: Polity Press, 2004).

35 E. F. Isin, 'Theorizing Acts of Citizenship,' in *Acts of Citizenship*, ed. E. F. Isin and G. M. Nielsen (London: Zed Books, 2008).

36 R. Basu, 'Negotiating Acts of Citizenship in an Era of Neoliberal Reform: The Game of School Closures,' *International Journal of Urban and Regional Research* 31, 1 (2007); E. F. Isin and M. Finn, 'Bombs, Bodies, Acts: The Banalization of Suicide,' in *War, Citizenship, Territory*, ed. D. Cowen and E. Gilbert (London: Routledge, 2007); E. F. Isin and E. Üstündağ, 'Wills, Deeds, Acts: Women's Civic Gift-Giving in Ottoman Istanbul,' *Gender, Place and Culture* 15, 5 (2008); A. McNevin, 'Political Belonging in a Neoliberal Era: The Struggle of the Sans-Papiers,' *Citizenship Studies* (2006); P. Nyers, 'The Accidental Citizen: Acts of Sovereignty and (Un) Making Citizenship,' *Economy and Society* 35, 1 (2006); M. L. Roberts, *Disruptive Acts: The New Woman in Fin-de-Siécle France* (Chicago: University of Chicago Press, 2002).

37 R. Miller, 'Is Wikileaks "the Press"?' *Econtent* 34, 2 (2011): 15.

38 WikiLeaks. 2011. What Is Wikileaks? 2011 [cited 22 January 2011]. Source: http://goo.gl/lclLg.

39 A. Star, ed., *Open Secrets: Wikileaks, War and American Diplomacy, Introduction by Bill Keller* (New York: New York Times, 2011).

40 S. Shane. 2011. 'Accused Soldier in Brig as Wikileaks Link Is Sought,' *The New York Times* 2011 [cited 22 January 2011]. Source: http://goo.gl/vmbJf.

41 E. Pilkington. 2011. 'Wikileaks's Alleged Source Bradley Manning Held in "Punitive" Conditions,' *The Guardian*, 5 February 2011 [cited 20 February 2011]. Source: http://goo.gl/1yvjf.

42 S. Rogers. 2011. 'Wikileaks Data Journalism: How We Handled the Data,' *The Guardian*, 31 January 2011 [cited 24 February 2012]. Source: http://goo.gl/uiByc.

43 G. Mitchell, 'Why Wikileaks Matters,' *Nation* 292, 5 (2011): 4.

44 WikiLeaks. 2011. Submissions 2011 [cited 22 January 2011]. Source: http://goo.gl/9ZjC2.

45 WikiLeaks. 2011. What Is Wikileaks? [cited 22 January 2011]. Source: http://goo.gl/lclLg.

46 M. Azzam. 2011. Opinion: How Wikileaks Helped Fuel Tunisian Revolution. CNN, 18 January 2011 [cited 18 January 2011]. Source: http://goo.gl/xVFcV.

47 J. Lynn. 2011. Wikileaks Founder Assange Slams Swiss Banker Arrest. Reuters, 23 January 2011 [cited 23 January 2011]. Source: http://goo.gl/zNQmi.

48 BBC. 2010. 'Cyber Attack Forces Wikileaks to Change Web Address. BBC, 3 December 2010 [cited 18 January 2011]. Source: http://goo.gl/MzaYr; BBC. 2011. LulzSec Hacking Group Announces End to Cyber Attacks: A Hacker

Group that Has Attacked Several High-Profile Websites over the Last Two Months Has Announced that It Is Disbanding. BBC, 26 June 2011 [cited 24 February 2012]. Source: http://goo.gl/8X7Us

49 J. Aron, 'Digital Conflict Spills into Real Life,' *The New Scientist* 208, 2791 (2010).

50 J. Assange, 'Of the People and for the People,' *New Statesman* 140, 5048 (2011): 21.

51 H. Sherwood. 2010. Gaza Aid Flotilla to Set Sail for Confrontation with Israel. *The Guardian* 2010 [cited 22 January 2011]. Source: http://goo.gl/fcVnH

52 P. Reynolds. 2010. Israeli Convoy Raid: What Went Wrong? 2 June 2010 [cited 22 January 2011]. Source: http://goo.gl/SpwaR

53 Ibid.

54 Al Jazeera. 2010. Another Aid Ship on Way to Gaza. Al Jazeera, 5 June 2010 [cited 22 January 2011]. Source: http://goo.gl/uT9Tx

55 Al Jazeera. 2010. Israel to Release Turkish Activists Al Jazeera, 4 June 2010 [cited 22 January 2011]. Source: http://goo.gl/tF8uv

56 Jerusalem Post. 2010. Navy Boards 'Rachel Corrie' Off Gaza. *Jerusalem Post*, 6 May 2010 [cited 23 January 2011]. Source: http://goo.gl/eGYlG

57 CNN. 2003. Israeli Bulldozer Kills American Protester. CNN, 25 March 2003 [cited 22 January 2011]. Source: http://goo.gl/PY9Ts

58 E. Said. 2003. The Meaning of Rachel Corrie. ZNET, 26 June 2003 [cited 22 January 2011]. Source: http://goo.gl/i3obR

59 Ibid. How right Said was. On 31 May, to protest against the raid on the Gaza Flotilla, an American student artist, Emily Henochowicz, lost her eye when hit by a canister fired by IDF. See E. Pilkington. 2010. Emily Henochowicz: Artist to Pro-Palestinian Activist. *The Guardian*, 21 August 2010 [cited 30 May 2011].

60 Foucault, 'Useless to Revolt?' in *Power*, ed. James D. Faubion (New York: New Press, 2000), 449.

61 Ibid.

62 Ibid., 451.

63 L. France. 2008. She Was a Girl from Small-Town America with Dreams of Being a Poet or a Dancer. So How, at Just 23, Did Rachel Corrie Become a Palestinian Martyr? *The Guardian* 2 March 2008 [cited 23 January 2011]. Source: http://goo.gl/RXyN4

64 Ibid.

65 The original declaration is written in Turkish. Ozan Zeybek kindly provided me an English version. The Turkish version can be found along with all known declarations since 1989 in C. Başkent, ed., *Vicdani Ret Açıklamalari Almanağı, 1989–2010 [Declarations of Conscientious Objections (Turkey): An Almanac, 1989–2010]* (Istanbul: Propaganda Yayınları, 2011), 77–9.

66 Amnesty International. 2011. Landmark ECHR Ruling Recognizes Right to Conscientious Objection. Amnesty International, 7 July 2011 [cited 25 September 2011]. Source: http://goo.gl/y5V9O. The other state that does not recognize conscientious objection is Azerbaijan.

67 Başkent, ed., *Vicdani Ret Açıklamalari Almanağı, 1989–2010 [Declarations of Conscientious Objections (Turkey): An Almanac, 1989–2010]*.

68 Amnesty International, Landmark ECHR Ruling Recognizes Right to Conscientious Objection [cited 25 September 2011]. Source: http://goo.gl/y5V9O

69 See a collection of essays that further analyze the history and development of conscientious objection in Turkey Ö.H. Çınar et al., eds., *Conscientious Objection: Resisting Militarized Society* (London: Zed, 2009).

70 Amnesty International, *Out of the Margins: The Right to Conscientious Objection to Military Service in Europe* (London: Amnesty International, International Secretariat, 1997); H. Takemura, *International Human Right to Conscientious Objection to Military Service and Individual Duties to Disobey Manifestly Illegal Orders* (Berlin: Springer, 2009).

CHAPTER TWO

'We, the People'

If you travel and are asked to produce your passport to enter a country you experience sovereignty.[1] It is this act of entry that gives the most potent sense of the sovereignty of a nation-state in control of 'its' territory, perhaps comparable to the experience of looking at a map of political boundaries. There are many other ways through which sovereignty is enacted and we are made to believe in the potency of the sovereign nation-state in control of its borders.[2]

There has been intense disagreement about 'globalization' and its effects on the 'nation-state' and the control it exercises over its borders. The disagreement concerns whether the nation-state in a given territory is losing at least some of that control when multinational corporations and international organizations, on the one hand, and regional and local movements, on the other hand, challenge it. Are these developments making it impossible to maintain such control or at least maintain that potent sense of it?[3] If we add to these developments the increasing flow of people across borders not only for travel but also for relocation, education or business, and the increasing flow of goods, services and images, sounds and ideas, it seems as if the writing is on the wall for nation-state sovereignty understood as control over a given territory and its population.[4] In the 1990s, the prevailing view was that the sovereignty of the nation-state was indeed waning. In the 2000s, this was mitigated by arguments that the nation-state was 'asserting' its sovereignty by establishing various new forms of control.

What is called sovereignty?

Although some terms used so far such as 'territory', 'sovereignty' and 'nation-state' as well as 'control' (of whom, what and where) are vague, the waxing or waning of nation-state sovereignty has been largely articulated as the crisis of sovereignty. The positions for and against 'globalization' reflect this basic understanding of sovereignty. Yet, there are some complicating issues involving the performative creation of 'we, the people' and its relation to sovereignty, the nation-state and citizenship. Two are especially important.

First, when we speak about sovereignty as control over territory, it implies different things depending on *what* is being controlled and *how*. There are significant differences in what and how different types of things are controlled over a given territory.[5] Controlling the movements of people in order to separate citizens from non-citizens, reducing health risks, managing environmental resources, regulating financial capital (and its global transactions), controlling pollution, preventing the spread of diseases, confiscating 'illegal' substances or guns all mobilize and require vastly different strategies and technologies of government. Moreover, they result in vastly different controls, or, more accurately, control-spaces; each poses a unique challenge to the ability of the nation-state to control its territory. Obviously, my concern here is with those that involve controlling the movements of people in order to separate citizens from non-citizens. Even then, and inevitably, such controls are implicated and intertwined with other types of control and regulation. At least analytically, we must therefore qualify the what and how of controls when we use the term sovereignty. This is important because the *what* and *how* of controls literally shape the *whereness* of territory; territory is not merely given and fixed borders but also change and response to the *whatness* and *howness* of control, of regulation, and of government. Controlling illegal substances or regulating financial transactions both literally create different spaces that come into focus as objects of control. These spaces do not always, if ever, map exactly over the political borders of the state. To put it in more stark terms when the nation-state is said to be controlling substances, the territories over which such controls govern, though overlapping, are quite different from those it is said to be controlling finance; these differences only come into focus through the mobilization of specific strategies and technologies of government appropriate to the object of control – whether it is drugs or finance or whatever.[6]

Second, we also need to make a separation, and indeed this is the aim of this chapter, between citizenship and nationality and, by extension, between citizens and nationals, and, by dissension, between the state and the nation. So far, I have used 'nation-state' in this chapter but henceforth I will separate them. The so-called crisis of sovereignty affects the state-form and the nation-form differently.[7] When the term sovereignty is used in conjunction with one or the other, it has completely different effects. Clearly, sovereignty of the state will designate such issues as borders, law, force and order. By contrast, sovereignty of the nation will raise issues such as self-determination, peoplehood and nationality. Of course, these are related and overlapping issues but they are significantly different. Taken together, these two issues lead me to emphatically state that the idea of 'sovereignty of the nation-state' is as empty of meaning as the idea of 'sovereignty of the moon'. Keeping these two issues in mind – that control can make sense only in relation to its object and that nation and state are very different things – we need to briefly understand how nation and state have become associated.

Narrating sovereignties

These two issues make it very difficult to succinctly reflect on sovereignty with coherence and consistency. But our concern is not with sovereignty or at least not as such. Rather, we want to comprehend how a particular understanding of sovereignty came to function as a grand narrative – a narrative that becomes an imperceptible blueprint through which we interpret our own experiences as well as that of others. Whether this narrative corresponds to something that can be described as the truth of sovereignty is not our concern. Instead, we are concerned with the effects of believing in such truths. How sovereignty was once considered as embodied in the king's body, how it was transferred from the king's body to that of the body of the state, and eventually to that of the body of the people is the narrative that concerns us since it is that narrative that makes us believe in the identification of nation with the state and nationality with citizenship. To put it differently, I am concerned with demonstrating how the nation as the people became the state and how citizenship became nationality. It is this fusion that is the problem I want to identify and it is this fusion that I think is under stress in our age.

It is a common assumption that for a long time in the history of European states, the king's body had come to embody and represent sovereignty.[8] The king was called the sovereign in the sense that inhabitants of his kingdom were subjects of and to his command.[9] This does not mean that the king's command as the sovereign was without checks and balances since making good on sovereign claims would mean nothing if the means of force and coercion were not in place and such means often meant negotiating with those who commanded them.[10] Moreover, the health and wealth of the king's subjects were part of this negotiation.[11] Yet, between roughly the twelfth and seventeenth centuries, the development of the European state, with considerable variations, *essentially* involved articulating the sovereignty embodied in the king's body into the body of the state. According to the sovereignty narrative, it was during the English (1689), American (1776) and French (1789) revolutions, which ostensibly ushered in Euro-American political subjectivity, that the king was disembodied (and decapitated). The king's body was replaced with the body of the people. The invention of the people as the embodiment of sovereignty has become the gift (or curse depending on your point of view) of modern political subjectivity. This was the shift or transition from royal sovereignty to popular sovereignty. Once 'we, the people' replaced the king as sovereign with popular sovereignty, what constitutes a people became *the* problem of sovereignty. That problem was effectively solved by the birth of the nation, or rather, by the invention of the people as the nation. The *ficta persona* of the king became the *ficta persona* of the people. That is how, more or less, the state became the nation-state.

This sketch compresses an immense history into a simple narrative. It is important though to isolate a narrative that we have inherited, or rather through which we see ourselves as heirs, of how the sovereign became the people and then was constituted as a nation.[12] Through this narrative we inherit (and inhabit) the idea that to each people corresponds a nation, to each nation corresponds a state and to each state corresponds a territory. However much the truth of the sovereignty narrative is called into question, its truth effects persist. The sovereignty of the people is often expressed only insofar as it claims a state with a territory and it invents nationhood and peoplehood as corresponding entities.

All of this perhaps sounds quite abstract in the sense of being remote from our lived experience but if you follow international events, you recognize how many struggles for nationhood are entwined if not equated with struggles of statehood. If you followed the debates leading to the Palestinian National Authority submitting a formal request to the United Nations, you will have seen how the words 'Palestinian people', 'Palestinian nation' and 'Palestinian state' were used as synonyms.[13] Although not everyone agrees that there should be a state for 'Palestinian people' and a state for 'Jewish people', it is still considered somewhat 'normal' that there should be a corresponding state for each people. Presumably, such an equation between nationhood (peoplehood) and statehood is also the guarantee of sovereignty.

Given the two issues mentioned earlier, we may wonder whether we are posing the question of sovereignty appropriately. Can we pose it properly from within this narrative, if you like, the overlap between sovereignty, people and nation-state? What is the crisis about? Is it about the sovereignty of the state? Or, is it about the sovereignty of the nation? Or, rather, is it not perhaps about the sovereignty narrative that equates state with nation, nation with people and people with territory? It may well be that the sovereignty narrative is losing its credulity precisely because the state is no longer able to control and contain its territory despite its desperate attempts (missile defence shields and separation walls are two different examples). That is why to pose the question from within this narrative is perhaps to evade and elide the essential question of how we have come to believe in this narrative and what is now making us incredulous about it. I am using the term 'crisis' to designate this moment when a narrative is becoming incredulous and not a state of affairs in which a decisive change for better or worse is imminent. That, I think, is what constitutes the essence of the crisis of sovereignty. The question about citizenship is not about whether sovereignty is waning or waxing. It is that the narrative of the nation–state–people–territory has become contested to the point where it is losing its credibility. If it has become increasingly difficult to maintain the narrative that in each territory occupied by a state, there exists a body of people that defines a nation ('we, the people'), this may be the moment to ask: How does it function? The conquest of the state by the nation, as Hannah Arendt described it, is the question we need to revisit.[14] How the nation became the subject of history, as Michel Foucault called it, is the next question we need to grapple with.[15] Both Arendt and Foucault appear rather abruptly here but they made the most engaging attempts to understand historically how the nation and state became associated through the invention 'we, the people'.[16] I shall shortly turn to their respective genealogies of this question of the fusion between the state and the nation and ask further questions with Derrida's work on the sovereign and the beast.

Two further questions arise. If 'we, the people' is having trouble constituting the sovereignty of the state how do we understand the transformations that are making this possible? What narrative is displacing the narrative of sovereignty? It turns out that what I assumed to be a simple proposition has become more complicated. Yet, it is impossible to discuss 'citizens without frontiers' without a discussion of the state–nation–people narrative or what is defined as 'we, the people'.

How did the nation conquer the state?

If we ask 'what is sovereignty', we will always find ourselves producing a list of features of the nation-state that ostensibly define it such as supremacy, perpetuity, decisionism, absoluteness, non-transferability and completeness.[17] These features then are said to define 'sovereignty'. This assumes that we can give a description of 'sovereignty' without describing the problem that is driving us to define it in the first place.[18]

Following Derrida, albeit with a twist, let us now return to the problem of the king's body briefly.[19] It perhaps goes back to the twelfth and thirteenth centuries when Europeans thought that the king had two bodies: corporeal and spiritual.[20] The corporeal body was the actual body of the sovereign while the body politic was the state. The body politic was embodied in the body of the king. The will of the sovereign was sovereignty over the will of the body politic. The sovereignty of the king was proclaimed by the grace of God. This history is quite well trodden but when and how did the body of the people replace the king's body politic? Of course, the greatest symbol of this is the beheading of the king during the French Revolution, which also invented the idea, along with the American Revolution, 'we, the people'. Clearly, this transformation was neither limited to France nor even Europe. Throughout the nineteenth and twentieth centuries, new 'we, the people' formations burst into history: Decolonization and the emergence of postcolonial nations attest to that. Fast forward to the 1989 revolutions in communist Europe and you will see similar 'we, the people' formations. In fact, still today, we witness the emergence of 'we, the people' throughout the world. The narrative of the sovereign people is not exhausted – yet.

Derrida illustrates that there is a long tradition of representing the sovereign as the beast, at least in European political practice. This is worth remembering. In fact, reading Derrida, we can appreciate how we have come to consider it 'normal' that rulers for centuries have been described with bestiality. Surely, a genealogy of the beast should give us a different perspective on the development of the sovereignty narrative. That is at least what Derrida seems to have attempted.[21] I will not provide even the briefest outline here: As is often the case with Derrida, his lectures amount to no more (or less) than a challenge to think about a genealogy (and deconstruction) of the thing, rather than making an argument about that thing. Be that as it may, it is the gist of his lectures that led me to connect the sovereign beast to 'we, the people' and it goes something like this.

Rather than thinking that sovereignty is somehow an expression of animality or bestiality, as is often done, we ought to understand why the figure of the animal for so long penetrated political thought as a beast. Derrida provides a bewildering list of features such as cruelty, cunningness and feigning that ostensibly defines the animality or bestiality of the sovereign's behaviour. So the relationship is not that the sovereign *is* the beast but how animality and bestiality have been used to define the figure of the sovereign to make, give and take power.[22] As Derrida implies, it is tempting to describe the sovereign beast as a figure of being-above-the-law or being-outside-the-law.[23] But what makes the sovereign beast an effective figure is precisely its double meaning of being-outside-the-law and the boundary of the law.[24] Thus, it can be said that the figure of the sovereign as the beast achieves this effect (and affect) that it is at once the commandment and commander of the law, and the force that enforces it. The list of animals associated with the figure of the 'sovereign as the beast' is also bewildering: It includes actual (e.g. elephant, fox, wolf, tiger, lion, bull, hippopotamus and serpent) and imaginary (werewolf) animals. But the point here, at least in my view, is not that the beast lives inside the sovereign. Rather, for centuries, the sovereign modelled itself after beastly beings it could find or conjure. So the Derridean attempt, it seems to me, is not to find features of the sovereign in animals but to give an account of how the sovereign persistently found itself in animals. That is why the sovereign beast always appears beyond the rational and irrational distinction as it straddles and embodies these two conditions, as the circumstances will dictate.[25]

Given that for so long the figure of the sovereign (king, prince, ruler, head, dictator, president, director) has been founded in the figure of the beast, can we imagine popular sovereignty – invested in and by 'we, the people' – without the qualities of animality and bestiality? The answer Derrida gives is negative since the concept of sovereignty always implies the possibility of positing the self as the originating ruler.[26] The transfer of sovereignty through revolutions from the body of the king to 'we, the people' will be equally suspected in terms of whether this transference will succeed in overcoming the beast.[27] To put it another way, despite the transference from 'people' into 'popular', 'we, the people' or popular sovereignty, rather than cutting the king's head, replaces it with leadership and continues the centuries-long habitus of modelling it after the figure and qualities of the beast. Again, this is not to suggest that political leadership inherits already existing and natural qualities of the sovereign beast but to demonstrate that the institution of political leadership continues to build itself upon qualities that it interprets as natural. This insight is political. It is not biological and does not depend on the independent existence of the qualities of animality and bestiality but how those qualities are produced politically.

We can use Derrida's insight on transference to retrospectively interpret Arendt's account that the invention of the people was a political argument. Arendt offers her analysis in the context of discussing the difference between the rights of man and those of the citizen – a difference introduced during the French Revolution.[28] Briefly, the rights of man refer to the rights that are due to man by virtue of being human. By contrast, the rights of the citizen are those that derive from being a member of a state. Arendt's argument about the futility of this distinction is quite complicated but well known.[29] What concerns me here is her related but separate argument that it was in the nineteenth century that the nation ('we, the people') conquered the state. While many of her contemporaries took it for granted that the prevailing order was of nation-states, Arendt investigated how we come to accept the nation *and* state combination. She identified nationalism as a social movement through which the 'nation conquers the state'.[30] This is an intriguing and promising phrase, yet Arendt did not elaborate on it since perhaps for her its causes were quite self-evident. Instead, she was much more interested in the consequences of this conquest:

> while the state as a legal institution has declared that it must protect the rights of men, its identification with the nation implied the identification of the citizen as national and thereby resulted in the confusion of the rights of men with the rights of national or with national rights.[31]

So the conquest of the state by the nation was of interest to Arendt only insofar as it demonstrated how the rights of men and rights of citizen became confused. But our interest here is different. Arendt also thought that this conquest was related to the rise of liberalism.[32] More specifically, as she later argued, liberalism invented an individual who had liberties only insofar as he (it was a 'he' when it was invented) was a member of a people, a nation. Only when the sovereignty of the king was transferred to the entity called the people ('we, the people') was it possible to imagine the sovereignty of the people *and* of the individual. For Arendt

> the people's sovereignty (different from that of the prince) was not proclaimed by the grace of God but in the name of Man, so that it seemed only natural that the 'inalienable' rights of man would find their guarantee and become an inalienable part of the right of the people to sovereign self-government.[33]

What concerned Arendt was that '. . . man had hardly appeared as a completely emancipated, completely isolated being who carried his dignity within himself without reference to some larger encompassing order, when he disappeared again into a member of a people'.[34] This is a fascinating insight with so much allegorical force that we will return to it at the end this book as a central theme. But let us dwell on it here a bit longer. That Man was discovered at the turn of the nineteenth century was a major accomplishment for Arendt. Not as Man a product of God, not Man as a member of human species, and not Man as a member of any tribe, clan, caste or kinship, and not Man as a member of any class, profession or club; but Man as a political being and as a member of the state. Yet, it is this Man that ever so briefly appeared as a possibility that became absorbed in the entity called 'we, the people'. For Arendt then the emergence of 'we, the people' is the problem of sovereignty as it denied the possibilities of the emancipation of Man.

This insight is crucial and yet it remained rather mysterious as Arendt moved on to the question of minorities, statelessness and human rights.[35] Surely, we cannot simply assume, as Arendt does, that the nineteenth century was marked by a confusion between the rights of man and those of the citizen and between citizenship and nationality. Besides, what exactly does it mean to refer to Man as an emancipated and dignified being without reference to an encompassing order? Can we define Man without reference to any encompassing order? Is this the sovereign subject? Arendt assumes that the state is not such an order but a contractual arrangement ('a legal institution') to which the sovereign subject consents with his free will. To maintain such an image of the state is commendable but did it ever, however briefly as Arendt contends, exist? Anyway, the point is that as soon as man emancipated himself from the command of one beast (king), he was absorbed into the command of another beast ('we, the people'). It is this insight, which Derrida elaborates, which is addressed by Foucault's lectures on sovereignty, and to which we now turn.[36]

The logic as outlined by Foucault proceeds as follows. During the formative years of the state, in the seventeenth and eighteenth centuries, the discourse on the state is dominated, on the one hand, and unsurprisingly, by the sovereignty of the king, on the other, by the history, glory and continuity of the state itself. Foucault says the state incessantly provides a narrative of itself. Yet, by the eighteenth century, the discourse on the state begins to provide a different narrative.[37] It is not so much the content of this narrative that is quite different as the voice with which or the perspective from which it is told: The king's voice was gradually being replaced with that of the nation.[38] Foucault considers this as the birth of a new subject of history in the sense that it begins to tell the history of the state from the perspective of the nation. Yet, in the eighteenth century, the nation is not a unified sovereign entity – 'we, the people' is not yet articulable or sayable. Various social groups call themselves nations. The nobility calls itself a nation. The bourgeoisie calls itself a nation. This fluid, shifting and vague notion of the nation persisted well into the nineteenth century. Foucault shows the paradoxical ways in which the nation was constituted as a subject of history by briefly tracing the struggles between the nobility and monarchy on the one hand and between the nobility and bourgeoisie on the other and with comparative remarks on England and France.[39]

Foucault then describes how the bourgeoisie constituted itself as *the* nation by reworking the idea of the nation.[40] Once the nation was already understood as a sovereign body to replace the king's body, an autonomous body whose existence was neither associated with nor created by the king's body, the question then became what constituted a nation. It was now seen that the existence of a multitude of people, laws, customs, habits, language and institutions was necessary but was not a sufficient condition for the existence of a nation.[41] It was recognized, for example, that just because France has laws, customs and language, this does not make it into a nation. The answer that gradually emerged was that what constitutes a nation in a given territory is its capacity to act as a collective subject to ensure the substantive and historical existence of that nation.[42] As mentioned earlier, until the late eighteenth century, many different groups called themselves 'nations' though that nominally never meant more than a social group, collective or even a club. Yet, while Marx may have defined the emerging bourgeoisie as a dominant class, the bourgeoisie began describing itself as *the* nation.[43] Foucault illustrates how the emergence of the bourgeoisie as a social class was related to its ability to constitute itself as the new subject of history. That it did so by writing its own history as the nation capable of sustaining and enhancing the life of the species-being among other nations within the state is really a key to understanding the relationship between the state and nation. While the aristocracy was dependent on a discourse that allowed the existence of multiple nations within the species-being, the bourgeoisie as a social class articulated itself as the *only* subject of history.[44] In Foucault's words, the bourgeoisie was obliged to assert that 'we are more than one nation among other individuals. But the nation [bourgeoisie] that we constitute is the only one that can effectively constitute the nation [France].'[45] Accordingly, 'the essential function and the historical role of the nation is not defined by its ability to exercise a relationship of domination over other nations' but '. . . its ability to administer itself, to manage, govern, and guarantee the constitution and workings of the figure of the state and of state power'.[46] What Foucault begins to describe here is how *a* nation becomes *the* nation of the state. To put it in Arendt's terms, this is Foucault's account of how the nation conquers the state. If citizenship is understood as membership in the nation, then, this is how citizenship becomes nationality.

To me what Derrida, Arendt and Foucault demonstrate is that the performative force of the sovereignty narrative derives from the invention of 'we, the people' as the subject of history. The question then concerns less the waxing and waning of sovereignty as authority over territory and more how 'we, the people' became its locus. Yet, neither Derrida nor Arendt, and nor Foucault really gives an account of the invention of 'we, the people' as a political event: Arendt perhaps because she is interested in human rights against citizenship rights and Foucault perhaps because he is interested in population and territory, and the apparatus that emerged in the nineteenth century. Elsewhere, Derrida comes close to articulating this question as a genealogy of fraternity but does not pursue it.[47] Yet, Foucault also mentions in passing that rather than being an event that ends the sovereignty of the king, the French Revolution may have 'completed' the work of the sovereign that preceded it.[48] Balibar does indeed make this connection later. Considering the function of race in nationalism, Balibar argues that the invention (which he calls production) of the people was crucial in the birth of the nation.[49] How so?

The invention of 'we, the people' as the nation

The birth of any people is arguably an invention. The birth of *the* people is especially so. Both suggestions are rather controversial and, in certain situations, can be dangerous to make. When Shlomo Sand went as far as to argue that one of the most durably constituted peoples in human history, the Jewish people, was an invention, he courted both controversy and danger.[50] The argument is not that '*a* people' or '*the* people' do not exist. To argue that something is invented is not to argue that it is inexistent. Eric

Hobsbawm and his colleagues, when they argued that all traditions were invented, also met with criticisms though perhaps not the dangers Sand faced.[51] Why? Why is it so difficult to accept that traditions and peoples can be invented entities? Part of the answer is, of course, investments that have been made in such entities and their durable, if not enduring, qualities. If I feel I belong to a people and have made investments throughout my life, not to mention sacrifices to protect it in wars, I probably would not want to hear that being of that people is a recent social invention. It just does not feel right, does it? Yet, the question of why inventions of traditions, peoples and nations are so resisted is not so mysterious if we begin to think a little differently. The fact that they are recent and social creations does not necessarily make them less desirable. Yet there are good reasons why we cannot endure their contingency and fragility.

To reflect on this analytically, Ian Hacking's striking phrase 'making up people' is pertinent. Hacking is concerned with how knowledge classifies people. He wants to know whether we can develop a general theory of making up people for each historic episode of making up people has its irreducible or non-generalizable qualities.[52] Hacking's striking phrase resonates with words so far used such as 'invention' or 'creation'.[53] This phrase sets up an opposition between realism that would have us believe that entities that are of concern to us have always existed and nominalism that would have us believe that these entities are socially constructed and named.[54] Hacking finds both alternatives equally implausible. He speaks, for example, about the avalanche of numbers in the nineteenth century on various categories of people: murderers, prostitutes, drunks, vagrants, the insane, the poor and all sorts of deviants. Where did these come from? Did they not exist before the nineteenth century in some form? Hacking says – and this is what he calls 'dynamic nominalism' – things that people *did* to get classified existed historically but how those things were used to describe, enumerate and classify people are made up and change often. He says

> even national and provincial censuses amazingly show that the categories into which people fall change every ten years. Social change creates new categories of people, but the counting is no mere report of developments. It elaborately, often philanthropically, creates new ways for people to be.[55]

It is the phrase 'new ways for people to be' that is of crucial value for thinking about 'we, the people'.

The categories that Hacking mentions involve many different 'ways to be' such as those of sexuality or ethnicity. Hacking says 'the homosexual and the heterosexual as kinds of persons (as ways to be persons, or as conditions of personhood) came into being only toward the end of the nineteenth century'.[56] Historically, there were sex acts between male and female individuals but it came under familiar and recognizable (sayable and visible) descriptions only in the nineteenth century. And there is no guarantee that these descriptions will live forever. So

> the claim of dynamic nominalism is not that there was a kind of person who came increasingly to be recognized by bureaucrats or by students of human nature, but rather that a kind of person came into being at the same time as the kind itself was being invented.[57]

All this sounds very promising but is Hacking's dynamic nominalism applicable to 'we, the people'? When Hacking talks about 'making up people', he means kinds of people. They are divisions or groups of people such as murderers, dandies, flaneurs, blacks and so on. But can we assume that 'the people' as such is also invented? Can we use a new phrase 'making up we, the people'? Perhaps. While dynamic nominalism is useful to think about the questions posed earlier about why people are so resistant to thinking about entities and themselves as inventions, it does not exactly answer the question of the invention of 'we, the people'. Admittedly, the invention or creation of 'we, the people' is more complicated, involving in some cases centuries of inventive practices. It is one thing to see how the category of murderers has come about; it is another to understand how the category Jewish people was invented. In short, we are concerned with not only the invention of kinds of people but also with the invention of *the* people, more precisely, 'we, the people'. The significant difference is that dandies and murderers as categories of people have never claimed sovereignty. When a group of people claims sovereignty, it fundamentally alters its relationship to itself and others.

Nevertheless, the problem, in essence, is the same. We can argue that versions of dynamic nominalism were present in accounts that we discussed by Arendt and Foucault. Each is trying to investigate how 'we, the people' came to replace the body of the sovereign. Arendt lamented that just when Man emerged from his subject status, he was absorbed back again into being a member of 'we, the people.' For Arendt, it is almost as if Man missed his chance of being a sovereign subject though he had a glimpse of it. By contrast, Foucault does not really lament it but demonstrates that this was how the sovereign subject became possible in the first place. This still leaves open the question of how 'we, the people' was invented and became synonymous with the nation. We must follow Hacking here and insist that there is probably no generalizable process by which we can claim to know how 'we, the people' was created everywhere. While we can draw some general lessons, the invention and creation of each people is irreducible to a generalized schema and must be genealogically investigated.

That is why Sand's argument mentioned earlier about the invention of the Jewish people is so important. But rather than being drawn into the specific genealogies that he traces in the invention of the Jewish people, I will limit myself here to the broader conclusions that he draws from his own account as they are helpful in understanding the association between 'we, the people' and nation. Unsurprisingly, Sand begins with the observation that almost all history books in Israel use the word 'people' (*am* in Hebrew) as a synonym for 'nation'.[58] Although sharing a biblical lineage with European languages and the terminology of 'people' such as the German *folk*, the French *peuple*, and the English *people*, Sand argues that modern Israeli Hebrew *am* does not have a direct association with the word 'people'.[59] Rather, it implies an indivisible unity. This probably explains why it becomes the preferred word to describe the nation as it aims to be an indivisible unity – one of the meanings of sovereignty. By contrast, Sand argues, actual historical connotations of the word people in many languages have been fluid; *am*, for example, means clan, tribe, community, throng or even force in different contexts. This is, in fact, the main conclusion Sand draws from his study: People came to define the (indivisible) nation only in the nineteenth century. Before the nineteenth century, throughout Europe, the word 'people' was used in much more fluid ways to describe various different human gatherings and groupings rather than being a description of *the* people. Mary Poovey documents, for example, how when working men published the People's Charter in 1838 in London (which is considered as the moment of birth of the Chartist movement), it brought into public consciousness working men as *a* people.[60]

The essential point here is that the invention of the people involves inviting us to invest ourselves as though we belong to a unified, singular, homogenous entity from which we draw strength and our identity. Peoplehood, if you like, is what gives stability and endurance to our own selves. It may be easier to make a transition from being a dandy to queer but it is no mean feat, if possible at all, to transform oneself from being, say, Turkish to British. Yet, are such categories as 'Turkish' or 'British' as stable as we think?[61] That Britishness is as fickle as dandyism becomes an unbearable thought. It is this insight that Lie generalizes with a broad-ranging study of what he calls peoplehood. Lie finds modern peoplehood absurd not because it is senseless but because it is hopeless.[62] That is, as he shows, it is hopelessly impossible to gather different groups under a category 'we, the people' as they display heterogeneous features. For Lie, 'we, the people' is absurd *analytically* but it becomes a credible narrative *politically* in which people invest themselves. The question is how the sovereignty narrative institutes its credibility to become an object and subject of this investment.

Counter-narratives of other peoples, *popolo, peuple* and populism

The genealogies provided by Arendt and Foucault, and the inventions of people traced by Sand and Lie are significant contributions towards understanding the birth of 'we, the people'.[63] Yet, these genealogies are strangely silent about the counter-narratives of 'we, the people'. There is also a significant history that runs from the ancient Greek *demos* to Roman *plebeians* to medieval Italian *popolo*.[64] Theirs is a history of those who constitute themselves as claimants of rights against dominant social groups – against which and through which they are defined – often as patricians or aristocrats. It is curious that these two histories (*demos*, plebs and popolo) and 'we, the people' are never analytically brought or staged together. There is a revealing tension between these histories and 'we, the people' narratives often differentiate or distance themselves from these unruly, rapturous and eruptive formations. The respectable, unified and virtuous stories of 'we, the people' are narrated against the unruly mob or herd.[65] Agamben notes this tension is essential to political thought. Agamben insists that

> any interpretation of the political meaning of the term people ought to start from the peculiar fact that in modern European languages this term always indicates also the poor, the underprivileged, and the excluded. The same term names the constitutive political subject as well as the class that is excluded – de facto, if not de jure – from politics.[66]

But, citing Arendt, Agamben notes that 'people' is associated with the excluded not because of compassion though it accounts for why '. . . the term became the equivalent for misfortune and unhappiness . . .'[67] From the beginning of political thinking about 'people', there is an ambiguity whether it means the constitutive dominant or the dominated or both. For Agamben then 'such a widespread and constant semantic ambiguity cannot be accidental: it surely reflects an ambiguity inherent in the nature and function of the concept of people in Western politics'.[68] According to Agamben,

> this also means, however, that the constitution of the human species into a body politic comes into being through a fundamental split and that in the concept of people we can easily recognize the conceptual pair identified earlier as the defining category of the original political structure: naked life (*people*) and political existence (*People*), exclusion and inclusion, *zoē* and *bios*.[69]

Agamben concludes that

> *The concept of people always already contains within itself the fundamental biopolitical fracture. It is what cannot be included in the whole of which it is a part as well as what cannot belong to the whole in which it is always already included.*[70]

Thus, 'If this is the case – if the concept of people necessarily contains within itself the fundamental biopolitical fracture – it is possible to read anew some decisive pages of the history of our century.'[71]

It is this fundamental biopolitical tension that is central to Jacques Rancière and Ernesto Laclau in their understanding of politics and political subjectivity. For both of them, a tension exists between 'we, the people' as a whole and people or peoples as its parts. Thus, a brief discussion of their usage of 'people' is needed but, to give the plot away in advance, I will try to show that their insistence on defining parts with the whole unintentionally inherits the sovereign beast as they search for a politics which is the relation between the whole and its parts.

Always against the background of the ancient Greco-Roman beginnings of modern politics, Rancière identifies a paradox in the Greek polis that scandalizes politics. Politics arises from this paradox or scandal. Rancière deploys a specific language of whole and parts to describe this scandal. The 'whole' is a political community and 'parts' are its constitutive elements. This language enables Rancière to avoid more established sociological and anthropological categories such as 'classes' and 'social groups' since these categories are given names that decide the distribution of parts that constitute the whole. For Rancière, what gives rise to politics is the dispute about what counts as parts. He says that dominant interpretations of ancient politics hitherto read this politics arising from an already constituted community and its already existing conflicts; however, he says, it is actually the other way around. Community is founded on politics that arises from what he calls counting the parts that constitute a community. Politics arises from the counting of parts; and it is disputes on what counts that constitute a political community.

For Rancière, there are two ways of counting: arithmetic and geometric. An arithmetic counting assumes that all is accounted for (hence always a false count); a geometric counting counts those parts that have no part. When counting is arithmetic (as in what is counted), it accounts for what is given; when it is geometric (as in what counts), it accounts for what is not given. Yet, and this is crucial, counts are always false counts as they fall short of taking into account of what actually counts. Politics arises from this paradox of being unable to and yet need to count parts.[72] The scandal arises from those who have no part actually making themselves count.[73] What is scandalous about making themselves count is that the parts that have no part identify themselves to be the whole of the community. It is this audacious identification that is the scandal of politics. This is, for example, the historical significance of demos in Athenian politics. The claim of demos is not only to make itself count but also to constitute itself as the whole. So then the language of those who have no part is not about an essential struggle between the rich and the poor, between this and that class or between this and that social group. Politics is not an opposition between the rich and the poor. Rather, politics is the interruption of an order of domination by the institution of a part of those who have no part.[74]

All of this is intriguing, you might say, but where is the people, let alone 'we, the people', you might ask. For that, Rancière introduces two terms: equality and wrong. The struggles of those who have no part to institute themselves as a part is based on their claims to equality and their declaration of wrong. The claim to inequality is necessary for the declaration of wrong and that declaration is impossible without the assumption of equality of speech and capacity, an equal part in dispute. If indeed 'politics exists wherever the count of parts and parties of society is disturbed by the inscription of a part of those who have no part', it begins when the equality of anyone and everyone is inscribed in the liberty of the people.[75] And 'this liberty of the people is an empty property, an improper property through which those who are nothing purport that their group is identical to the whole of the community'.[76] So the enactment of liberty as the people, its claim, is simultaneously the origins of politics and its scandal.

What is this whole, that the people identifies with? Is it 'we, the people'? Rancière is ambiguous on this point. Sometimes, 'the people' means simply any people. Other times, it means 'we, the people' though Rancière never makes this distinction. Elsewhere, Rancière does indeed say that 'the people' has a double embodiment: It is both the name of a whole community and the name of a part of that community. The gap between these two names of the people is the site of a grievance.[77] While ancient politics understood this gap, says Rancière, modern politics cannot tolerate it. Modern politics cannot accept that the people simultaneously can be both sovereign and not sovereign, whole and part.[78] For Rancière, in modern politics, 'the appearance of the people must be strictly confined to the attributes of sovereignty or the appearance of sovereignty dissolved in favour of the realities of the people as producers'.[79] Yet, as far as I can discern, this distinction remains ambiguous in Rancière when he uses the category 'the people' to elaborate a concept of politics. Clearly, from our perspective, we need a clarification on this point. Without distinguishing between peoples and 'we, the people' and by assuming that 'we, the people' is constituted by a people with an identification – however scandalous – then the appearance of the people in the scene may be nothing other than that of the sovereign beast. I strongly suspect that it is.

Although not concerned with the ancient origins or lineages of modern politics, Laclau seems very close to Rancière in conceptualizing politics. At the centre of his argument is the category of sociopolitical 'demands' articulated by the dominated to the dominant (hegemonic) order. They articulate an exclusion or deprivation as their grievance and it is such demands that constitute a people.[80] As with Rancière then the people is not a given sociological category but something that arises with and from politics. This recognizes that there is a constitutive asymmetry between the political community understood as a whole (the *populus*) and the dominated as its part (the plebs). For Laclau, as for Rancière, it is crucial that the plebs identify themselves with the *populus* as the community as a whole.[81] Thus, as in Rancière, the plebs function both as part of a whole and a part that is the whole.[82] The logic of hegemony that arises from this tension between the part and the whole implies that the whole is 'contaminated' by the part and the part contains the whole. The analytical distinction between the universal and the particular as though they are mutually exclusive opposites is thus false and belies the logic of hegemony.[83] The ambiguity of 'the people' both as the *populus* and the plebs is not a logical contradiction but expresses the logic of hegemony. Where Laclau differs from Rancière is that while Rancière seems to assume that the constitution of the part that has no part will always invoke a politics of emancipation, Laclau does not think that can be determined theoretically.[84] Laclau also differs from Rancière in insisting on limits of philosophical analysis and the necessity of sociological investigation of the ways in which the logic of hegemony constitutes a people.[85]

What is agreeable with both Rancière and Laclau, from our point of view, is their insistence on taking the tension between parts and the whole as the beginnings of politics. What is disagreeable with both is their insistence that politics inevitably if not essentially involves the construction or formation of peoples either as a whole or as parts. More specifically, the requirement that parts must identify with the whole to take part gives the sovereign beast its licence. If, as Rancière says, there is no politics beyond and outside this configuration of the whole and its parts and that 'there is only the order of domination or the disorder of revolt', then how does the configuration itself get disrupted?[86] If we follow Rancière and Laclau in insisting that the whole ('we, the people') and its parts (peoples) are implicated in each other, then to what extent can we imagine politics without the sovereign beast? Both Rancière and Laclau define politics as rupture in a given order but why this rupture should be conceived as the formation of a people, as identification with the whole, is never explained. Laclau says that the formation of a people involves an act of institution and as an act it does not derive its force 'from any logic already operating within the preceding situation' and that 'what is crucial for the emergence of "the people" as a new historical actor is that the unification of plurality of demands in a new configuration is constitutive and not derivative.'[87] It sounds like Laclau is finding a way out of the configuration and we can, with some modifications, agree with him. But he then adds 'it constitutes an *act* in the strict sense, for it does not have its source in anything external to itself'.[88] If this is not Arendt's Man without reference to an encompassing order, then who is Laclau's Man who can act without anything external to himself? In any case, why is the people the one and only 'actor'? Can there not be politics without identification with the people? That sounds odd not because it is impossible but because we are so accustomed to think of ourselves as parts belonging to a whole. We perhaps cannot even bear hearing the sound of 'politics without people'. That is to say, politics without desiring to belong to a whole. Perhaps, there are not two (arithmetic and geometric) but three ways of counting. We shall see in Chapter 3 that perhaps in addition to arithmetic and geometric ways of counting, there is another way of counting.

Sovereignty as a question of a whole and its parts

So far, rather than following the sovereignty question as authority over a given territory, we have been following the problem of absorbing the sovereign subject in a 'we, the people' narrative. The sovereignty narrative defines the political subject as a member of 'we, the people'. Following the figure of the 'sovereign beast', we imagined how it inhabits the political subject called the citizen who has political existence only insofar as it is a member of 'we, the people'. The crisis of sovereignty is not about authority over a given territory but about absorbing the subject into 'we, the people'. In other words, the crisis of sovereignty is not about the supremacy, perpetuity, decisionism, absoluteness, non-transferability and completeness of the state. It is the inability to forge a 'we, the people' and narrate it into a unified entity called the nation. It is not that this is not being tried. It is that this has become difficult – hence the sense in which it is a crisis. Of course, the question arises as to why it has become difficult to sustain the credulity of the sovereignty narrative of 'we, the people'. It is tempting, as many have shown, to jump into words such as post-modernization, globalization and their attendant consequences such as migration, immigration, multiculturalism, diversity and the like and consider this crisis as derivative of these seemingly independent trends. Yes, it is tempting to 'explain' why incredulity towards the sovereignty narrative is getting stronger with external, if extraneous, phenomena. But rather than participating in recounting these extraneous and independent trends, I now want to indicate how we can give an account of ourselves at the beginning of the twenty-first century not merely as members of 'we, the people' but as 'we, the connected'. The point of the next chapter is to illustrate that 'we, the connected' reinstitutes 'we, the people' by shaping our experiences in relation to already existing norms, thus stifling creative, inventive and autonomous enactments of politics without people as a whole and its parts. To put it another way, we have a chance to rescue the political subject from the claws and the pangs of the sovereign beast by naming it as a 'citizen without frontiers'; but just at that moment of possible rescue, we are delivering to the beast the soul of the political subject.

ACT 4. OF DEFENCE: MINUTEMAN CIVIL DEFENSE CORPS

On 30 May 2009, Raul Flores, 29, and his daughter, Brisenia, 9, of Arivaca, Arizona, were murdered by Shawna Forde and two men who were dressed as police officers.[89] Forde was reportedly expelled in 2007 from the Minuteman Civil Defense Corps (MCDC), a national volunteer group which was founded to patrol and monitor US borders against illegal immigrants; it founded a splinter group Minutemen American Defense (MAD). Ostensibly an act of murder became nestled within acts of protecting or defending frontiers against invading aliens by founding a force of violence. Are there no limits when the sovereign beast inhabits the soul of the citizen?

MCDC arose from a fear that too many illegal immigrants are being allowed to pass the US–Mexico border, that many work for drug cartels and participate in drug smuggling and that these aliens commit violent crime. It aims 'to secure United States borders and coastal boundaries against unlawful and unauthorized entry of all individuals, contraband, and foreign military'. The US–Mexico border has become a site of struggle not only because of drug trafficking, illegal labour and suffering, but also because it has come to crystallize the state, sovereignty and people regime more poignantly than any other.

For Minutemen, it is the duty of an American citizen to protect and defend the borders especially when the citizen feels that the state is failing to fulfill its duty. Who does speak when Minutemen say '[w]e, as citizens, are the government, are acting within the social contract of our right to freedom, and we will apply our efforts within the limits of the laws we have created'?[90] However we interpret the thought that 'citizens are the government', the repertoires of action it has enabled are unmistakable. Minutemen emphatically state that

> Composing letters, e-mails and faxes did not make an impression on our public servants. Now we will assert ourselves as citizen representatives of the government. We are citizens who set the example, of the people for the people and by the people.[91]

It is this assertion, this representative claim that reveals the sovereign beast in the soul of the citizen.

But the historical reference point is also as symbolic as it is instructive. We may well remember that the Minuteman is a revolutionary figure etched in the American mind not only through revolutionary imaginaries but also memorialized in statues throughout American cities and towns. The Minutemen were part of the militia that could be 'ready in a minute' for battle.[92] Typically young men, they were self-equipped, decentralized yet well-organized companies that were called into action as elite battle units.[93] Their origins go further back to early colonies, especially in Massachusetts and Plymouth, where the Minutemen were crucial in organizing battles against 'Indians'.[94] So the poignancy of the Minuteman as a figure of battle against invaders and enemies derives from being present in both colonial settlement and revolution.

This figure was enacted during the 2005 monitoring of the US–Mexico border across a 23-mile stretch in Arizona. Minutemen volunteers were recruited and equipped with binoculars and mobile phones. The co-founder, Jim Gilchrist, claims that their early efforts succeeded in preventing border crossing.[95] Minutemen worked by surveying the borders and tracking the movements of those whom they identified as aliens and alerting authorities about these movements through tip-offs.[96] But what happened after that became increasingly a source of frustration for them. For the Minutemen became convinced that their movements were also being monitored by the government and that the government was sharing this information with Mexican authorities.[97]

What kind of figure is the new Minuteman? Although they work within the confines of the law, there have been incidents of guns being brought on patrols and the detaining of migrants at gunpoint. Is this vigilantism acting beyond the law? Or is it the symbolic outsourcing of the sovereign beast? Some scholars argue that the increased militarization of the border creates an acceptable social environment, which legitimates the Minutemen to exact forms of surveillance and violence.[98] It can perhaps be argued that the new Minutemen becomes an extension of the state rather than existing outside its legality (which they themselves deny) or in opposition to the government (as they often claim). The fact that they see themselves operating within the parameters of legality shows them not to be vigilantes but as part of the law-enforcement machine. This becomes evident in their sophisticated technological approach (which mimics Homeland Security), their rhetoric and collaboration with public officials. The Minutemen make the distinction between where the state ends and civil society begins increasingly problematic.[99]

Can what the Minutemen enacted be considered as 'safe citizenship'?[100] Simcox (one of their founders) presents the Minutemen as such.[101] Expelling illegal immigrants makes American citizenship safe, which itself has always been an imaginary which shapes a narrative that would create the aura of the safe citizen as something to be and to return to. This becomes particularly poignant when Gilchrist and Coris use the Trojan horse as an analogy to state 'we have allowed into our midst an army of illegal immigrants who will cause our downfall unless we do something about it.'[102] If we follow this analogy, it also unwittingly functions to provide the view of America as besieged by a more powerful yet culturally inferior foe. Yet, it is also possible to invert the analogy. What if the Minutemen were the people hidden in the belly of the beast? After all, was not the very frontier that they are ostensibly protecting once invaded and occupied by the sovereign beast, which now inhabits their souls?

The acts that produced the 23-mile stretch border as a site of contestation of the sovereignty, state and people regime complicate more than the monopoly of violence or the protection of the physical borders of the state. These acts constitute a racialized border of invisible whiteness. Despite claims by the national executive director that the Minuteman is a non-racist organization,[103] sovereignty of the state is said to be threatened by Mexicans by virtue of their cultural differentiation.[104] What is protected is not so much borders as the frontiers of peoplehood.

Yet, the figure of the new Minutemen remains unstable. Once defined by an act of defiance to oppression from an expropriating state, it now denotes a reversal: a response to the threat of invasion. It is not enough to state nation-alism expresses itself in benevolent or virulent forms, but the very symbol of the patriotic revolutionary through which Minutemen orient themselves can be separated from its 'original' meaning. The flexibility of the term becomes more evident when individuals within the wider project of anti-illegal immigrant vigilant-ism threaten the very sovereignty of the state they cherish. Here the exceptional act of Shawana Forde becomes significant. The act of murder revealed her as the sovereign subject. This is where the Minutemen expose an ambivalent relation-ship to state sovereignty as they are pulled apart in two directions: on the one hand towards civic action, in perhaps the most nationally exemplary sense, and on the other against the state's monopoly of violence.

ACT 5. OF CENSORING: THE GOLDEN SHIELD PROJECT

In November 2000, 300 companies from over 16 countries attended a trade show in Beijing called Security China 2000. The Chinese Communist Party Central Committee Commission for the Comprehensive Management of Social Security was listed among the organizers. It became clear that a central aim of the show was the Golden Shield Project, launched to promote 'the adoption of advanced information and communication technology to strengthen central police control, responsiveness, and crime combating capacity, so as to improve the efficiency and effectiveness of police work'.[105] The show then was the occasion when China's security apparatus announced an ambitious plan: to build a nationwide digital surveillance network, linking national, regional and local security agencies with a panoptic web of surveillance. The act of creating what later came to be called 'The Great Firewall of China' involved creating a massive infrastructure with a management employing thousands of security officers. But it also featured a massive involvement of Western companies to provide hardware, software, logistic and protocol support. It turned out that the act of creating the Golden Shield was not merely a Chinese but a global experiment in creating a sovereign bubble.

In 2009, it was estimated by the China Network Information Center that the number of Chinese internet users had reached 338 million people, surpassing the entire population of the United States.[106] The world leader in internet usage (generally seen as a space of free exchange and uncontrolled access to expression and information) also became a world leader in technologies of restricting access to the internet.

In the 1990s, China Telecom had inaugurated a monumental state project of establishing phone lines and fibre optics across urban centres and actively encouraged internet usage as a strategy of economic development.[107] In the wake of the Tiananmen Square massacre, it is inconceivable that the Chinese security apparatus did not anticipate that this usage would result in anti-government movements. Rather, the Chinese state has attempted to contain a modicum of political criticism within a controlled space. It can be said that it achieved this objective through 'reterritorializing' internet usage by mediating all internet content and service through state-owned (and controlled) corporations.[108] This act by the Chinese state creates unparalleled restrictions on both content and access and is a break with the technologically deterministic norms of internet transactions as a symbol of democratic rights and freedoms. Yet, at the same time, the Golden Shield project is an impossibility. When, for example, serious breaches of health and safety or public official negligence are aired (such as the 2003 HIV crisis in Henan), local pressure follows, information barriers begin to crumble and convictions follow, thus demonstrating the pressure or 'supervisory role' online spaces provide.[109]

Two functions thus emerge from this act whose consequences are contradictory: stymieing political dissent and curbing corruption.[110] This process of filtering limits expression when it is perceived a threat to the central state or the state's vision of the good life (i.e. the blocking of vices, national unity and 'socialism').

It is the unparalleled act of filtering the most expansive conduit of information in human history and offers a more pervasive form of political exclusion than physical borders allow.

How should we name such an act? That it has been named by borrowing a historical figure that has a physical counterpart probably shows the limits of thinking about sovereignty in the present. How can the Great Firewall operate like the Great Wall when the networked infrastructure of the internet constantly implicates the actions of the Chinese state itself in cross-border activities? In 2002, this was manifest in the 'Public Pledge on Self-Discipline for the China Internet Industry' where self-censorship was encouraged, which resulted in even greater regulation to ensure that one was on the right side of government.[111] How long can the Chinese government continue to open markets for direct investment and consumption while at the same time coercing and cajoling Western companies to conform to its internet standards? So far, Google, Yahoo, Microsoft and Skype have all conformed to the 2002 Chinese laws but not without contradictions that maintain a fragile relationship.[112]

What are the boundaries between conformism and complicity? The acts of the Great Firewall and the Great Wall of China here present fundamentally different forms of territorialization and deterritorialization. One may cross a border and become a citizen, sometimes leaving behind certain values or rights one had before while gaining others. However, when a body such as Google is allowed to cross the firewall and enters the world of government regulation, it dynamically interacts and further entrenches the sovereign will.[113] A clear example of the consequences of this was in 2006. By providing incriminating data to authorities, Yahoo contributed to the arrest of Shi Tao, a journalist who disseminated information about government warnings to journalists to stay away from sensitive issues.[114]

It may be that the self-styled vanguard corporations of the internet age see themselves as subverting the Chinese laws. Yet this is always to be compromised if the state itself does not sympathize with the corporation. Google, which has taken a relatively conformist approach to Chinese laws, has recently decided to challenge its restrictive information laws by reshaping its services.[115] While this may initially threaten the firewall, it also reinforces the sovereign will. Is Google acting as the conformist or complicit? Thus, we find Baidu (China's Google-like service) economically competing with Google when the latter takes a politicized stance that contradicts censorship rules.[116] The loss of a market such as China is simply unfathomable even if Google periodically threatens to withdraw (but not disavow) and yet continues to assert its presence in China.[117]

The Golden Shield may be the last gasp of the sovereignty principle and it may buckle under its own weight or succeed in convincing other sovereign beasts to follow, if they have not already done so. Various movements have developed to undermine this possibility both in China and elsewhere and that is why the entire internet infrastructure has now been declared as a site of cyberwar.

ACT 6. OF ESPIONAGE: STUXNET

In June 2010, a malicious code or software called Stuxnet was discovered in Iran. It worked by recalibrating the speed of centrifuges at nuclear power plants to damaging levels while disrupting the monitoring of these levels.[118] Its aim was to damage the progress of uranium enrichment in Natanz, and hinder the progress of the Iranian nuclear programme. According to media reports, expertise from Israel and America helped contribute to the development of the virus.[119] Within 10 months of its initial discovery, the virus was said to have 'spread' to five industrial facilities in Iran.[120] It appears that up to 60 per cent of the infections were located in Iran, with infections also discovered in Indonesia and India.[121]

We are so used to the production and release of malicious code into the internet that we no longer think of it as an act. It is now routine. Yet, when a state produces malicious code to destroy facilities in another state and enacts this with utmost secrecy, we are on a new terrain. The production and dissemination of the Stuxnet virus exemplifies how states traverse frontiers with absolute impunity. It is an act though it is difficult to name it. It is made even more difficult by the fact that we know very little about this act since its subjects never appear. Instead, with the help of internet security professionals and journalists, we have to piece it together from its effects.

Researchers at Symantec, an internet security firm, provided a detailed report on how Stuxnet was created and distributed. Their conclusions are instructive. They surmise that

> attackers would [have needed] to setup a mirrored environment . . . in order to test their code. The full cycle may have taken six months and involved five to ten core developers and numerous other individuals, such as quality assurance and management personnel.[122]

In other words, considerable investment went into the production of this code and it would have been beyond the scope of independent hackers. This was in fact the first sign that there was a sovereign beast behind this code. More tellingly, the researchers also think that 'the attackers would have needed to obtain the digital certificates from someone who may have physically entered the premises of the two companies and stole them, as the two companies are in close physical proximity'. This is another sign of the beast in the sense that the production of the code required more than employing a few geeks, it needed a sophisticated espionage operation. Moreover,

> to infect their target, Stuxnet would need to be introduced into the target environment. This may have occurred by infecting a willing or unknowing third party, such as a contractor who perhaps had access to the facility, or an insider. The original infection may have been introduced by removable drive.

This is yet another sign that the actual release of the offspring of the beast would have been done actually and not simply virtually.

Of course, industrial espionage and sabotage have long been features of how states operate to disrupt, without detection, the critical infrastructure of their enemies without ostensibly threatening their sovereignty. It is clear that the current US administration wishes to end Iran's uranium enrichment programme, and so far it appears that the virus successfully helped stymie the possibility of air strikes.[123] The Stuxnet virus exemplifies a new mode of cyber warfare that cannot be encompassed by traditional warfare categories, and offers possibilities which exceed traditional warfare. According to North Atlantic Treaty Organization (NATO), cyber attacks do not constitute a military action and thus the article concerning self-defence is not immediately extended to the recipient country.[124] When the sovereignty of a state is breached by cyber warfare, it therefore appears that the sovereign will of the offending state remains unrecognizable in its offence. Stuxnet breaches sovereignty, but the conclusive evidence is still elusive.[125] As Farwell and Rohozinski note, Stuxnet means 'states can sidestep culpability even for an event occurring in a segment of cyberspace over which they exert sovereign regulatory authority and jurisdiction'.[126]

There has been much discussion about the meaning of Stuxnet for the future of warfare. But Mary Wollstonecraft Shelley's modern Prometheus, who is horrified by the beast he brings into life, perhaps best captures its truly original aspect as an act.[127] We may well remember that Shelley does not refer to the beast by its name in the title but variously as 'monster', 'demon' and so on. Moreover, it is the cruel and irresponsible creator and not its creation that is the real 'monster' or 'beast' of Shelley's tale. Unlike its modern counterpart, our postmodern beast is not horrified at all and is very pleased with itself to have brought an offspring into this world that it cannot possibly control. Truly, once created, the potential impact and dissemination of such code is beyond the control of anyone and that is why even rather innocuous ones have wrought such havoc over the years. That states are now engaged in the production of code that they cannot control has far-reaching consequences that we have yet to digest.

Apparently, Stuxnet exploits (but also creates) weaknesses that did not exist and such codes have provoked the formation of new virtual borders that do not comply with our images of actual borders. The act produces paradoxical outcomes. On the one hand, it is now argued that the demand for international recognition of sovereignty inaugurated by modern states is in need of extension to hitherto unprotected domains of cyberspace in order to match the new 'cyber conflict age'.[128] The Pentagon's Cyber Command exemplifies this trend where it is offered as a measure of protection of that which it cannot see.[129] On the other hand, Stuxnet severely disrupts sovereignty as cyber-attacks reside and emanate from unknown or at least undisclosed territories.[130] Yet, it becomes woefully inadequate to still try to fit these developments into a Westphalian framework by adding the 'cyber' qualifier to it as Demchak and Dombrowski seem to do: 'Distinguishing criminal laws and activity from national security missions and jurisdiction becomes enormously more manageable when the jurisdictional lines are drawn and recognized in a new cyber-Westphalian process.'[131] I am afraid the sovereign beast now lives in a much more clandestine, uncontrollable and tentacular form through its new offspring than the Westphalian image would have us believe.

ACT 7. OF ASSASSINATION: DRONES

On 18 June 2004, American forces in an air attack in South Waziristan, Pakistan, killed a Pashtun commander, Nek Muhammed Wazir. Until 3 October 2006, only a few people knew how this attack was carried out. On that date, a PBS Frontline programme revealed that it was by a Hellfire missile fired from an unmanned Predator airplane.[132]

The United States has long been involved in 'targeted killings' operated from its various bases around the world. But the use of unmanned aerial vehicles to fire missiles operated from a base in the US mainland was new. When in 2004 the United States Air Force Unmanned Aerial Vehicle Battlelab unveiled its first UAVs (what came to be known as drones) capable of combat operations, experts suspected their actual was imminent.[133]

Since 2004, drones have been used in Northwest Pakistan to attack militants throughout the border region between Afghanistan and Pakistan – a vast site of battle for supremacy in Afghanistan and arguably in Pakistan. The attacks are controlled from the Creech Air Force base in Nevada, where pilots remotely operate the UAVs through joysticks and computer screens.[134] Some commentators have noted that this becomes a surreal situation where entrance and exit from the combat zone mimics more conventional patterns of a 'day job'.[135] Others have commented on the effectiveness of these attacks by focusing on killing.[136]

Yet, the appearance of a new species of acts – killing at a distance – and ostensibly protecting the boundaries of sovereignty while simultaneously stretching them from thousands of miles away, arguably has serious consequences for where the frontiers of a state begin and end. Although the drone attacks are seen as a new strategy that seeks to eliminate risk from war and improve combat capabilities, its consequences – intended or otherwise – reach farther and deeper than many acts of war with which we are familiar. A commander of one of the units, Colonel Felder, may think that killing at a distance will enable hitting targets without risking the lives of pilots; but the new risks that it creates are yet hardly imaginable.[137] In the name of 'we, the people' states have authorized themselves to act across frontiers and kill people, including their own citizens, at a distance.[138]

Acts of killing at a distance join the already existing repertoire of cross-border 'targeted killings' that are already sanctioned under International Humanitarian Law (under the right to self-defence against those who are participating in hostilities). Although acts of killing at a distance technically come into conflict with Human Rights Law concerning the prevention of 'arbitrary deprivation of life', this conflict is not isolated to drone attacks. President Clinton's authorization of cruise missile strikes in the 1990s can be said to pose similar issues.[139] The notion that drones penetrate airspace that hasn't been penetrated before renders these acts of killing somewhat different from other forms of cross-border strikes. What is particularly unique about drone attacks, coupled with the war on terror context, is the issues they raise in terms of sovereignty and accountability. These are attacks that mimic sustained conventional patterns of targeted killings during times of war rather than singular retaliation incidents.

These drone attacks could be interpreted as an enactment of the rights bestowed under Article 51 of the United Nations Charter that

> Nothing in the present Charter shall impair the inherent right of individual or collective self-defence if an armed attack occurs against a Member of the United Nations, until the Security Council has taken measures necessary to maintain international peace and security.[140]

Arguably, the drones do not represent any significant departure from the sovereign will exercising self-defence.[141] Yet, the United States is not at war with Pakistan but is conducting military operations within Pakistan. To assert this as a violation of sovereignty neglects the way sovereignty is performed through complex territorial arrangements and the struggle over Afghanistan traverses frontiers.[142] Praust provides a hypothetical example to illustrate the justification of why a state can breach sovereignty in such situations. He surmises that if non-state terrorists operate from within Mexico and attack the United States from across the border with rockets, the United States should not wait for permission to defend itself if such actions cost further loss of life.[143] The logic here is that the priority of self-defence supersedes territorial sovereignty. To put it differently, states consider traversing frontiers as also their sovereign right.

What such logic legitimates is that the state can perform itself beyond its borders through acts of killing without occupation, invasion or even conventional air attacks with manned vehicles. The acts of killing at a distance with drones provide a telling comparison with no-fly zones that were invented in the 1990s. The first no-fly zone, used against the Iraqi regime in 1991 and citing United Nations Security Council Resolution 688, prohibited Iraqi planes flying into an area protecting the Kurdish population. Since 1991, no-fly zones have been used in Bosnia and Herzegovina, from 1993 to 1995 and more recently in Libya in 2011.[144] Although each sovereign state has an internationally recognized right to establish no-fly zones within its territorial borders, its use for regulating actions of another state is a new development and its legal foundations are obscure. Considered together with drones the control of no-fly and fly zones gives a topological image of how sovereign frontiers are enacted, one which departs from the neatly drawn borders of a topographical map.[145]

ACT 8. OF WRITING: BANKSY

When Banksy arrived in early August 2005 in the occupied territories of the West Bank as 'an ultimate activity holiday destination for graffiti writers', the Israeli security apparatus must have wished he had gone to Ibiza instead. Apparently at gunpoint and with Israeli forces shooting in the air, Banksy drew nine stunning images on what the International Security Council deems is an illegal separation wall stretching for 425-miles (680-kilometres) and made of high concrete walls and razor-wire fences.[146] The images depict a blue sky through the wall, a beach, a ladder, a girl being uplifted by balloons and a cutout.[147] Banksy considers this an act of defiance against a wall that effectively turns the West Bank into the world's largest open air prison.

Given that Banksy was risking the wrath of security forces but also his own very identity – Banksy remains an anonymous artist – it is quite a poignant act. It effectively turns a site of oppression into a site of contestation by symbolic and cultural capital that are not available to those who are engaged in the struggle itself. It is an act of solidarity traversing frontiers, which calls into question the borders that are being erected. When Banksy depicts cracks in the wall, it translates imagination into action. Banksy's act is not simply mocking, it deliberately reflects the limits of art in the face of the sovereign beast. The sovereignty of the state is rendered brutal through the deceptively peaceful images that reflect a perfect Israel beyond the wall, which the sovereign beast can only fantasize about (thus not a depiction intended for Palestinians). It is perhaps not the images themselves but Banksy's interruption in the concrete, breaking the continuous grey, that awakes us to the prison of sovereignty.

Yet, Banksy's act is not without its ambivalences. On his website, Banksy recalls that when he thanked a Palestinian man for positively commenting on his art, he was met with the response '[w]e don't want it to be beautiful, we hate this wall. Go home.'[148] Where do the boundaries of aesthetics cross those of politics?

How did the wall come about in the first place? What is the originary act that Banksy's act exposes? The idea that Israelis and Palestinians could be separated by a barrier circulated in the mid 1990s, reflecting the dampened support for economic integration and the continuation of productive political engagement on the part of the Israeli state. In 1995 Yitzhak Rabin established the Shahal Commission, which looked into the construction of a barrier to separate Palestinians and Israelis.[149] The plan faded with Shimon Peres, but was revitalized through Benjamin Netanyahu and Ehud Barak, and became implemented by an initially reluctant Ariel Sharon.[150] The building of a barrier between the West Bank and Israel began in 2002, together with an escalation of further roadblocks, gates and internal fences. The timing of this project was prompted by the 2001 al Aqsa intifada, an increase in suicide bombings and public support for the wall. Sharon became convinced that the wall was a viable solution.[151]

Is the wall a means to secure the sovereignty of Israel or is it a way of sequestering and confining the Palestinians within unlivable borders?[152] It is probably both and neither. This reframing of borders extends beyond the ceasefire line devised at the end of 1948–9 that led to the creation of Israel. According to B'Tselem, 85 per cent of the wall does not run along the Green Line, thus creating difficulties for Palestinians trying to gain access to farmland.[153] At the same time as the wall seeks to settle Israel's long-disputed borders, it makes the visibility of internal others particularly problematic. Some 10 per cent of the Palestinian population falls on the Israeli side without being included into the Israeli population, while their farmland is annexed into Israeli territory.[154] In 2003, the UN General Assembly passed a resolution calling for Israel to cease construction of the wall.[155] Israel ignored the resolution and the matter was taken to the International Court of Justice (ICJ). The ICJ decided that the barrier was 'contrary to international law'.[156] Israel did not recognize the jurisdiction of the ICJ.[157] This act of defiance symbolizes the reassertion of territorial sovereignty against an international court of law.

Why has this wall become existential to Israel? The wall functions to separate Israel from Palestine. But it also regulates the 'enclosed' populations within the Israeli state to fortify its sovereignty against those without and also those within. The wall is doing more than fixing a border between Israel and Palestine; it also isolates towns such as Bethlehem, Qalqilyah and Tulkarm from both the West Bank and Israel.[158] It is possible to argue that Israel is following a 'logic of encystation': that simultaneously the wall reflects the sovereign power with its de facto borders and projects an imagined community through the idea of the 'Land of Israel' and the Law of Return.[159] It can also be argued that while the wall acts as a technology of 'discipline' and 'containment' for the Palestinians, it acts as a 'technology of freedom' for those on the Israeli side in the sense of promising movement without fear.[160] The wall constitutes Palestinian subjects as illegal in their movements, and through this, an illegal economy intensifies as vendors travel to Jerusalem from towns where there is little market for their products (though their presence and infiltration is a testament to resisting normalization).[161] Moreover, it also functions to ease concerns facing settlers who have come to direct the agenda, thus giving it the label of a 'Settlers Wall'.[162] The wall also ostensibly prevents illegal immigration from across the Egyptian border. This is one of the reasons why the border will be split in two, with one running from Eilat and the other by the Gaza strip.[163] The wall currently constitutes roughly 50–60 per cent of Israel's borders.[164]

Yet, after all these justifications, rationalizations and reasons, the wall may well represent something else, the sovereign beast. This became most clear when Netanyahu stated that '[t]his is a strategic decision to secure Israel's Jewish and democratic character.'[165] Isn't that the sovereign beast speaking? The impossible dream is purification: to create a people without contamination, a demos without difference and democracy without argument.[166]

ACT 9. OF SOLIDARITY: STRANGERS INTO CITIZENS

On 7 May 2007, an unprecedented rally took place in Trafalgar Square, London. Thousands of migrant workers, faith groups, trade unions and civic organizations assembled together in what was claimed to be one of the 'largest ever call[s] for migrant justice'.[167] Their demands were simple and modest: illegal(ized) migrants who have resided in the United Kingdom for 4 years or more should be granted a 'two-year work permit'.[168] After the permit expires, subject to appropriate references, they are to be given leave to remain.[169] The organizers of the rally agreed with the Home Office that immigration should be restricted but argued that some '300,000 people already in the UK. . . should be given the legal right to stay'.[170] Essentially the protest was about creating a 'pathway to citizenship' for long-term undocumented migrants residing in the United Kingdom.[171] As the argument goes, those who have become economically and socially settled in the country are entitled to the same rights as citizens.

Although unprecedented, these demands could hardly be called radical or revolutionary since they essentially accept 'we, the people' and its birthright principle. Their simplicity and modesty become both their performative force and constative conservatism. Nonetheless, what makes them not only unprecedented but also potentially transformative is their declaration: a demand to open citizenship to strangers and the shift of discussion from roots to rights.

The 2007 protest was organized by Strangers into Citizens. The campaign seeks to transform irregular migrant workers who are denied citizenship status, into full-fledged citizens who have legal avenues to both work and pay taxes.[172] The campaign was launched in November 2006 by the Citizens Organizing Foundation, a civil society organization which consists of various faith groups, unions and community organizations.[173] The effective and expressive aim of Strangers into Citizens is the regularization of long-term undocumented migrants in order to integrate them into the mainstream economy. This is justified in terms of the benefits procured by the residents, lessening their vulnerability to the informal labour market.[174] Regularization is also justified as a benefit to the British economy, saving costs on 'removal' while also bringing some £3bn to the economy.[175]

Another purpose to regularization is to free the UK border authority's resources so as to better direct their attention to migrants involved in criminal activity,[176] while simultaneously enabling local authorities to keep an account of the existence, and thus the needs of, local populations.[177] As the campaign argues, both of these functions are increasingly difficult to achieve if unmanageably large sections of the population are (or become) criminalized to the point of non-existence before the law by the fact that they do not have the correct papers. Furthermore, the UKBA's exponential growth in spending on detention and deportation has not even caused a dent in undocumented migration, and successive governments have failed to deport the majority of undocumented people. Together these surface as major economic reasons (setting the political positioning) to adopt the process of regularization.[178] The campaign argues that more money can be saved through amnesty. Strangers into Citizens 'offers a solution to that problem [of undocumented migrants], in a way that is compatible with – indeed supports – the enforcement measures being taken by the Government'.[179] The aforementioned amnesty or 'path to citizenship' is thus both for the benefit of the state and the individual.

The moral impetus of the campaign, coupled with a growing need to address state and public concerns about immigration and the economy, has led to increased support in mainstream politics. Subsequently, six councils, including the Greater London Authority, passed 'motions in favour of Strangers into Citizens'.[180] With regards to the 2007 protest, its political visibility was intensified by one of the speakers at the rally, the Labour MP for Dagenham Jon Cruddas. A month after the protest, Jon Cruddas highlighted his support for the Strangers into Citizens campaign during a Commons Debate, stating that the regularization measures would save public expenditure, would not be causally linked to a rise in illegal immigration and would benefit migrants.[181]

Nevertheless, the act of the 2007 protest transcends both this new largely unimplemented managerial policy for dealing with the problem of undocumented migrants and how the issues manifested in parliament. It contextualizes Squire's assertion that Strangers into Citizens questions who has the right to shape a social movement.[182] British unionism has been historically active and movements demanding a deepening of social rights are nothing new. What sets the 2007 protest apart are the participating subjects. This protest was specifically geared towards a shared recognition of social and civil rights regardless of one's country of origin or status. In spite of the 'worker-citizen'[183] being a crucial figure in the Strangers into Citizens narrative, the act of the protest challenged the nationality of this figure.

Yet, the act also shows the paradoxes (and perils) of participating in the 'we, the people' narrative. Why the organizers of the 2007 protest felt the need for migrants to show their belonging to Britain is perhaps clear. But why the established symbols of the narrative were chosen reveals how an act that can potentially produce counter-narratives can reproduce perhaps the worst symbols of the dominant narrative. That the organizers called on those taking part 'to wave the Union Jack' is both misguided and misjudged.[184] In an age of 'British jobs for British workers', we can assume that this claim to Britishness was meant to be the icing on the cake for politicians and the public who deploy politico-cultural identity to further justify denying opportunities to those without British citizenship. Yet many workers chose to 'wave flags from their own countries' as if to demonstrate that playing with flags for political symbolism amounts to playing with fire. This illustrates what Squire calls the blurring between 'citizens and irregular migrants'.[185]

This act of migrants demanding rights in the streets of London was a presentation of subjects who could choose to speak on their own terms for inclusion, yet in the process redefine the criteria of inclusion. But the act of citizens demanding rights for others is an illustration of the capacity of citizens to act without frontiers not for humanitarian but for political reasons. As such these acts join others across other states in a growing movement towards recognizing that *sans-papiers* (those 'without papers') have the right to have rights.[186]

Notes

1   M. B. Salter, *Politics at the Airport* (Minneapolis: University of Minnesota Press, 2008); M. B. Salter, *Rights of Passage: The Passport in International Relations* (Boulder, CO: Lynne Rienner Publishers, 2003); J. Torpey, *The Invention of the Passport: Surveillance, Citizenship and the State* (Cambridge: Cambridge University Press, 2000).

2   It is not too provocative to assert that there is no such thing as the state as Dunn says. K. C. Dunn, 'There Is No Such Thing as the State: Discourse, Effect and Performativity,' *Forum for Development Studies* 37, 1 (2010).

3   S. Sassen, *Losing Control?: Sovereignty in an Age of Globalization* (New York: Columbia University Press, 1996). Sassen was among the first to make the case for a critical evaluation of the question as a zero-sum game. H. Spruyt, *The Sovereign State and Its Competitors: An Analysis of Systems Change* (Princeton, NJ: Princeton University Press, 1996). Spruyt was also a notable contribution. Cooley and Spruyt, for example, define sovereignty 'in strict terms it denotes that the people within recognized territorial borders are masters of their own fate. No higher juridical authority exists above that of the national government. And all states are equal in international law. . . . [Yet] the world is replete with instances where sovereignty appears fragile'. A. Cooley and H. Spruyt, *Contracting States: Sovereign Transfers in International Relations* (Princeton, NJ: Princeton University Press, 2009), 1.

4   Admittedly, there are various and contested conceptions of sovereignty. It is not only a contested but also a fluid concept changing over time. But its basic definition as authority and control over a given territory and its population is the one that is increasingly being challenged by globalization. J.-M. Guéhenno, *The End of the Nation-State* (Minneapolis: University of Minnesota Press, 1995).

5   R. Prokhovnik, *Sovereignties: History, Theory and Practice* (Basingstoke: Palgrave Macmillan, 2007).

6   This is, of course, not an original argument and many geographers and political sociologists have made it. P. Banerjee, 'Frontiers and Borders: Spaces of Sharing, Spaces of Conflict,' in *Space, Territory and the State: New Readings in International Politics*, ed. R. Samaddar (Hyderabad: Orient Longman, 2002); S. Elden, *Terror and Territory: The Spatial Extent of Sovereignty* (Minneapolis: University of Minnesota Press, 2009). Yet, it is easily neglected in debates over globalization, sovereignty and citizenship.

7   I am referring to B. R. Anderson, *Imagined Communities: Reflections on the Origin and Spread of Nationalism* (London: Verso, 1983). It has become more difficult to imagine nations as communities as unified and homogeneous peoples.

8   F. H. Hinsley, *Sovereignty* (Cambridge: Cambridge University Press, 1986); A. Linklater, 'Citizenship and Sovereignty in the Post-Westphalian State,' *European Journal of International Relations* 2, 1 (1996); Spruyt, *The Sovereign State and Its Competitors: An Analysis of Systems Change*.

9   A classic study is by J. R. Strayer, *On the Medieval Origins of the Modern State* (Princeton, NJ: Princeton University Press, 1971). Also a significant

study is now a standard classic: E. H. Kantorowicz, *The King's Two Bodies* (Princeton, NJ: Princeton University Press, 1957).

10 G. Poggi, *The Development of the Modern State: A Sociological Introduction* (Stanford, CA: Stanford University Press, 1978); G. Poggi, *The State: Its Nature, Development, and Prospects* (Cambridge: Polity Press, 1990); Strayer, *On the Medieval Origins of the Modern State*; C. Tilly, *Coercion, Capital, and European States, Ad 990–1992* (Cambridge, MA: Blackwell, 1992); C. Tilly, *Reflections on the History of European State-Making*, ed. C. Tilly (Princeton, NJ: Princeton University Press, 1975).

11 Foucault meticulously illustrated the importance of the wealth and health of its subjects in the development of great European monarchies. M. Foucault, *The Birth of Biopolitics: Lectures at the Collége de France, 1978–79*, ed. M. Senellart (Basingstoke: Palgrave Macmillan, 2008); M. Foucault, *Security, Territory, Population: Lectures at the Collége de France, 1977–78*, ed. M. Senellart and A. I. Davidson (Basingstoke: Palgrave Macmillan, 2007).

12 I am using the term 'narrative' when 'discourse' or 'ideology' would also be alternatives. But I shall stay with the term 'narrative' for both its scholarly and popular connotations and for evading a discussion on the difference between discourse and ideology.

13 UN News Centre, Security Council refers Palestinian application to UN membership committee, 28 September 2011, http://goo.gl/MsbiS [cited 4 November 2011].

14 H. Arendt, 'The Nation,' in *Essays in Understanding 1930–1954: Formation, Exile, and Totalitarianism* (New York: Schocken Books, 2005), 209.

15 M. Foucault, *Society Must be Defended: Lectures at the Collège de France, 1975–76*, ed. M. Bertani and A. Fontana, trans. D. Macey (New York: Picador, 2003), 203.

16 Arendt and Foucault were the first to provide genealogies of 'we, the people' and yet these were preliminary and tentative. This is not because they lacked analytical tools but because the crisis that has become more transparent to us was only dimly visible in the 1940s and 1970s. We are still part of this crisis and we cannot foresee what is yet to come but we can contribute to it by sharpening the images of the crisis and continuing with the genealogies that Arendt and Foucault initiated.

17 Brown, *Walled States, Waning Sovereignty*, 22.

18 See Q. Skinner, 'The Sovereign State: A Genealogy,' in *Sovereignty in Fragments: The Past, Present and Future of a Contested Concept*, ed. H. Kalmo and Q. Skinner (Cambridge: Cambridge University Press, 2010).

19 The representation of the sovereign as beast has a long tradition. As Walker says 'Hobbes already knew [sovereignty] to be a very strange beast indeed'. R. B. J. Walker, *After the Globe, before the World* (London: Routledge, 2010), 194. But Derrida drew attention to the mutual constitution of the sovereign and the beast. He insists repeatedly that the sovereign and the beast implicate each other. J. Derrida, *The Beast & the Sovereign*, ed. M. Lisse et al., trans. G. Bennington, vol. 1, *The Seminars of Jacques Derrida* (Chicago: Chicago University Press, 2009).

20 Kantorowicz, *The King's Two Bodies*.

21 There are 13 lectures that range from Aristotle to Machiavelli, Hobbes and
    Bodin and also discussions of modern figures such as Lacan, Deleuze and
    Agamben.
22 Derrida says 'We should never be content to say, in spite of temptations,
    something like: the social, the political, and in them the value or exercise of
    sovereignty are merely disguised manifestations of animal force, or conflicts of
    pure force, the truth of which is given to us by zoology, that is to say at bottom
    bestiality or barbarity or inhuman cruelty. It would and will be possible to
    quote a thousand and one statements that rely on this schema, a whole archive
    or a worldwide library. We could also invert the sense of the analogy and
    recognize, on the contrary, not that political man is still animal but that the
    animal is already political . . .' Derrida, *The Beast & the Sovereign*, 14.
23 Ibid., 16–17.
24 Ibid., 17.
25 Derrida illustrates this with an example from N. Chomsky, *Rogue States: The
    Rule of Force in World Affairs* (London: Pluto, 2000). He takes a United States
    Strategic Command, Stratcom, document to show that scaring the enemy with
    irrational behaviour is among its *rational* strategies. Derrida, *The Beast & the
    Sovereign*, 80.
26 Derrida says With argues that since sovereignty implies this possibility whether
    it is a prince, a dictator, a subject-citizen, or the people will make no difference
    since the figure of the master sovereign will be transferred. Derrida, *The Beast
    & the Sovereign*, 67.
27 Ibid., 290. 'As for the transfer of sovereignty, for example, the revolution as
    transfer of sovereignty, however violent and bloody it might be as a taking of
    power (and a political revolution that was not a revolution of the political and
    a poetic revolution in the nonrestrictive sense I was defining the other day – a
    political revolution without a poetic revolution of the political is never more
    than a transfer of sovereignty and a handing over of power) – what I am here
    designating as transfer of sovereignty clearly situates the essential features
    of the problem.' Similarly, 'The trial of the king and his decapitation would
    be, in my opinion or according to one of the readings I would be tempted to
    propose, one of these transfers of sovereignty, a transfer that is at one and the
    same time fictional, narrative, theatrical, representational, performative, which
    does not for all that prevent it from being terribly effective and bloody. In all
    these deployments of ceremonial representation and theatrical cult, in all these
    simulacra, blood flows nonetheless, no less cruelly and no less irreversibly – the
    blood of the elephant like the blood of the absolute monarch. The beast and
    the sovereign bleed, even marionettes bleed.'
28 There have been discussions about Arendt's insight by G. Agamben, *Homo
    Sacer: Sovereign Power and Bare Life* (Stanford, CA: Stanford University Press,
    1998); É. Balibar, '(De)Constructing the Human as Human Institution: A
    Reflection on the Coherence of Hannah Arendt's Practical Philosophy,' *Social
    Research* 74 (2007); É. Balibar, *Masses, Classes, Ideas: Studies on Politics and
    Philosophy before and after Marx*, trans. J. Swenson (London: Routledge,
    1994); J. Derrida, *On Cosmopolitanism and Forgiveness* (Routledge, 2001);
    J.-F. Lyotard, 'The Other's Rights,' in *On Human Rights*, ed. S. L. Hurley
    and S. Shute (New York, NY: Basic Books, 1993); J. Rancière, *Dissensus:*

On Politics and Aesthetics, ed. S. Corcoran, trans. S. Corcoran (London: Continuum, 2010), 62–75; S. Žižek, 'Against Human Rights,' *New Left Review* 34 (2005). I do not need to discuss this literature here as my point is about Arendt's much more specific insight about the relationship between the nation and the state.

29 See C. Douzinas, *The End of Human Rights: Critical Legal Thought at the Turn of the Century* (Oxford: Hart, 2000).

30 Arendt, 'The Nation,' 206–8.

31 Ibid., 208.

32 Ibid., 209.

33 H. Arendt, *The Origins of Totalitarianism* (New York: Harcourt Brace Jovanovich, 1951), 291.

34 Ibid.

35 Ibid., 292.

36 I say Foucault returns to this insight not because I have evidence but because Foucault poses these questions in his Collège de France lectures on 18 February and 10 March 1976. Foucault, *Society Must Be Defended: Lectures at the Collège de France, 1975–76*, 141–66, 215–38.

37 Ibid., 141–2.

38 Ibid., 142.

39 Ibid., 143–4.

40 Ibid., 215.

41 Ibid., 220.

42 Ibid., 221.

43 K. Marx and F. Engels, *The Communist Manifesto: A Modern Edition* (London: Verso, 1998).

44 Foucault, *Society Must Be Defended: Lectures at the Collège de France, 1975–76*, 221.

45 Ibid., 222.

46 Ibid., 223.

47 See J. Derrida, *Politics of Friendship* (London: Verso, 1997).

48 Foucault, *Society Must Be Defended: Lectures at the Collège de France, 1975–76*, 232.

49 Balibar says 'In the last analysis, the overlapping of [nationalism and racism] goes back to the circumstances in which the nation states, established upon historically contested territories, have striven to control population movements, and to the very production of the "people" as a political community taking precedence over class divisions.' É. Balibar, "Racism and Nationalism," in *Race, Nation, Class: Ambiguous Identities*, ed. Immanuel Wallerstein and Étienne Balibar (London: Verso, 1991), 48.

50 S. Sand, *The Invention of the Jewish People* (London: Verso, 2009).

51 E. Hobsbawm and T. Ranger, eds, *The Invention of Tradition* (Cambridge: Cambridge University Press, 1992).

52 I. Hacking, *Historical Ontology* (Cambridge, MA: Harvard University Press, 2002), 100.

53 Hacking calls his approach 'dynamic nominalism'. Ibid.; I. Hacking, 'Kinds of People: Moving Targets,' *Proceedings of the British academy* 151 (2007).

54 I. Hacking, *The Social Construction of What?* (Cambridge: Harvard University Press, 2000).

55 Hacking, *Historical Ontology*, 100.

56 Ibid., 103.

57 Ibid., 106.

58 Sand, *The Invention of the Jewish People*, 24.

59 Ibid., 24–5.

60 M. Poovey, *Making a Social Body: British Cultural Formation, 1830–1864* (Chicago: University of Chicago Press, 1995), 126.

61 For an insightful study of how young people negotiate such unbearable thoughts, see V. Ware, *Who Cares About Britishness: A Global View of the National Identity Debate* (London: Arcadia Books, 2007).

62 J. Lie, *Modern Peoplehood* (Cambridge: Harvard University Press, 2004), 11.

63 Bamberg and Andrews, *Considering Counter-Narratives: Narrating, Resisting, Making Sense*, x.

64 Although there are voluminous literatures about each of these peoples (demos, plebs and popolo), stunningly Max Weber's genealogies of the transformations of these things still remain as evocative and authoritative as ever. See M. Weber et al., *Economy and Society: An Outline of Interpretive Sociology*, ed. G. Roth and C. Wittich, trans. E. Fischoff, 2 vols (Berkeley: University of California Press, 1978). It is this trajectory that inspires much of critical political theory. See J. Rancière, *Disagreement: Politics and Philosophy*, trans. J. Rose (Minneapolis: University of Minnesota Press, 1998).

65 Ernesto Laclau calls this 'the denigration of the masses'. See E. Laclau, *On Populist Reason* (London: Verso, 2005).

66 G. Agamben, *Means without End: Notes on Politics* (Minneapolis: University of Minnesota Press, 2000), 29.

67 Ibid., 30.

68 Ibid., 31.

69 Ibid., 31–2.

70 Ibid., 32 (italics original).

71 Ibid., 33.

72 Rancière, *Disagreement: Politics and Philosophy*, 6.

73 Ibid., 9.

74 Ibid., 11.

75 Ibid., 123.

76 Ibid., 123–4.

77 J. Rancière, *On the Shores of Politics*, trans. L. Heron (London: Verso, 1995), 97.

78 Ibid., 99.

79 Ibid.

80 Laclau, *On Populist Reason*, 123.

81 Ibid., 224.

82 Ibid., 225.

83 Ibid., 226.

84 Ibid., 246.

85 Ibid., 248.

86 Rancière, *Disagreement: Politics and Philosophy*, 12.

87 Laclau, *On Populist Reason*, 228.

88 Ibid.

89 BBC. 2011. Activist Shawna Forde Guilty of Migrants' Murder. BBC, 15 February 2011 [cited 20 February 2011]. Source: http://goo.gl/u46He

90 C. Mercer. 2010. About Us. MinutemanHQ.com 2010 [cited 29 January 2011]. Source: http://goo.gl/Kegx3

91 Ibid.

92 J. R. Galvin, *The Minute Men: The First Fight: Myths & Realities of the American Revolution*, 2nd ed., rev. ed. (Dulles, Virginia: Brassey's Book, 1989).

93 Ibid., 6–7.

94 Ibid., 7–8.

95 J. Gilchrist and J. R. Corsi, *Minutemen: The Battle to Secure America's Borders* (Los Angeles: World Ahead Publishing, 2006).

96 Tucson Chapter Leader. 2007. Minutemen Shock and Awe in Green Valley, Az [web page]. The Minutemen Civil Defense Corps Border Operations Headquarters 2007 [cited 29 January 2011]. Source: http://goo.gl/Km9vs

97 Gilchrist and Corsi, *Minutemen: The Battle to Secure America's Borders*.

98 S. H. Kil et al., 'Securing Borders: Patriotism, Vigilantism and the Brutalization of the American Public,' *Immigration, Crime and Justice* 13 (2009).

99 Ibid.

100 R. L. Doty, 'Do You Know if Your Borders Are Secure?' *International Political Sociology* 4, 1 (2010); C. Weber, 'Citizenship, Security, Humanity,' *International Political Sociology* 4, 1 (2010).

101 R. L. Doty, 'Do You Know If Your Borders Are Secure?' ibid.

102 Gilchrist and Corsi, *Minutemen: The Battle to Secure America's Borders*, 20.

103 J. Shacat. 2008. Radio Show Focuses on Immigration Douglas Dispatch, 26 July 2008 [cited 20 February 2011]. Source: http://goo.gl/xVLLT

104 J. Grimm, 'Patrolling Whiteness: Framing the Minuteman Project on the Evening News,' in *Annual Meeting of the International Communication Association* (Montreal, Canada, 2008).

105 G. Walton, *China's Golden Shield: Corporations and the Development of Surveillance Technology in the People's Republic of China* (Toronto: International Centre for Human Rights and Democratic Development, 2001).

106 C. Arthur. 2009. China's Internet Users Surpass Us Population. *The Guardian*, 16 July 2009 [cited 5 February 2011]. Source: http://goo.gl/jsYcA

107 R. J. Deibert, 'Dark Guests and Great Firewalls: The Internet and Chinese Security Policy,' *Journal of Social Issues* 58, 1 (2002).

108 Ibid.

109 G. Yang, 'The Internet and Emerging Civil Society in China,' in *Debating Political Reform in China: Rule of Law vs. Democratization*, ed. S. Zhao (New York: M. E. Sharpe, 2006).

110 T. R. Shie, 'The Internet and Single-Party Rule in China,' ibid.

111 B. Liang et al., 'Internet Development, Censorship, and Cyber Crimes in China,' *Journal of Contemporary Criminal Justice* 26, 1 (2010).

112 Ibid.

113 BBC. 2006. Google Censors Itself for China. BBC, 25 January 2006 [cited 5 February 2011]. Source: http://goo.gl/1mp9F

114 P. S. Goodman. 2005. Yahoo Says It Gave China Internet Data. *Washington Post*, 11 September 2005 [cited 5 February 2011]. Source: http://goo.gl/DG4ey

115 D. Goldman. 2010. Congress Slams China and Microsoft, Praises Google. CNN Money, 24 March 2010 [cited 20 February 2011]. Source: http://goo.gl/5B1w

116 M. Lee. 2011. Baidu's Profit Rises after Making Gains on Google in Advertising in China. Bloomberg, 31 January 2011 [cited 20 February 2011]. Source: http://goo.gl/lDpFB

117 Y.-H. Kim. 2011. Update: Google to Continue to Invest in China; Sets Sights on Se Asia Wall Street Journal 2011 [cited 20 February 2011]. Source: http://goo.gl/xJzKu

118 C. Williams. 2011. Stuxnet: Cyber Attack on Iran 'Was Carried out by Western Powers and Israel'. *The Telegraph*, 21 January 2011 [cited 6 March 2011]. Source: http://goo.gl/Vprym

119 BBC. 2011. Us and Israel Were Behind Stuxnet Claims Researcher. BBC, 4 March 2011 [cited 13 March 2011]. Source: http://goo.gl/RCZ5p

120 J. Fildes. 2011. Stuxnet Virus Targets and Spread Revealed. BBC, 15 February 2011 [cited 6 March 2011]. Source: http://goo.gl/R7Mh1

121 N. Falliere et al., 'W32.Stuxnet Dossier' (Symantec, 2011).

122 Ibid., 3.

123 E. MacAskill. 2011. Stuxnet Cyberworm Heads Off Us Strike on Iran. *The Guardian*, 16 January 2011 [cited 13 March 2011]. Source: http://goo.gl/Unkfp

124 I. Traynor. 2007. Russia Accused of Unleashing Cyberwar to Disable Estonia. *The Guardian*, 17 May 2007 [cited 6 March 2011]. Source: http://goo.gl/1kctK

125 J. P. Farwell and R. Rohozinski, 'Stuxnet and the Future of Cyber War,' *Survival* 53, 1 (2011).

126 Ibid.

127 M. W. Shelley, *Frankenstein, or, the Modern Prometheus* (London: Thomas Davison, Whitefriars, 1823).

128 C. C. Demchak and P. Dombrowski, 'Rise of a Cybered Westphalian Age,' *Strategic Studies Quarterly* 5, 1 (2011).

129 J. F. Brenner, 'Privacy and Security Why Isn't Cyberspace More Secure?' *Communications of the ACM* 53, 11 (2010).

130 Demchak and Dombrowski, 'Rise of a Cybered Westphalian Age,' 36.

131 Ibid., 44.

132 PBS. 2006. The Return of the Taliban: Nek Mohammed 2006 [cited 28 May 2011]. Source: http://goo.gl/3QHxz

133 C. Ramey. 2004. Uav Battlelab Stands up at Indian Springs. U.S. Air Force, 23 June 2004 [cited 3 February 2011]. Source: http://goo.gl/yxfyA

134 M. Pitzke. 2010. Remote Warriors: How Drone Pilots Wage War. Spiegel Online, 3 December 2010 [cited 2 March 2011]. Source: http://goo.gl/ZQGyI

135 Ibid.

136 P. Bergen et al. 2010. The Hidden War. Foreign Policy, 21 December 2010 [cited 2 March 2011]. Source: http://goo.gl/QDFEY

137 Ramey, Uav Battlelab Stands up at Indian Springs [cited 3 February 2011]. Source: http://goo.gl/yxfyA

138 W. Saletan. 2011. Drones Are Death Warrants: Can the U.S. Send Drones to Execute American Citizens Like Anwar Al-Awlaki without Trial? You Bet. Slate, 3 October 2011 [cited 14 February 2012]. Source: http://goo.gl/WBJXl

139 P. Alston. Report of the Special Rapporteur on Extrajudicial, Summary or Arbitrary Executions (United Nations, 2010); J. Bennet. 1998. U.S. Cruise Missiles Strike Sudan and Afghan Targets Tied to Terrorist Network. *The New York Times*, 21 August 1998 [cited 29 May 2011]. Source: http://goo.gl/BOhxW

140 Charter of the United Nations. Chapter VII, Article 51. Source: http://goo.gl/tL4ic

141 J. J. Praust, 'Self-Defence Targetings of Non-State Actors and Permissibility of U.S. Use of Drones in Pakistan,' *Journal of Transnational Law & Policy* 19, 2 (2010).

142 Ibid., 240.

143 Ibid., 260.

144 A. J. Williams, 'Hakumat Al Tayarrat: The Role of Air Power in the Enforcement of Iraq's Boundaries,' *Geopolitics* 12, 3 (2007): 515.

145 A. J. Williams, 'Reconceptualising Spaces of the Air: Performing the Multiple Spatialities of UK Military Airspaces,' *Transactions of the Institute of British Geographers* 36, 2 (2011): 260.

146 BBC. 2005. Art Prankster Sprays Israeli Wall. BBC, 5 August 2005 [cited 30 May 2001]. Source: http://goo.gl/46VwP

147 T. Guardian. 2005. Banksy at the West Bank Barrier. *The Guardian* 2005 [cited 30 May 2011]. Source: http://goo.gl/DoCiM

148 S. Jones. 2005. Spray Can Prankster Tackles Israel's Security Barrier. *The Guardian*, 5 August 2005 [cited 30 March 2011]. Source: http://goo.gl/6Rxj6

149 D. Makovsky, 'How to Build a Fence,' *Foreign Affairs* 83, 2 (2004).

150 Ibid.

151 Ibid.

152 N. Chomsky. 2004. A Wall as a Weapon. *The New York Times*, 23 February 2004 [cited 20 February 2011]. Source: http://goo.gl/JMx27

153 B'Tselem. 2011. Separation Barrier. B'Tselem, 21 March 2011 [cited 21 March 2011]. Source: http://goo.gl/fDgPu

154 L. Farsakh, 'The Political Economy of Israeli Occupation: What Is Colonial About It?' in *Comparative Occupations: Chechnya, Iraq, Palestine*, Department of Political Science (Jerusalem: 2006).

155 UNOCHA. 2007. Three Years Later: The Humanitarian Impact of the Barrier since the International Court of Justice Opinion. United Nations Office for the Coordination of Humanitarian Affairs 2007 [cited 23 March 2011]. Source: http://goo.gl/IjKee

156 Advisory Opinion. 2004. Legal Consequences of the Construction of a Wall in the Occupied Palestinian Territory. International Court of Justice, 9 July 2004 [cited 21 March 2011]. Source: http://goo.gl/9CH85; S. Shamir et al. 2004. Israel Firmly Rejects Icj Fence Ruling Haaretz, 11 July 2004 [cited 15 February 2011]. Source: http://goo.gl/qWUX3

157 UNOCHA. Three Years Later: The Humanitarian Impact of the Barrier since the International Court of Justice Opinion [cited 23 March 2011]. Source: http://goo.gl/IjKee

158 G. Bowman, 'Israel's Wall and the Logic of Encystation: Sovereign Exception or Wild Sovereignty?' *Focaal – European Journal of Anthropology* 50 (2007).

159 Ibid., 133.

160 S. Alatout, 'Walls as Technologies of Government: The Double Construction of Geographies of Peace and Conflict in Israeli Politics, 2002–Present,' *Annals of the Association of American Geographers* 99, 5 (2009).

161 Ibid.

162 Al Jazeera. 2007. West Bank Wall Divides Neighbours. Al Jazeera, 27 November 2007 [cited 21 March 2011]. Source: http://goo.gl/bmPQN

163 J. Elgot. 2011. Israel to Build Egypt Security Wall. *Jewish Chronicle*, 11 January 2011 [cited 21 March 2011]. Source: http://goo.gl/Th8K8.

164 Al Jazeera. 2011. Israel Plans Wall for Egypt Border. Al Jazeera, 11 January 2011 [cited 21 March 2011]. Source: http://goo.gl/CUq5v.

165 Elgot, Israel to Build Egypt Security Wall [cited 21 March 2011]. Source: http://goo.gl/Th8K8

166 Brown, *Walled States, Waning Sovereignty.*

167 UNISON. 2007. Supporting Migrant Workers. UNISON, 4 May 2007 [cited 6 July 2011].

168 L. Baker. 2007. Illegal Immigrants March for More Rights. Reuters, 7 May 2007 [cited 5 July 2011]. Source: http://goo.gl/ck68H

169 Ibid.

170 BBC. 2007. Rally Call for Migrant 'Amnesty'. BBC, 7 May 2007 [cited 5 July 2011]. Source: http://goo.gl/bFEpd

171 UNISON, Supporting Migrant Workers [cited 6 July 2011].

172 K. Smith. 2007. 'Strangers into Citizens' – for the Regularisation of UK People without Status. IRR, 11 January 2007 [cited 5 July 2011]. Source: http://goo.gl/5FYLd

173 Citizens UK. 2010. Citizens UK Is the Home of Community Organizing in Britain. Citizens UK 2010 [cited 6 July 2011]. Source: http://goo.gl/mnbt2.

174 Strangers into Citizens. 2011. Why Regularisation? Strangers into Citizens 2011 [cited 6 July 2011]. Source: http://goo.gl/DuyJC

175 Ibid.

176 L. Z. Fernández. 2010. Regularisation: Practical and Humane. Strangers into Citizens 2010 [cited 6 July 2011]. Source: http://goo.gl/bohR4

177 T. Brady. 2010. Borough Welcome for 20,000 Illegals. *Harrow Observer*, 3 February 2010 [cited 6 July 2011]. Source: http://goo.gl/DU8nG.

178 Fernández. Regularisation: Practical and Humane [cited 6 July 2011]. Source: http://goo.gl/bohR4

179 Strangers into Citizens. 2010. Brent Council Backs Strangers into Citizens. Strangers into Citizens, 8 February 2010 [cited 6 July 2011]. Source: http://goo.gl/bJNyF

180 Ibid.

181 Hansard. 439wh Parl. Deb. H.C. 20 June 2007 (House of Commons, 2007).

182 V. Squire, 'From Community Cohesion to Mobile Solidarities: The City of Sanctuary Network and the Strangers into Citizens,' *Political Studies* 59, 2 (2011).

183 J. Newman, 'Regendering Governance,' in *Remaking Governance: Peoples, Politics and the Public Sphere*, ed. J. Newman (Bristol: Policy Press, 2005).

184 A. Bhattacharyya. 2007. Strangers into Citizens Rally: 'We Are All Citizens'. Socialist Worker Online, 8 May 2007 [cited 5 July 2011]. Source: http://goo.gl/hFFwf

185 Squire, 'From Community Cohesion to Mobile Solidarities: The City of Sanctuary Network and the Strangers into Citizens,' 7.

186 A. McNevin, *Contesting Citizenship: Irregular Migrants and New Frontiers of the Political* (New York: Columbia University Press, 2011).

CHAPTER THREE

'We, the Connected'

It was during beta testing in 2011 that Google+ was forced to be closed to new user registration because of intense demand.[1] LinkedIn had already been floated on the market with a valuation double that of what analysts expected. Perhaps, these are less known forms of what have come to be known as 'social media' such as Facebook and Twitter. That Google+ and LinkedIn did not require introduction must tell you something. 'Who doesn't have a social media account?' – we are now often invited to ask. I do not have one. (Though I experimented with all that, and you can hack your way into traces I must have left.) The reasons why I find social media troubling will become clear in this chapter but I have already hinted at why at the end of the last chapter. To put it bluntly, notwithstanding (or rather perhaps because of) their 'cool' ideologies, Google+, Twitter, Facebook and LinkedIn are the new habitats of the sovereign beast. To put it differently, while 'we, the connected' opposes itself to 'we, the people', it has developed and incorporated many elements of 'we, the people'. Or, at least, this is what I now set out to illustrate in this chapter. Doing so would amount to addressing the question Chapter 1 elaborated: Why is it so hard to imagine citizens without frontiers?

This chapter highlights the emergence of connectivity as a new narrative and its association with sovereignty. I will name this narrative 'we, the connected' and illustrate how its metaphors are being mobilized to capture incipient political subjectivities on the internet and 'elsewhere'. I will also discuss how this narrative attempts and (often and increasingly) succeeds in domesticating and inhabiting these subjectivities of the sovereign beast. The internet, or more popularly and broadly cyberspace, not only becomes more centralized, securitized and privatized but also embodies sites of wars and battles over rights and knowledge. This itself is a vast subject and its interpretation and appropriation are ongoing intellectual, political and social struggles. What concerns us in this chapter is twofold. First, we want to consider whether and to what extent connectivity becomes opposed to peoplehood. At first glance, it looks like they are radically opposed ways of becoming political. But, as you can guess from my choice of symmetrical designation – 'we, the people' and 'we, the connected' – we want to consider to what extent subjectivities in cyberspace are being cultivated along similar paths by inviting people to become part of a whole. Second, we want to know whether the emerging counter-narratives of 'we, the connected' provide the means to develop and cultivate creative, inventive and autonomous political subjectivities. These two issues clearly concern the concept 'citizens without frontiers' since their practices traverse frontiers and simultaneously deterritorialize and reterritorialize the sites through and over which they are constituted. These two also parallel the argument in Chapter 2 'We, the People'. There we began with the emergence of a dominant narrative, discussed how it gradually absorbed (or, more accurately, attempted to absorb) 'rogue' or 'unruly' subjectivities into a unified and homogeneous whole, and how these rogue and unruly subjectivities articulated themselves as counter-narratives to the dominant whole, 'we, the people'. Similarly, this chapter begins with the connectivity narrative and proceeds to consider various emergent political subjectivities as possible counter-narratives. Along the way, we expand our repertoire, as it were, and consider various ways of counting the parts that have no part in the whole.

Are we all connected?

If the crisis of sovereignty is not only one of authority over territory but of 'we, the people' or, rather, the formations of a 'we, the people', then what account of ourselves are we giving in the present? If the sovereign beast inhabited the political subject through the formation of 'we, the people', what are the dominant narratives through which political subjects are summoned today? Or, how is the political subject being formed in the present? What stories are we increasingly telling ourselves? To address these questions, we cannot return to a moment when the nation had not yet conquered the state. Arendt's moment of justice when the sovereign subject emerged as a bearer of the right to have rights and came to inhabit 'we, the people' (or the sovereign beast) is not the moment to which we can now contemplate a return. The sovereign beast inhabited both the sovereign citizen and the sovereign people and, in fact, only insofar as it could inhabit the latter did it successfully inhabit the former. How then do we conceive political subjectivity at present? What images are being produced? What metaphors are being mobilized?

It is now a mantra that people are more 'connected' than ever before. It is not enough to counter this mantra with statistics showing still only a fraction of world population is connected. The mantra grows, becoming a grand narrative. The emergence of new social media aided by ever-changing information and communication technologies, and their relationships with economic and social transformations have been discussed, analyzed and debated extensively. The question that concerns us is how all these transformations are producing a subject that is not only summoned by these changes but is also appropriate to them. Since we are especially interested in the formation of political subjectivity, the question that arises is how new political subjectivities are being described now that the sovereignty narrative, which relied on the sovereignties of the individual and the people, is being rearticulated. I propose to name this emerging grand narrative as 'connectivity' or, more precisely, 'we, the connected' and will compare it to counter-narratives of connectivity as struggling modes, metaphors and allegories of political subjectivity: the network and the multitude.

Over the past few years, the subject, especially the political subject, is increasingly imagined in terms of connectivity. Obviously, this is partly because of the predominance of the internet as the medium of communication and the emergence of so-called social media models of communication. The most prominent mode of interpretation of connectivity has been a networked understanding of both the individual and society. Some have gone as far to declare our present as the rise of a network society.[2] Others have announced the rise of a network economy.[3] Whether a new society or economy has emerged on the basis of a networked model of communication is debatable. Commentators have often derived political implications from the networked models of society, proposing ways in which democracies might work under the networked model. Two of the most interesting interpretations in this vein are by William Mitchell and Darin Barney.[4] Mitchell projects the emergence of a cyborg model of subjectivity where the networked subject becomes one with the network, not imagined as the entire network but a node in a web of relations in which the subject is embedded. Barney is much less convinced about the prospects for democracy of such a networked subject though he too is persuaded about the emergence of a networked subjectivity. Of course, among the best-recognized images of the networked model of subjectivity is Bruno Latour's approach to actor-network theory.[5] Despite his protests to the contrary, a networked image of the subject still pervades approaches to actor-network theory, so much so that Latour himself suggests changing its name to actant-rhizome theory. I am not sure if this renaming helps but I shall return to Latour when discussing a perspective on social space. Anyway, in this approach, while connectivity is used to describe the networked subject and his, her or its subjectivity, the image that still remains is of the network organized as a recognizable whole. The image that pertains is a topographical one since the actual hardware and software that constitute the network is itself based upon topographical properties. That is, the node, hub and spokes that organize networks as lattices and their mechanisms and protocols of transmission are pretty much modelled on the physical properties we find in computer networks. The technology provides the model for thinking about the image of the subject whereas the challenge is to think about the image of the subject that provides a model for the network to develop. As we shall see later when discussing Annemarie Mol and John Law, the consequences of this difference are significant.

If connectivity seems tied to communication technologies that is because these technologies have come to dominate our views of the world and our relationship to and place in that world. But connectivity has also become a dominant narrative because of the increasing integration of the world, or its time–space compression to use David Harvey's early and insightful phrase to define 'globalization'.[6] So when we encounter ideas about the network that does not mean only the virtual (e.g. social media, communications, devices) but also implies actual movements, relationships and affinities across frontiers. The emergence of global or transnational activism is of course among the most important developments of a political subjectivity through connectivity. The emergence of international non-profit organizations, humanitarianism, struggles against global injustices and the development of transnational networks of activists have been interpreted as 'activists beyond borders' or as 'transnational networks'.[7] On this view, globalization is not only a phenomenon from 'above' led by elites but also from 'below' led by activists. As Allen says

> the ability to mobilize across borders, to conduct transnational campaigns through extensive activist networks and to 'jump' the territorial, jurisdictional authority of states, has, it would appear, empowered many across the globe who previously found themselves constrained in some kind of zero-sum game.[8]

The network metaphor captures this phenomenon of connectivity across borders or moving beyond borders.

Another contending metaphor is the multitude coined by Hardt and Negri.[9] They do not derive the political subject from a network model based on technologies of communication but trace the emergence of a political subject from transnational movements: the multitude. Unlike global or transnational activism, however, the multitude is opposed to Empire, a new kind of sovereignty. Hardt and Negri argue that the concept of multitude, although irreducible to the revival of the Left, nevertheless can contribute to the task of resurrecting or reinventing the Left by naming simultaneously a political subject *and* project. Rather than being a directive to form a project, the concept aims to be an expression of actual developments of the multitude. The multitude is foremost an expression of a political project and is based on a human, all too human, and thus noble instinct for autonomy against rule. The political understanding of the multitude is based on an ontological understanding of being human as autonomous subjects. (The reason it is called a noble instinct is not because it is biological but social.) Although the ontological multitude already exists (produced over a very long period), the political multitude is the product of political projects and struggles in the present. These two multitudes are inseparable:

> If the multitude were not already latent and implicit in our social being, we could not even imagine it as a political project; and, similarly, we can only hope to realize it today because it already exists as a real potential.[10]

Hardt and Negri reject that the multitude therefore can be understood as a spontaneous project. The very fact that it is used as the name of a political project already rules out such criticism. 'The multitude is created in collaborative social interactions.'[11] Nor is it a kind of vanguardism (of an intellectual and political elite) since it is committed to the development of a common project together. The multitude emerges from multiple struggles and spaces. If Hardt and Negri use the singular multitude rather than multitudes, it is not because the singular is preferred over plural but because the multitude acts in common. It is this common aspect that determines its singularity and not that it is a unity opposed to multiplicity.[12] This may expose themselves to a criticism for reviving the dichotomy between the One and the Many when they use the term in relation to global struggles between Empire and the multitude. But, Hardt and Negri say that this is a misunderstanding of *their* project since the multitude is neither the One nor the Many. Thus, Empire and the multitude are not symmetrical.[13] Empire as world order is dependent on the multitude and its social productivity. The multitude is, by contrast, potentially autonomous and has the capacity to independently move across and beyond borders. Yet, this does not mean that the multitude does not create its own exclusions, its own subaltern, if you like. These are open questions and the multitude is potentially open insofar as it includes all those who can act in common and across borders. The multitude includes those who believe that another world is possible and it is meant to be an emblem for that desire.[14] What acting in common and across borders means then is to identify with the desire that another world, a better democratic world, is possible and to participate in creating it. So the multitude becomes a kind of political subject that is invariably collective, though formed through various places and durations, and resisting Empire.[15]

Although having very different social and political objectives, what is shared in these contending metaphors of network or the multitude is political subjectivity understood as integrated modes of identification that derive from and owe their existence to a whole or common. If you recall the discussion of counter-narratives of 'we, the people', the question was precisely how to understand such uncommon or rogue peoples as demos, plebs and popolo against and outside 'we, the people', as a whole. As long as we imagine that the uncommon or the rogue identifies with and eventually stands for the whole as its integrating and integrated element, then we are neglecting crucial aspects of the rogue that is not the whole or the common. It is this thought that we now need to develop with a focus on Foucault and Deleuze, or, more precisely, Deleuze's Foucault, as I find Deleuze–Foucault closest to the image I have in mind; closest but not close enough though. That is why we then need to turn to the most recent developments in genealogical and topological thinking about power and space.

Of ethical and political subjectivities

The connectivity narrative about the formation of new political subjectivities is something much more mundane, quotidian and open than the term 'grand narrative' may imply. That is not only because 'connectivity' is rather a recent narrative (hence it is open and contested) but also its dominance does not arise from a unified and centralized source. It is here that Foucault's use of subjectivation is much more useful than those theories that derive the subject, such as the networked or multitude, from supposedly independent and external developments such as post-modernization and globalization. In other words, I would like to discuss connectivity as a matter of subjectivation through which we inhabit and are inhabited by social practices and, in the process, form relatively durable habits (or dispositions) that become embodied such that we can repeat, iterate and cite them without thinking. (How much thinking do people do before they tweet?)

Before discussing subjectivation though we need to consider where subjectivation fits in Foucault's *oeuvre*. It is important to hear Foucault say that the question that he always investigated was how humans produce practical knowledges to govern themselves and others.[16] He defined such investigations as a 'historical ontology of ourselves'.[17] Such knowledges are implicated in technologies invented for governing selves and others. But his use of the term 'technologies' does not mean technologies such as hardware or engineering protocols. Technologies are assemblages of *episteme* (know-how) and *techné* (how-know) that enable humans to create relatively durable dispositions, institutions and knowledges. Foucault outlined four types of technologies of government: (1) technologies of production that involve the manipulation and shaping of material things – such technologies can range from giant bulldozers digging out oil sands in Alberta (Canada) to print technologies that embed microchips in films that can act like human skin with processing power; (2) technologies of communication that involve the transmission and codification of images, ideas, symbols and signs – such technologies can include routers and switches that disassemble and reassemble digital information as well as protocols for negotiating flows of such information; (3) technologies of power that involve affecting, manipulating, controlling or dominating the conduct of others – such technologies can range from laws, rules and regulations to ethical codes of conduct as well as disciplines in the military, school, work and leisure (yes, there was a time when people *did not* know how to watch a film or listen to a concert together in public; it had to be learned through disciplinary practices) and (4) technologies of the self that involve acting 'on their own bodies and souls, thoughts, conduct, and way of being, so as to transform themselves in order to attain a certain state of happiness, purity, wisdom, perfection, or immortality'.[18] For Foucault, these four technologies never function separately but each implies a particular form of domination, control or mastery over things, others and selves. Another insight Foucault provides is that when each works in tandem with another, the resultant pairs constitute specific modes of government. Foucault, for example, identifies Marx as working on the relationship between (1) technologies of production and (3) technologies of power, where the changes in the former require modification in the latter. Fordism, for example, as a mode of producing commodities in large quantities, would not have been possible without the discipline of workers in factories. Foucault identifies much of his own work as being about the relationship between (3) technologies of power and (4) technologies of the self and he calls this specific mode of government as 'governmentality'. The later Foucault was almost entirely dedicated to the question of technologies of the self or what he also calls the hermeneutics of the subject.[19]

It is this later work on 'subjectivation' and the relationship between (3) technologies of power and (4) technologies of the self that became increasingly prominent in his work yet remained incomplete. Deleuze reconstructed the concept of subjectivation and its relationship to other technologies in an especially effective and poignant manner – effective because it places the concept within the context of Foucault's *oeuvre* on knowledge and power and poignant because he later revisits the concept to provide new insights on the history of the present.[20] Deleuze insists that what appears to be an emphasis in Foucault's later *oeuvre* on technologies of the self and on subjectivism should not be interpreted as an interest in humanism. Deleuze insists, if Foucault is driven to investigate the inside of the subject (the relations of the self to the self), it is because Foucault does not consider the outside as a fixed limit or frontier rather the inside as a fold of the outside.[21] Deleuze called these 'foldings' to capture how the outside folds the inside and how the inside folds the outside. Put another way, foldings are the insides *of* the outside and outsides *of* the inside.[22] Deleuze says Foucault was always haunted by the issue of the inside as an operation of the outside throughout his work, which often appeared as the question of the double. The double was never a projection of the interior or the mirror of the exterior but a fold, a particular interiorization of the outside.[23] The doubling in Foucault, Deleuze insists, 'is not a doubling of the One, but a redoubling of the Other. It is not a reproduction of the Same, but a repetition of the Different'.[24] On this immanent concept of subjectivation, the other and distant are always also the same and the near. The fold as doubling gives an image of subjectivation that, on the one hand, requires the claim to govern others, and, on the other hand, is possible only insofar as one can govern oneself.[25] Thus, subjectivation is not subjectivity as it insists that it is not a relation of already constituted subjects but it is the relation to oneself insofar as it is a relation to the other as its fold or double.[26] Already, you can begin to see how my title 'citizens without frontiers' is indebted to this idea of subjectivation and the self as a fold. In particular, my use of the term 'traversing frontiers' indicates that the self is already a double of that which it traverses and by which it is traversed. This is fine but it is still pretty abstract and that is why we need to consider modes or ways through which subjectivation as folding of the inside of the outside works.

Deleuze identifies four modes of subjectivation.[27] The first concerns how we interiorize the material world that surrounds us and how it is enfolded. We can, for example, argue that we interiorize the material world of protocols, switches and machines of the internet or cyberspace through devices such as laptops and smartphones with which we have affective relationships. These devices become our affective embodiments or the interiorization of our life on the internet. What that involves is that when the media, family or friends speak about the internet or cyberspace, our relationship to it is not to an external object but already interiorized experiences mediated by devices with which we have affective and effective relations. We are oriented towards cyberspace already as its subjects through this interiorization. The second mode of subjectivation concerns the fold of relations between forces and how these forces are negotiated. To continue with the internet illustration, the interiorization that we inhabit involves those devices we develop affective relationships with as well as the protocols that we choose. But both the devices and protocols are sites of competitive struggles among various forces: corporations (e.g. Google, Facebook, Twitter, Myspace, Apple), governments, organizations and various other groups. We are implicated in the dynamic relations between these forces and are folded into how they negotiate their fields of influence, reach and effect. That is why two corporations such as Samsung and Apple would have seemingly paradoxical relationships as competitors and suppliers to each other, mounting multimillion court challenges around the world and at the same time intensely using each other's services and products. When we make decisions about this or that device, these forces pass through us as we actively engage with others through them. We are at once both objects and subjects of these competitive struggles between and among forces that constitute a field in which we find ourselves. The third mode of subjectivation is the fold of knowledge or how relations to oneself are constituted through telling truths. Being affectively and effectively engaged with others through them, we tell truths about both devices and protocols: how Facebook is making it easier to keep up with families; how Twitter is causing revolutions; how Google is becoming our second memory and so forth. These are truths not in the sense that they accurately describe reality (each of those cited above are contestable claims) but in the sense that they are becoming increasingly self-evident and referential by citation, repetition and iteration. It is these citations, repetitions and iterations that produce truth effects not because we have the means and wherewithal to study and evaluate them. The fourth mode of subjectivation is the outside itself where the subject constitutes itself in relation to immortality, salvation, eternity, freedom or death. The presentation of ourselves on the internet, the traces that we leave and the images that we portray of ourselves become our investments as beings in the world relating to others and their worlds. Through these, we constitute ourselves as free or unfree, mortal or immortal, private or public selves and we tell ourselves that these are our ways of being in the world.

These four modes of subjectivation always operate together in dynamic rhythms but not in harmonious and consistent ways.[28] Now, Deleuze distils these four modes of subjectivation from Foucault's main concern, which he calls the formation of the ethical subject, and generalizes this in the concept of subjectivation. I did not mention specific examples that Deleuze gives since Foucault's focus is ancient Greek and early Christian practices; instead, I inflected them with illustrations from our lives on the internet. Foucault offers his genealogy of the ethical subject in order to consider the relationship among moral code, ethical conduct and ethical work upon ourselves.[29] Rather than conceptualizing action as 'following a rule' Foucault offers what Deleuze calls four modes of subjectivation whereby a subject acts upon and monitors, assesses, improves and transforms himself or herself into an ethical subject.[30] He argues that for 'action' to be moral or ethical, it should not be reduced to an act conforming to an already existing rule, law or even value.[31]

Are these insights on the ethical subject applicable to the political subject? Can we use these insights on 'ethical subjectivity' to understand 'political subjectivity'? Foucault does not provide any guidance on this question though he does provide a fascinating but brief genealogy of 'Greco-Roman' political subjectivity after the classical age of the Greek polis and during what is often called the era of the decline of polis.[32] He argues against the idea that the decline of the polis also meant the decline of politics. He considers it questionable to reduce political subjectivity to the decline of a political form such as the city.[33] He insists that

. . . the organization of the Hellenistic monarchies, then that of the Roman Empire, cannot be analyzed simply in negative terms of a decline of civic life and a confiscation of power by state authorities operating from further and further away.[34]

In an insight that is central to *Citizens without Frontiers*, Foucault says that perhaps 'apprehension before a universe become too vast and having lost its constituent communities could well be a feeling that has been imputed retrospectively to the people of the Greco-Roman world'.[35] Rather than seeing an inexorable decline, especially if it is imputed retrospectively, Foucault insists that 'instead, one should see in this interest the search for a new way of conceiving the relationship one ought to have with one's status, one's functions, one's activities, and one's obligations'.[36] If 'the new rules of the political game made it more difficult to define the relations between what one was, what one could do, and what one was expected to accomplish', then 'the formation of oneself as the ethical subject of one's own actions became more problematic'.[37] But what about the political subject? Foucault seems to be switching back and forth between ethical and political subjectivity. But his discussion of ethical subjectivity provides us with a sense that restlessness and uncertainty can also be sources of new experimentations and new relations to ourselves rather than lamenting the disappearance of the old and the familiar. This insight is crucial because our incredulity towards the 'we, the people' narrative is unfolding at such a moment of restlessness and uncertainty; and, rather than lamenting its disappearance, we are experimenting with inventive, creative and autonomous acts through which we are constituting ourselves as ethical and political subjects. Yet, the emergence of 'we, the connected' as a unifying and integrating narrative in a space dominated by a few corporations and governments and as a site through which we make ourselves is, I suggest, a political problem. The significance of identifying this problem precisely lies in the argument that we are in that space between 'no longer' and 'not yet'.

Counter-narratives of connectivity: Cyberhackers and hacktivists

The question for us, as Deleuze puts it, is 'what are our four folds?'[38] What can we say about our own modes and relations to ourselves in the present? At first glance, these are not so different questions than those asked by the struggling metaphors of the present: the network and the multitude. But we cannot proceed by collecting as many facts as possible to interpret our present. Our facts and interpretations are unfolding simultaneously and we are not observing phenomena of which we are not a part. Although we illustrated these four folds with examples from our lives on the internet, these illustrations are just that. They give no answer to Deleuze's question. Deleuze does not answer it either. But in his 'postscript on control societies', he provides a glimpse. By interpreting Foucault's earlier work on discipline, punishment and incarceration in light of his later work on subjectivation, Deleuze announces 'control societies'.[39] While this short piece has been discussed widely, his use of 'control' to describe a new mode of subjectivation has been misleading or misunderstood. Perhaps against his intentions of using it to mean *modulation*, it has been mostly understood as *control* in the traditional sense, which places an overemphasis on discipline and surveillance. If we replace 'control' with 'modulation', it opens up new ways of answering that question Deleuze posed regarding Foucault's modes of subjectivation. To put it briefly, Deleuze's point in 'control societies' is that *disciplines* that worked on bodies in specific sites such as hospitals, asylums, schools, prisons, barracks and even cities that Foucault investigated as technologies of power (as actions upon actions) are being displaced (not replaced since disciplines have not 'disappeared') with *controls* that are creating protocols of modulation through which conduct is shaped. To return again to the internet here is appropriate. If, Deleuze seems to suggest, the internet was operating with the same logic as the disciplines that Foucault investigated, we would be seeing the education and training of bodies about the 'illegal' downloading of copyright music and videos. That, of course, happened to an extent. But, we can argue along with Deleuze that what tipped conduct against 'illegal' downloading was the provision of a convenient and quality alternative provided by iTunes: a paid, closed and regulated service. It is this service that liberated users and rendered them as willingly paying subjects. The radical behaviour change was modulated rather than simply regulated or controlled. Of course, this is too simple a comparison and it ignores many legal and political complexities. But the point is that the complex struggle over governing subjectivities on the internet could scarcely be understood by focusing on discipline alone and that is what modulating conduct or control societies is meant to emphasize.

Having discussed Deleuze's interpretation of Foucault, his reformulation of the question *of* the present and his glimpse of control societies, we can now return to the connectivity narrative. We discussed earlier that two images of political subjectivity in contemporary politics emerged and struggled for dominance. One is the image of the networked political subject. This image portrays the subject as a node in a network of relations much like a computer that belongs to local or global networks. From this image then is derived an image of the political which ostensibly this subject gives rise to. There are variations on this theme and the most prominent have been the ideas of 'network society', 'actor-network theory' or 'transnational activism'. Although there are differences, the similarity with these images is that each interprets the subject from a unifying whole from which the subject derives its attributes and to which it orients.

Another image of the new political subject is the 'multitude' – a kind of collective subject that emerges as a political project. This is the key aspect: Since it is envisaged explicitly to address the question of reviving a political project called the 'left', it develops an integrated image of the subject as a constituent power of a project. The subject is integrated into this project and the subject derives its features from the project itself. It is quite telling that the main figure of this collective subject is the militant, joyful communist rather than the activist.[40] For Hardt and Negri, activists serve Empire and its requirements.[41] Yet, surprisingly, the most radical demand that this militant as opposed to the activist is able to make is global citizenship.[42]

Both networked and integrated images of the subject – especially the political subject – is too calculative and derivative to allow for the kind of analysis Foucault, let alone Deleuze's Foucault, would have performed. It is too calculative to imply intentionality and too derivative to imply a unified, integrated whole from which the subject derives its character and to which it orients. To put it another way, both images are still topographical rather than topological and thus cannot comprehend subjectivity in its multiple modes of formation.

How could we develop a topological understanding of political subjectivity? Just consider the images we have been given during the Arab Spring throughout Iran, Tunisia, Egypt, Libya, Yemen, Bahrain and Syria in 2010 and 2011. The media was awash with images of young activists using Twitter, Facebook and other social media to communicate, organize and mobilize their activism. It was also awash with arguments for and against the ostensible impact or effects of the social media in mobilizing these activisms. These images are relevant but they give a unified if not totalizing view of very complex social and political processes through which political subjects came into being and articulated demands. Understanding these complex processes requires the analysis of forces and their problematizations (power), statements and their distributions (knowledge) and the kinds of subjects that these forces and statements both interpellate and condition (subjectivation). Moreover, it requires investigating the four technologies of government: (1) production, (2) communication, (3) power and (4) the self; and especially exploring the relations between (2) technologies of communication and (4) of the self. As Foucault was more concerned with the relations between (3) technologies of power and (4) of the self (governmentality), we do not even have an illustration of how we might investigate those between (2) technologies of communication and (4) technologies of the self (connectivity). Finally, we would also need to explore four modes of subjectivation in the present as they unfold through the relations between technologies of communication and of the self.

Clearly, all that lies beyond the scope of this book and my capabilities. Besides, the aim is to get to the question of 'we, the connected' so that we can develop some idea of the political subject without 'we, the people'. So it will be a brief outline. The forces that have shaped our present over the past decade or so are complex and heterogeneous. But taking guidance from some of the best accounts, we can outline the following elements. The geographic shift of industrial production from the west to the east and from the north to the south was accompanied by the proliferation of new industrial forms from electronics to pharmaceuticals that required different principles of production, consumption and exchange. With the rise of new logistic systems, the world has become a vast demand and supply chain system for the production and consumption of commodities. But this is not 'global capitalism' or a 'world order' driven by a singular and identifiable logic. As Bourdieu insisted, these fields of production involve multiple forms of capital (economic, cultural, symbolic) and their accumulation precipitates the emergence of multiple classes and groups as forces shaping our world. Just as the accumulation of different forms of capital requires appropriation of a world composed of demand and supply chains, flows and transactions, the emerging classes and social groups become mobile within these chains as opportunities become attached to them. It is not that a 'global elite' emerges and roams the world as often-dominant images assert. These chains implicate all emergent classes and their segments and become connected to them. So then the logics of these fields of accumulation implicate everyone, and their connectivity to these chains also implies their connectivity through actual and virtual networks including communications technologies and social media. Such technologies are not emerging independently from the accumulation of different forms of capital. Both movements and acts of people crossing and traversing frontiers respectively are implicated in these chains in often paradoxical ways. Being connected may mean literally being connected to social media but the social media connects us to actual fields of opportunities through which we become subjects.[43]

It is in this sense and against this background that connectivity (or 'we, the connected') functions as the dominant mode through which we become subjects. Consider some of the modes through which we are becoming political subjects. Unlike the networked or integrated images of subjectivity, we are becoming political subjects that can exist and in fact must exist in multiple spaces and multiple times: We simultaneously relate to here and there (spaces) as we simultaneously relate to now and then (times). To repeat, as Deleuze insists, the outside is more than any exterior and is folded or doubled by an inside that is traversal rather than an enclosed interior.[44] This is neither intersubjectivity nor intentionality both of which presuppose a topographical space that 'prevents it from understanding itself, and must be surpassed by another, "topological", space which establishes contact between the Outside and the Inside, the most distant, the most deep'.[45] It is this image that captures the relations between technologies of communication and technologies of the self in the present, being simultaneously connected to here and there and now and then. As John Allen says

> a topological appreciation of power in the contemporary global era would have drawn attention to the fact that neither social justice movements nor any other type of global actor actually 'jump' scale, they merely connect more or less directly with others elsewhere. Distanciated relationships, direct ties and real-time connections displace the notion of geometric scale and the idea that actors move up and down them, from the local to the global and back.[46]

If Foucault named the relations between (3) technologies of power and (4) technologies of the self 'governmentality', should we not consider naming the relations between (2) technologies of communication and (4) technologies of the self as 'connectivity'? Can we not consider connectivity as a dominant rationality through which we govern ourselves and others here and there, now and then, almost all the time and all at once?[47] This, at any rate, is what I have been moving towards from the beginning of this chapter, if not the book. Modern political subjectivity depends on a homogeneous topographical space (state) that closes upon itself as 'we, the people'. It provides the outside of the inside. 'We, the people' functions as both the outside and the inside in the figure of the citizen, or, more accurately, citizen as national; it combines citizenship with nationality. But the politics of connectivity as the emerging (if not already dominant) rationality of governing others and ourselves already throws modern political subjectivity into crisis.[48] Again, I am using the term 'crisis' to designate the moment when a narrative becomes incredulous and not a state of affairs in which a decisive change for better or worse is imminent.

Genealogies, topologies, connectivity

How can we approach the politics of connectivity as a rationality of government? We just encountered the word topological above when quoting Deleuze on Foucault saying that it is a '. . . space which establishes contact between the Outside and the Inside, the most distant, the most deep'.[49] In Chapter 2, we used 'genealogies' to describe those studies by Arendt, Derrida and Foucault that have helped us understand the complex histories of sovereignty as 'we, the people'. I now want to turn our attention to 'topologies' to describe how we may understand complex geographies of connectivity as 'we, the connected'. I will briefly discuss Annemarie Mol,

John Law and John Allen who have drawn our attention, albeit for different purposes and in different fields, to complexities that spaces generate for understanding ourselves.

The studies by Mol and Law that spatialize truth are of interest in approaching connectivity. In a way, I can suggest an (not so far fetched) analogy between their question about the universality of truth and the question of sovereignty. They say that in social studies of science and technology, the idea of the universal truth became suspect once it was admitted that truth operates differently in different locations.[50] How can truth function differently in different locations? This 'discovery' owed much to the fact that many scholars turned their attention to the social spaces in which truth was produced and disseminated rather than trying to sort it out logically on paper as many other scholars had done. Once the attention turned away from logic on paper to logic in practice, the question of what kind of spaces is truth produced in became crucial. I have neither the expertise nor space here to discuss the fascinating examples Mol and Law provide from social studies of science to develop their vocabulary of social spaces through which science is practised.[51] My interest here is connectivity and how their spatial vocabulary, which they call topological, might help. I am also drawing upon John Allen who uses topological insights to understand how power is exercised in the present. It is this vocabulary that interests me as a description of how we are not only interpreting our experiences but also that of others. I am naming this description 'connectivity' or 'we, the connected' and the description that is becoming increasingly problematic as 'sovereignty' or 'we, the people'. As I argued, those who are producing contending metaphors to describe our experiences of connectivity, such as the network and the multitude, are continuing with assumptions that undergird descriptions of our experiences of sovereignty.

Admittedly, what Mol and Law study is just one domain of human activity: social studies of science and technology. Yet, as their argument also implies, there is no domain of human activity that can be isolated and there are always family resemblances in which social practices produce truths about the world and themselves.[52] Besides, as I just said, it is not too far fetched to assume that political language of sovereignty should have elective affinities with scientific language of universalism. As Allen says, it creates problems when we translate words meant to be used in specific domains to other domains especially if this translation is from science to social science.[53] Yet, it is also important to recognize these translations not for their transference value or to make them work as they were intended, but to allow them to do some evocative work where we feel our current vocabulary is failing us, in order to communicate things we see as novel or important.

To start with Mol and Law, they use a vocabulary that draws its inspiration from topology (a branch of mathematics) rather than topography to describe these spaces. They begin with the suggestion that social relations exist in multiple spaces that while coexisting, conjoining and overlapping with each other, also occupy parallel and distinct modalities. Mol and Law think that topology is appropriate for borrowing metaphors to describe these spaces, rather than relying on topographical descriptions that do not deal with these heterogeneous multiplicities.[54] But does that mean that Mol and Law somehow reject the existence of topographical spaces? No. Their point is that there are other spaces too and they conjoin and overlap. In fact, they initially define three such spaces: regions, networks and fluids. Regions are topographical and delimited entities in which things happen. Distance and proximity (nearness and farness) are metric. Networks are spaces through which things disseminate. Distance and proximity are not metric. While Mol and Law are indebted to what came to be known as actor-network theory, they are quick to identify both its critics as well as its limitations.[55] Moreover, 'here' and 'there' are not objects or attributes that fall inside or outside boundaries.[56] Fluids are spaces without boundaries or at least without *clear* boundaries.[57] Fluid spaces are never pure as they always include mixtures. Yet, while fluid, these spaces are also relatively robust in the sense that they maintain some stability and continuity. They add a fourth possible space later.[58] They call these fires. These are spaces that condense rather than disseminate social relations.[59] Through their intensity, they condense the global in the local as a space of conjoined alterity or otherness. Fires are spaces of enactment and enactments are complex associations between those things that are absent and those that are present. Fire spaces conjoin alterity and dissipate otherness – only if for a brief moment.[60]

While Mol and Law offer a vocabulary for understanding how truth is produced (universalized, globalized, localized) through four spaces (regions, networks, fluids and fires), it is relatively easy to conjoin these metaphors with studies of boundaries and borders that describe the worlds which we inhabit or the worlds that inhabit us at present. It is said so many times now that we have become accustomed to it: The topographically drawn and contiguous map of states no longer (though it is always added, if ever) correspond to the realities we experience through travel, migration, communication and labour that cross those borders. It is not so difficult to imagine our worlds through the metaphors that Mol and Law provide. We do live in a world of regions with neatly drawn borders voraciously protected by states that create opportunities for some and inhibit others. We continuously experience border controls such as checkpoints, visas, permits, papers and so on that attempt to maintain the integrity of regions. Yet, we also live through networks of proximity and distance that are not measurable or calculable (or controllable) with metrics. We are increasingly implicated in fluid spaces through which our bodies and subjectivities cross, form and interact. We do maintain (at least we try) relatively stable and continuous existences through these fluid spaces and form solidarities, agonisms, and alienations. Yes, we also get caught in fires through which, if only for a moment, the world condenses, intensifies, and ourselves and our alterities become reconfigured. None of these modes of being is mutually exclusive. All inhabit us simultaneously albeit in different intensities in different times.

Allen draws similar conclusions from thinking in topological rather than topographical ways in relation to power and space. Like Mol and Law, Allen also sees territorial, networked and topological spaces not as mutually exclusive and superseding but coexisting and overlapping. For Allen,

> the driving insight behind topology is that certain characteristics or properties of things retain their integrity despite being stretched or twisted out of shape. The way things hold or are connected together through space places an emphasis on the nature and form of the ties involved, their relatedness as it were, rather than upon the measurable distance between the points. It is the relationship between the points, not their distance from one another, that produces the space.[61]

When we translate this insight into understanding geographies of power, 'when such thinking informs geographical considerations rather than geometric problems, the sense in which government takes place at a distance, for example, prompts us to question the spatial relationships involved'.[62] Questioning rationalities of government or the politics of connectivity then moves to

> . . . disrupt our sense of what is near and what is far by eliding notions of physical and social proximity. Connections are no longer conceived as lines which cut across sovereign spaces, but rather as intensive relationships which create the distances between the powerful [or powerless] actors.[63]

All this makes understanding how subjects become political under conditions of connectivity profoundly complex. Yet, it is also rather simple if we are prepared to abandon thinking in terms of parts and whole or seeing ourselves one with 'we, the people' or 'we, the connected'.

Paradoxes, multiplicities, heterogeneities

We must end this chapter with a troubling paradox. The chapter attempts to illustrate how in the present we are experiencing a transformation in the way in which we give an account of ourselves as subjects. This transformation involves gradually though certainly not smoothly shifting from a narrative, which I called the sovereignty narrative, where we see ourselves or at least are invited (sometimes nicely) to see ourselves as members of a 'we, the people' to another narrative, which I called the connectivity narrative, where we increasingly see ourselves or at least are invited (often nicely) to see ourselves as connected beings or 'we, the connected'. Just as the sovereignty narrative was told in a thousand tales both before the nineteenth century when it was associated with the king's body and after when it was associated with 'we, the people', so is the connectivity narrative or 'we, the connected' is being told through the tales of Google+, Twitter, Facebook and others. There is a paradox here; are we providing a 'better' description of ourselves, when we describe ourselves as connected beings? The aim of the chapter is not to announce that we are now connected beings as described. That is why I called it the 'connectivity narrative' to indicate that this is the description under which we are increasingly being constituted and at the same time seeing ourselves as acting beings. As I hope to have also shown, this description is not without its struggles. Our descriptions neither shape nor represent the world we inhabit; rather, they participate in it, or, perhaps more accurately, we participate in it and struggle through these descriptions. The struggles among these descriptions are not about accurately representing the world (though to increase their chances of success, they are often presented as such) but finding ways to act in the world we are ceaselessly involved in creating. Just as I think investing in 'we, the people' or its counter-narratives of demos and plebs is problematic for understanding that political subjectivity called citizenship, it is equally suspect to invest in the 'we, the connected' narrative or its counter-narratives of hackers as the new plebs to recover an image of citizenship. That is why articulating an image of 'citizens without frontiers' is also about revealing a description under which we can act (and will) as citizens. This is why giving an account of what makes acts creative, inventive and autonomous is indispensable. It is their performative force that reveals the ways in which people can and are constituting themselves as political subjects.

Politics without 'we, the people'?

What explains the endurance or durability of a narrative such as 'we, the people'? Since the end of the eighteenth century, a complex and heterogeneous field of practices called the nation-state has expressed and was creatively performed by that narrative 'we, the people' and it became a dominant object of political identification. For all their differences, various strategies such as racism, sexism, nationalism, cosmopolitanism, multiculturalism, rather than being mutually exclusive and competing strategies, belong to this dominant field of political identification which the 'we, the people' grand narrative constitutes. The same can be said of various technologies such as sovereignties, borders and territories. That it is dominant does not mean that it does not produce counter-hegemonic practices, as some of the ideologies mentioned above can certainly be considered. Although cosmopolitanism is often considered counter to nationalism, they both belong to the 'we, the people' grand narrative. We have seen, especially in Rancière and Laclau, how their idea of politics depends on the identification of those who do not have a part with the whole ('we, the people'). By contrast, with the concept 'citizens without frontiers', we are seeking to understand a new form of politics that does not depend on that identification with the whole. Yet, it has its own logic, which I designate as traversal.

Just when 'we, the people' is losing its credibility (as witnessed by the increasing questions about its legitimacy), we are now experiencing 'we, the connected' as an emerging grand narrative that shapes or orders our political subjectivities. As with 'we, the people', it does not mean that it is the only narrative but it is becoming 'grand' in the sense that it is gaining credibility and legitimacy through performative practices. If territory was the operative principle arising from and enabling 'we, the people', we can argue that 'the cloud' has become the operative principle of 'we, the connected'. It is remarkable how quickly that term came to represent digital information stored in actual and massive data farms. But, just as territory gave the impression that it is *here*, the cloud gives the impression that it is *nowhere* – and, of course, both are illusions. Just as territory mobilized images of smooth togetherness, the cloud gives the impression of smooth connectivity. Yet, the cloud also gives shape to striated cyberspace. After all, the cloud is not the clear sky: boundless space without borders. We can learn from Wikipedia that clouds exist in different forms: cirriform, cumuliform and stratiform, with further species and varieties. What we cannot learn from it is that the cloud is emerging as the metaphor of the new internet against the striated, heterogeneous and complex entity called cyberspace and that the latter now is mostly identified with irregular and illegal activities (cyberhackers but not cloudmonsters). This perhaps illustrates the emerging dominance of 'we, the connected' and the end of the open internet.[64]

How can we conceive citizenship as political subjectivity without or against these two grand narratives?[65] This question was the key focus of Chapters 2 and 3. But the figure 'citizens without frontiers' not only aims to understand a politics without identification with 'we, the people' but also resists being inhabited by 'we, the connected' as an amorphous and shapeless world without borders. Clearly, I propose the figure of 'citizens without frontiers' in response to how citizenship is being reconfigured as political subjectivity *and* how we could think about citizenship as political subjectivity. This is to concede that, inevitably, reading Chapters 2 and 3 (how citizenship is being reconfigured as political subjectivity) required some understanding of the way in which I propose to think about citizenship differently as political subjectivity in Chapter 4.

ACT 10. OF IDENTIFICATION: WE ARE ALL KHALED SAID

On 6 June 2010, Khaled Said, a 28-year-old Egyptian, died after sustaining extensive injuries caused by two plain-clothed police officers.[66] Soon after his death post-mortem photos were distributed across the internet. This provided evidence of the torture he received as he was dragged from an internet café in Alexandria and publicly beaten. This event caught the attention of Wael Ghonim, an Egyptian Google Marketing Executive for the Middle East and North Africa.[67] Determined to keep the memory of Said alive, draw attention to the Egyptian police brutality and draw inspiration from the then ongoing Tunisian uprising,[68] Ghonim connected these events and established a memorial and dissident Facebook page named 'We are all Khaled Said'. The grounds of this act of identification and its consequences illustrate how an act produces political subjects traversing frontiers. The site gathered a significant following and by mid-June 2010, '130,000 joined the page'.[69]

'We are all Khaled Said' became a rallying point against the regime in Egypt set on achieving two aims: to bring an end to police brutality and President Mubarak's 30-year emergency rule.[70] With the outbreak of the Egyptian uprising, the Facebook page became an increasingly popular gathering point.[71] The success of the demonstrations on 25 January 2011 was in part due to mobilizations facilitated by the site as many of those protesting at Tahrir Square were also part of the online gathering.[72] Many protesters held placards displaying Khaled Said's disfigured body.[73]

Ghonim has been described as the spark that led to the outburst of protests; he stated that 'our role was to create the snowball, and once the snowball was created most of the Egyptians who were hurt by the regime started to join and broke the psychological barrier of fear.'[74] Arguably, what added a performative force to this act was the fact that, shortly after Ghonim launched the Facebook page, he was arrested and detained by Egyptian police for 12 days. We will never know if the act would have gained the same performative force without the arrest of an 'executive' of a global brand and the ideological interests of the brand to institute itself on the side against evil. Ghonim claimed that he was psychologically tortured, as he was kept blindfolded and was not allowed to talk to anyone.[75] An appearance by Ghonim on Egyptian independent television after his release served to galvanize his supporters, with fresh protests breaking out shortly afterwards. In a popular talk show on Dream 2, Ghonim burst into tears after being shown the beatings protestors received during the uprising and claimed it was the fault of authorities.[76] This display of emotion was said to have moved 'thousands of people to join the protests for the first time on Tuesday'.[77] Quickly, Ghonim became an unofficial spokesperson for the 'internet revolution', a role he has consistently and simultaneously denied and accepted by emphasizing its leaderless nature. In a television interview, Ghonim dubbed the protests 'the revolution of the youth of the Internet'.[78] Clearly, Ghonim gave every impression that he was caught in the act. Since then, there have been demands for Wael Ghonim to become identified as the leader of the revolution.[79]

What made Ghonim's acts of identification 'We are all Khaled Said', including other Twitter and Facebook pages, particularly effective in translating a movement from an online gathering to 'offline' political activism was how social networks operated in Egypt. Government-controlled communication meant that independent online forums became crucial sites for circulating news and programmes of action.[80] Attia et al. claim that the relationships forged online, based on the issue of change, was a significant catalyst in facilitating and translating trust, loyalty and direction to the forms of political activism witnessed on the streets of Cairo and Alexandria.[81]

In search of metaphors to describe the act in which he was caught, Ghonim calls the uprisings Revolution 2.0: 'Revolution 2.0 is . . . like Wikipedia, OK? Everyone is contributing content. You don't know the names of the people contributing the content . . . This is exactly what happened.'[82] He also told CNN's Wolf Blitzer 'if you want to liberate a government, give them the Internet.'[83] It is hard to tell whether this is the voice of a generation that mistakes all that happens online for *all* that happens, or the voice of an executive who becomes convinced that his company can only do good. For him, using Facebook becomes the tool that can challenge a despotic regime without any understanding of transformative practices that have been taking place in Egypt (or anywhere else) for decades and centuries.

Yet, there is still another paradox in Revolution 2.0. Ghonim's argument of decentralized openness can only sustain itself by appealing to an image of the internet that is fast disappearing, if it ever existed. An image of a free, open and deliberative Facebook, as opposed by its very structure to the patrimonial, closed and violent Mubarak's Egypt is ultimately an image that belies the control protocols that regulate social media networks with increasing intensity. It positions Facebook, Twitter and Google as inherently non-totalizing and benevolent democratic forces when, arguably, they are also serving the very opposite ends. Revolution 2.0 creates a fusion between contemporary lifestyle consumption and democracy, giving legitimacy to 'the notion that democracy is a byproduct of media products for self-expression and that the corporations that create such media products would never side with governments against their own people'.[84] This is further reflected when CNN's Wolf Blitzer asked: 'Tunisia, then Egypt. What's next?' Ghonim replied: 'Ask Facebook.'[85] Clearly, we can imagine situations, for instance in China, when Ghonim's company took a very different role of collaborating with the state in the suppression of internet activism.

It is easy to say that Revolution 2.0 instigated by sites such as 'We are all Khaled Said' is as totalizing as Revolution 1.0. Harder to detect is the difference in their logics. Mejias argues that as the internet becomes increasingly privatized and centralized, the monopolies of social media corporations become more susceptible to being shut down.[86] This became the case in Egypt where Twitter and Facebook were blocked shortly after the 25 January protests.[87] Although there were inventive ways to overcome these prohibitions, techniques of mobilization and the promise of democracy appear even more fragile within new social movements that rely upon Web 2.0 not only as their technologies but also as their ideologies. While in Egypt the battle is raging about who is 'we, the people', Revolution 2.0 has already declared that the winner is 'we, the connected'.[88]

ACT 11. OF HACKING: LULZSEC

Its audacity was brazen and apparently fearless. Among its high-profile victims were Sony, the CIA, the FBI, the US Senate and even the UK's Serious Organised Crime Agency. Exposing frailties in government and corporate networks, the group leaked hundreds of thousands of hacked passwords, and in the process garnered more than a quarter of a million followers on Twitter. But after just 50 days, on 25 June [2011], LulzSec suddenly said it was disbanding.[89]

Can a social group, even if it is a virtual group, disband itself? Can the will of its subjects enact its disappearance?

On 27 July 2011, a member of the elusive online hacktivist network LulzSec was arrested.[90] The 18-year-old Jake Davis, who allegedly used the online pseudonym 'Topiary', was later charged by police in connection with several cyber-attacks on government and police networks in the United Kingdom since May, which they claim were committed by the hacking network LulzSec.[91] It is alleged that LulzSec is a splinter group of another hacktivist group called Anonymous, which gained prominence when it attacked the financial institutions that suspended the transactions of WikiLeaks.[92] The attacks by LulzSec the week before Topiary's arrest consisted of redirecting individuals accessing *The Sun* website to a false story which claimed that Rupert Murdoch was dead.[93] Hacks in May and June targeted government and police websites, as well as Sony.

What is fascinating here is not so much its attacks but its final act. Only 50 days after its emergence, Topiary announced that LulzSec was disbanded. LulzSec left this message to the world: 'Our planned 50 day cruise has expired and we must now sail into the distance leaving behind, we hope, inspiration, fear, denial, happiness, approval, disapproval, mockery, embarrassment, thoughtfulness, jealousy, hate, even love.'[94] If life were only this straightforward. Soon, other consequences would follow.

The group was reported to consist between six and eight members.[95] Apparently, members of the group kept their affiliation deliberately vague.[96] Those arrested, including Jake Davis, have yet to be officially linked to their aliases.[97] Topiary described how the group came together in a very spontaneous fashion, and that they revelled in the fact that they 'weren't burdened by plans or board meetings'.[98] They acted as a group. The internet was used as a common ground for their attacks, with members spanning the globe from the Shetland Islands to Iowa and New York.[99] Topiary describes the decision to disband as a natural conclusion to their short burst of activity. The group had come together, agreed on a few objectives, achieved them and then disbanded. Gallagher reports Topiary as saying that the group was set up for the lulz (internet slang for 'laughs'). After the group decided to disband, the media reported that the pressure of being chased by government e-crime units in the United Kingdom and the United States influenced the group's decision.[100] Gallagher offers two alternative explanations for disbanding: that the group became too powerful when it acted together, and that they chose to disband to protect themselves; or they were teenagers who just got bored.

In many ways, LulzSec reflects Milone's description of hacktivist networks. Milone describes how the communication network of hacktivists can be seen as a 'full-matrix network' of 'collaborative networks of groups where everybody is connected to everybody else'.[101] Milone states that

> online activists consist of dispersed organizations – small groups and individuals who communicate, coordinate, and conduct their campaigns in a networked manner, often without a precise central command. Like netwar, the unifying element of the new activist is the use of networked forms of coordination, policy, and technology.[102]

This not only exemplifies the organization of LulzSec but also complicates its act of disbandment.

The act of disbanding could itself be another opportunity to reshape and reinvigorate further instances of hacktivism. This is perhaps the case since 'hacktivists are neither secret agents nor soldiers, neither terrorists nor netwarriors. Hacktivism aims to capture attention; it is calculated for maximum media effect, trying to raise the awareness of citizens regarding certain rights and liberties: free speech, privacy, access'.[103] Its effects then are in the act rather than the ostensible aims, intentions or purposes of a group. For that reason, disbanding may be a euphemism for relocation, dispersal or even traversing – moving across frontiers, moving onto something else. But it cannot be disappearance. Once an act produces subjects, intensifies sites, shifts scales, prepares ground and generates consequences, it is impossible to erase at will its traces. For state authorities that are used to dealing with ascriptive identities and fixed boundaries, a social group that can disband itself with a singular act is unsettling not because it is untraceable but because it becomes ungovernable.

Turning to the relationship between Twitter and disbanding, the disjointed nature of the attacks seems to reflect the personal affiliation of the hackers and their continued commitment: together and yet not together at the same time. The group's members are united not through an ideology but an agreement of targets. The identities of the group's members are extremely hard to confirm, with online interviews taking place via the group's Twitter feeds.[104] One such interview conducted by the BBC reports a LulzSec member with the alias 'Whirlpool' as representing the internet as a whole. After the person alleged to be Topiary, the lead Twitter spokesman, was arrested, another individual came forward named Batteye. In a Tweet, he cryptically remarks 'I'm not really with anonymous . . . but then again I sort of am, aren't I?'[105] He appears to be referring to the fact that he has been linked to the group by the media. The group seems to reinforce its unitary identity via Twitter. Yet the spokespeople regularly change. The group's decision to disband means very little if the act of tweeting reaffirms their existence.

An article about the hashtag phenomenon may shed some light on the connectivity versus disbanding of LulzSec through Twitter: 'Twitter emphasizes novelty over popularity. Twitter trends come from an algorithm that identifies topics that are being talked about more now than previously. So trends happen not because of cumulative interest but something much more ephemeral.'[106] It is uncertain whether this continuation through Twitter, despite the act of disbanding, is itself another act or catalyst for hacktivism.

Although Krapp observes that 'an act of hacktivism can involve many people or only one; it can forge links and coalitions between people whose politics may otherwise run the gamut', there is something qualitatively different about what LulzSec represents.[107] Krapp thinks that 'Essentially, hacktivism translates into the digital realm what disruptive or expressive politics have been using for centuries. . . . [and thus it is] . . . nothing more or less than digital demonstrations.'[108] Yet, the differences between Facebook and Twitter and LulzSec are dramatic. LulzSec perhaps indicates what being connected to the internet might look like without joining the 'we, the connected' narrative. That becomes perhaps both its promise and danger.[109]

ACT 12. OF DEFIANCE: NO ONE IS ILLEGAL

Of various movements and arguments for open borders, No One Is Illegal (NOII) has been the most creative, inventive and autonomous. Its founding as an act challenges immigration control regimes and campaigns for their total abolition. Rather than making immigration controls 'workable', it rejects any idea that there can be 'fair' or 'just' or 'reasonable' or 'non-racist' controls and makes no distinction between 'economic migrants' and 'refugees', between the 'legal' and the 'illegal'. In effect, and although it does not express it this way, NOII is a rejection of 'we, the people' as the foundation of the state. The case for open borders that it advocates barely registers in its powerful but simple message about the inherent injustice of population movement control exercised by the sovereign beast.[110] It has long been assumed that if immigration controls were removed, then immigrants would become citizens. As Hayter argues in his account of NOII,

> new residents need to not only have the right to work, but all the gains from the working class that exist in the country they migrate to. . . . they should have the right to vote and right to hold public office. . . . full access to social provision, including health provision and education for their children.[111]

NOII has become a movement that challenges immigration regimes as population control by campaigning for the legalization of all people deemed to be unlawfully entering or residing in a country. The movement began in Germany in 1997 and has since spread to the United Kingdom and Canada. The phrase 'No One Is Illegal' is derived during a speech in 1985 which defended the rights of refugees to live and work in America, made by Eile Weisel, a holocaust survivor.[112]

The founder of the organization, Steven Cohen, wrote the group's manifesto in 2003 after the publication of the book *No One Is Illegal: Asylum and Immigration Control, Past and Present*.[113] This book outlined much of the direction and ethos of NOII. It sought to identify how little has changed since the 1905 Aliens Act, with its proto-fascist basis, that targeted Jews, and contemporary immigration laws, which are supposedly colour-blind. He argued that immigration controls cannot be fair because they reiterate a Victorian notion of the deserving and undeserving with arbitrary judgement. Cohen stated that controlling immigration is necessarily 'racist' because it categorizes people 'between foreigner and native, between them and us, between alien and British'.[114] Lastly, he argued that immigration control is imperialistic in that it is 'about control of labour from the colonial and underdeveloped world into the imperial and developed world'.[115] These messages have become condensed and shaped into the mission statement of NOII. It is important to recognize that NOII 'rejects any idea there can be "fair" or "just" or "reasonable" or "non racist" controls, and the distinction between "economic migrants" and "refugees", and between the "legal" and the "illegal."' And that NOII 'supports free movement and equal rights for all, and unity between all.'[116]

As the name suggests, NOII's activities do not simply pertain to the figure of the international illegal migrant, but to groups facing eviction on grounds of their movements. For example, NOII supported the Gypsies and Travellers campaign to resist eviction from Dale Farm.[117] NOII advocates numerous strategies to achieve their ends such as organizing local groups, protests and giving lectures.[118] To realize their ends, they seek to work through existing organizations that have state recognition when campaigning for social democratic causes, such as trade unions.[119] NOII remains very much in the tradition of action by social movements for civil and economic rights. However, NOII also seeks to engage the social base of new social movements. NOII has mutual support from Lush, an ethical cosmetics company tailored to the more discerning middle-class shopper. It has published NOII's newspaper and invited shoppers to sign a 'No One Is Illegal declaration'.[120]

However, the claim 'No One Is Illegal' embeds an even more disruptive element. To understand this, we must first highlight the ambivalent, unrecognized, but rendered illegal, position of the unwanted migrant. Cohen highlights this through the peculiarity of immigration law:

> In other areas of law it is the deed that is unlawful. In immigration control it is the person who becomes illegal – an illegal, a pariah, a non-person. In this way the modern migrant, immigrant and refugee assumes and resumes the status of the medieval outlaw – outside of legal norms and beyond legal protection.[121]

It is through this non-personhood, or rather non-citizenship, that the claim 'No One Is Illegal' disrupts the very conditions of legality. It is illegal to claim that no one is illegal, yet by making this claim, the supposedly stable boundary of legality between citizen and non-citizen is brought into question. The apparent exclusion of the status illegal is not reversed and simply a matter of inclusion, but the claim is one which endangers the very logic of differentiation between citizen and non-citizen. Nyers argues that claims such as 'No One Is Illegal' or 'Status for all' can be heard as declarations that are generative of a political subjectivity. The process of subjectification in this context allows non-status groups to extract themselves from the hegemonic categories by which political identity is normally understood. It is quite a wonderful paradox to say that publicly self-identifying as a non-status migrant is to engage in an act of citizenship.'[122]

NOII produced a World Passport which exemplifies this 'wonderful paradox' inherent in the act of citizenship. A passport is the traditional differentiator between citizen and non-citizen, the documentation that can make or break a person's right to reside and work. However, on the first page of NOII's World Passport, it is stated that 'human beings should not need passports, and should be free to go wherever they like . . . . until then, this passport will reassure officials of your humanity whenever it is challenged'.[123] It uses an object of domination and differentiation for other purposes. The World Passport symbolically subverts the authority of the traditional passport by asking users to fill in details innocuous to current state concerns (such as one's sense of humour or ability to juggle). Yet it also retains the similar demands for visibility (in this case showing fidelity to a criteria of a law-abiding and pacifist human), although such terms disrupt the very criteria of exclusion (a foreign nationality).

Yet, framing its ethos as a 'world without borders', NOII is also conflating the image of a state without 'we, the people' and a world without states. There is a difference between creative, inventive and autonomous acts that disrupt our established ways of doing and thinking and those that generate impossible missions thereby frustrating the subjects that it produces. It is perhaps best to separate creative, inventive and autonomous acts as generating heterotopias – counter-hegemonic spaces and possibilities – and those that urge utopias as expressions of the sovereign beast. Those who traverse frontiers must be careful what they wish for when they imagine a world without borders; resolving a paradox into a utopia can have unintended and dangerous consequences. Such a utopia may well engender a global or cosmopolitan sovereign beast with the aim to capture all movements within its reach.

ACT 13. OF STAGING: CLIMATE CAMP

In mid-August 2007, protesters assembled on the perimeter of Heathrow Airport to register their opposition to the British Airport Authority's (BAA) proposed expansion with a new runway.[124] Aside from increased air and noise pollution, the construction of a third runway also meant that the towns of Sipson and Harlington would have to be destroyed.[125] The weeklong campaign officially began on 14 August, yet a trademark 'eco-village' was set up 2 days prior on private land between these two towns roughly a kilometre from Heathrow.[126] Once underway, the protest gathered 2,000 people (including local residents) with non-violent direct action as its central feature. Thus was born the Heathrow Climate Camp. We will shortly see the creative and inventive aspects of the camp. But it also illustrates how an act can become a repertoire without frontiers by borrowing tactics from its predecessors. Although originating in the United Kingdom (in 2006 as a method of non-violent direct action organized along 'anarchist' principles against pollution from the Drax coal-fired power station, and followed up in 2007 at London Heathrow Airport and in 2009 in London during the G20 Summit), the camp has now been enacted in Canada, Denmark, France, Ireland, The Netherlands, Belgium, Scotland, Wales and Australia.

While such an act can be judged on the basis of its explicitly stated aims as when John McDonnell (MP) declared that the actions of Climate Camp made a 'pivotal contribution' to stopping the construction of a third runway, equally important were the siting and staging of the act. These themselves became political interventions and demonstrations.[127] The choice of campsite was, for example, itself an act of defiance against antiterrorism legislation and a statement about rights of protest in even the most securitized spaces. In late July, tensions mounted when the proposed Climate Camp was met with legal action by BAA on the grounds of disruption and security.[128] BAA sought an injunction whose net was inevitably cast to cover the diverse organizations that the protesters represented. If it had been passed, then the 5 million members of organizations such as the Woodland Trust, Greenpeace and the Royal Society for the Protection of Birds (RSPB) would have been tarred and tagged as potential demonstrators and potentially subject to arrest not only at Heathrow but also across major expressways such as the M25 and M4.[129] The majority of the political leaders supported the decision of the court, due to the excessive curbing of civil liberties and impracticalities of BAA's proposal. So the siting or production of a site as the condensation of politics was a centrally creative aspect of the act.

The staging of the act was creative too. Once the Heathrow Climate Camp was launched on 14 August, it functioned as a base of operations to devise actions that could disrupt BAA. Literature on direct action was disseminated and suggested that people should create a roadblock with a scrap car and that protesters should chain themselves to barriers.[130] On 17 August, nine protesters glued themselves to the Department for Transport.[131] The 19th became a day of direct action. Some scaled a building near the BAA headquarters with a banner 'Make Planes History'.[132] Several protesters prevented an employee from entering BAA headquarters.[133] Campaigners also practised civil disobedience by refusing to move from BAA headquarters.[134]

Just before siting and staging the act, Anna Jackson, the spokesperson for Climate Camp, stated the camp was '100 per cent democratic, run through consensus. It will be down to individuals' judgement as to what they think is the best way to take action.'[135] This inventive ethos struck a chord with George Monbiot, who argued that the actions of Climate Camp instantiated 'a genuine participatory democracy of the kind that you will never encounter in British public life'.[136] Monbiot found this to be a necessary challenge to the 'elaborate theatre of consultation and democracy . . . . designed only to hide the fact that the decision has already been made.'[137] Non-institutionalized, leaderless decision-making and 'taking democracy in your own hands' practices are clearly important spaces that have been created through the act of Climate Camp. So arguably the act was autonomous as well as being creative and inventive. It showed how to experiment with political deliberation without or against the rules that sanction what political deliberation should entail. Heathrow 2007 was as much a protest against the ineffectiveness of the government's response to climate change as it was an exemplification of what 'Climate Campers' considered ethical living and political engagement.

The act of Climate Camp functions with at least four aims. It seeks to exemplify an ethical living, implement a programme of education about climate change (and its associated causes), engage in 'movement-building' and undertake direct action.[138] In the majority of Climate Camp protests, the four aims become intertwined. The educational programme provides one of the bases for this combination. It produces a political subject that is not only aware of economic and environmental exploitation but also able to act in an ethical manner in relation to the environment. This manifests as compost toilets, solar power and vegan curries.[139] Far from being a privatized matter, the individual is taught that averting ecological catastrophe can only be realized if change is effectively traversal, crossing between personal and political, local and global and environmental and social. The staging works effectively as it demonstrates that activists can write their own scripts collectively and produce forms of engagement that are dramatic and illustrative. The London 2009 Climate Camp, for example, exemplifies this through an extensive workshop programme ranging from Yoga, direct action training and anti-capitalist marches to creating sustainable communities.[140]

Since forming in 2006 through a protest against pollution from the Drax coal-fired power station, the movement has increasingly raised the stakes. After Heathrow 2007, Climate Camp took its protests to London, this time against the G20 summit in 2009. Climate Camp's subsequent target was what they considered to be the ineffective 2009 Copenhagen Climate Summit: a conference aimed at bringing together state, business and NGO leaders from across the world in an effort to secure a consensus on the best means of dealing with climate change and the responsibilities each state should hold.[141] Climate Camp proposed holding an alternative assembly in the Bella Centre in Copenhagen where the United Nations Climate Change Conference (2009) was taking place.[142] This assembly brought together Climate activists from the North with grassroots movements of the South and discussed solutions such as food and energy sovereignty.[143] Oliver, a Climate Camp activist, expressed the rationale for this alternative assembly: '[I]t was to affirm practically our RIGHT to break in and hold an Assembly to talk of the peoples' solutions. To make it impossible to ignore that there IS an alternative agenda.'[144]

We can note two further lessons from the Climate Camp. First, it resignifies the camp against an image of a passive space of punishment and detention. It creatively and inventively produces an activist meaning for the word. Second, it literally brings into being a new space of politics by siting and staging an act in prohibited locations and thereby questioning both the prohibition itself and those spaces where politics is supposed to be staged. And it does all this at a time when political leaders and interpreters bemoan the decline of politics. The enactment of a citizen able to form alliances and solidarities without frontiers, local or international, and protest for environmental and social justice has been central to Climate Camp agenda since 2006.

Notes

.1 Google+ is a connection platform that is widely seen as a professional
Facebook. It was first tested by invitation-only accounts, which exceeded
its capacity. All this was probably a marketing technology to create hype by
driving expectations. But even then, it shows how such platforms have come to
dominate what it means to be connected. See D. Grant. 2011. Google+ Shuts
Down Invites . . . for Now: Is the Latest Social Network Playing Hard to Get,
or Just Worried About More Privacy Lawsuits? Salon, 30 June 2011 [cited 20
January 2012]. Source: http://goo.gl/b3Q02

2 One of the most prominent (and perhaps earliest) of such interpretations is
that by M. Castells, *The Rise of Network Society*, vol. 1, *The Information
Age: Economy, Society and Culture* (Cambridge, MA: Blackwell, 1996).
But there have been many more since such as J. Barkhoff and H. Eberhart,
*Networking across Borders and Frontiers: Demarcation and Connectedness
in European Culture and Society* (Frankfurt am Main: Peter Lang, 2009);
D. Barney, *Prometheus Wired: The Hope for Democracy in the Age of
Network Technology* (Vancouver: University of British Columbia Press,
2001); W. J. Mitchell, *Me++: The Cyborg Self and the Networked City*
(Cambridge, MA: MIT Press, 2003); D. Tambini, 'Civic Networking
and Universal Rights to Connectivity: Bologna,' in *Cyberdemocracy:
Technology, Cities, and Civic Networks*, ed. R. Tsagarousianou et al.
(London: Routledge, 1998).

3 See A.-P. de Man, *The Network Economy: Strategy, Structure and Management*
(Cheltenham: Edward Elgar, 2004).

4 Barney, *Prometheus Wired: The Hope for Democracy in the Age of Network
Technology*; Mitchell, *Me++: The Cyborg Self and the Networked City*.

5 B. Latour, *Reassembling the Social: An Introduction to Actor-Network-Theory*
(Oxford: Oxford University Press, 2005).

6 D. Harvey, *The Condition of Postmodernity: An Inquiry into the Origins of
Cultural Change* (Cambridge: Butterworth, 1989).

7 D. Della Porta, *Globalization from Below: Transnational Activists and Protest
Networks* (Minneapolis: University of Minnesota Press, 2006); Keck and
Sikkink, *Activists Beyond Borders: Advocacy Networks in International
Politics*; Reitan, *Global Activism*; Tarrow, *The New Transnational Activism*.

8 J. Allen, 'Powerful Geographies: Spatial Shifts in the Architecture of
Globalization,' in *The Sage Handbook of Power* (London: Sage, 2009), 169.

9 M. Hardt and A. Negri, *Empire* (Cambridge: Harvard University Press, 2000);
M. Hardt and A. Negri, *Multitude: War and Democracy in the Age of Empire*
(London: Penguin, 2005).

10 Hardt and Negri, *Multitude: War and Democracy in the Age of Empire*, 221–2.

11 Ibid., 222.

12 Ibid., 223.

13 Ibid., 225.

14 Ibid., 227.

15 A. W. Gouldner, *The Two Marxisms: Contradictions and Anomalies in the
Development of Theory* (London: Macmillan, 1980).

16 M. Foucault, 'Technologies of the Self,' in *Technologies of the Self: A Seminar with Michel Foucault*, ed. L. H. Martin et al. (Amherst: University of Massachusetts Press, 1988), 224.

17 Ian Hacking uses the phrase 'historical ontology' as a title for a book. He says 'Ontology has been dry and dusty, but I lift my title from an author whom none consider arid, even if he has now fallen from grace in some quarters, into a mire of unkind refutations. In his remarkable essay "What Is Enlightenment?" Michel Foucault twice referred to "the historical ontology of ourselves". This could be the name of a study, he said, that was concerned with "truth through which we constitute ourselves as objects of knowledge"; with "power through which we constitute ourselves as subjects acting on others" and with "ethics through which we constitute ourselves as moral agents": He calls these the axes of knowledge, power, and ethics.' Hacking, *Historical Ontology*, 2.

18 Foucault, 'Technologies of the Self,' 225.

19 Foucault, *The Care of the Self*; M. Foucault, *The Government of Self and Others* (Basingstoke: Palgrave Macmillan, 2010); M. Foucault, *The Hermeneutics of the Subject: Lectures at the Collège De France 1981–1982* (New York: Palgrave MacMillan, 2005); Foucault, *The Use of Pleasure*.

20 G. Deleuze, *Foucault* (Minneapolis, MN: University of Minnesota Press, 1988), 94–122. He later revisits it in G. Deleuze, 'Postscript on Control Societies,' in *Negotiations* (New York: Columbia University Press, 1990).

21 Deleuze, *Foucault*, 96–7.

22 Ibid., 97.

23 Ibid., 98.

24 Ibid.

25 Ibid., 100.

26 Ibid., 104.

27 Deleuze, ibid., suggests that this formulation is an outline of Foucault's discussion in Foucault, *The Use of Pleasure*, 25–32. However, Foucault's discussion does not exactly match Deleuze's four modes of subjectivation. The reason is, I think, that Deleuze is keen to place subjectivation within the broader work of Foucault and he was more concerned with the double than Foucault was in *The Use of Pleasure*.

28 Deleuze, *Foucault*, 105.

29 Foucault, *The Use of Pleasure*, 26–7.

30 Ibid., 28.

31 Ibid., 27.

32 Foucault, *The Care of the Self*, 81–95. The chapter is in the third volume and it is called 'the political game'. Here Foucault gives an image of how he would use the four modes of subjectivation in analyzing the political subject.

33 Ibid., 81.

34 Ibid., 82.

35 Ibid., 82–3.

36 Ibid., 84.

37 Ibid.

38 Deleuze, *Foucault*, 105.

39 Deleuze, 'Postscript on Control Societies'.

40 Hardt and Negri, *Empire*, 412. 'We are thinking of nothing like that and of no one who acts on the basis of duty and discipline, who pretends his or her actions are deduced from an ideal plan. We are referring, on the contrary, to something more like the communist and liberatory combatants of the twentieth-century revolutions, the intellectuals who were persecuted and exiled in the course of anti-fascist struggles, the republicans of the Spanish civil war and the European resistance movements, and the freedom fighters of all the anticolonial and anti-imperialist wars.'

41 Ibid., 36. 'The term [international NGOs] refers to a wide variety of groups, but we are referring here principally to the global, regional, and local organizations that are dedicated to relief work and the protection of human rights, such as Amnesty International, Oxfam and *Médecins sans Frontiéres*. Such humanitarian NGOs are in effect (even if this runs counter to the intentions of the participants) some of the most powerful pacific weapons of the new world order – the charitable campaigns and the mendicant orders of Empire.'

42 Ibid., 399–400. 'What specific and concrete practices will animate this political project? We cannot say at this point. What we can see nonetheless is a first element of a political program for the global multitude, a first political demand: *global citizenship. . . . The general right to control its own movement is the multitude's ultimate demand for global citizenship.*'

43 D. Bigo, 'Pierre Bourdieu and International Relations: Power of Practices, Practices of Power,' *International Political Sociology* 5, 3 (2011).

44 Deleuze, *Foucault*, 110.

45 Ibid., 110–11.

46 Allen, 'Powerful Geographies: Spatial Shifts in the Architecture of Globalization,' 171.

47 This is what Ash Amin calls the politics of connectivity. A. Amin, 'Spatialities of Globalisation,' *Environment and Planning A* 34 (2002); A. Amin, 'Towards a New Politics of Place,' *Geografiska Annaler. Series B, Human Geography* 86, 1 (2004).

48 Perhaps the rules of the political game are changing. Can we not say that, recalling Foucault, the new rules of the political game make it, once again, more difficult to define the relations between what we were, what we could do and what we are expected to accomplish?

49 I do not remember when I first encountered the word 'topological' but I was awakened to it when Annemarie Mol asked me after a lecture I had given on method whether I saw any parallels between how genealogical method deals with time and how topological method deals with space. This was on 1 September 2010 during a CRESC conference in St Hugh's College at Oxford University. I do not recall my answer but it could not have been intelligible. I am indebted to Annemarie Mol and John Law as well as John Allen whose works enabled me to draw these parallels between genealogical and topological.

50 Mol and Law state it much more eloquently: 'The old idea was that scientific truth was more than global, it was universal. Once it was established then it was like God: everywhere without any need to move. But in the last thirty years science has been brought down to earth. Technoscience studies have

given it a place on earth. A place, for instance, in the laboratory. In the first stages of this work, science was *regionalized*.' J. Law et al., 'Situating Technoscience: An Inquiry into Spatialities,' *Environment and Planning D: Society and Space* 19 (2001): 618.

51 Ibid.; A. Mol and J. Law, 'Regions, Networks and Fluids: Anaemia and Social Topology,' *Social Studies of Science* 24 (1994).

52 Besides, I would make a similar argument regarding the turn towards social practices in the social science over the last few decades. Arguably, a similar turn away from the universality of truth to its effects in social practices has been taking place. A parallel transformation can also be suggested in history where 'genealogical' studies have made a major impact. In fact, it would be interesting to draw comparisons between 'topological' understandings of space and 'genealogical' understandings of time in the social sciences and humanities.

53 J. Allen, 'Three Spaces of Power: Territory, Networks, Plus a Topological Twist in the Tale of Domination and Authority,' *Journal of Power* 2 (2009).

54 Mol and Law, 'Regions, Networks and Fluids: Anaemia and Social Topology,' 643.

55 For Latour, subjectivity of the subject cannot be limited to the human subject but must be expanded to things that constitute the networked space that we inhabit. Thus, things will also have subjectivity if not political subjectivity as evinced by the term 'the parliament of things'. I would not object to 'things' having agency among their properties even their ability to cause other things happen. But the attribution of political agency or, more precisely, political subjectivity to things glosses over the performative force of social and political beings such as ourselves.

56 Mol and Law, 'Regions, Networks and Fluids: Anaemia and Social Topology,' 649.

57 Ibid., 659. As Mol and Law put it 'In a fluid space it's not possible to determine identities nice and neatly, once and for all. Or to distinguish inside from outside, this place from somewhere else. Similarity and difference aren't like identity and non-identity. They come, as it were, in varying shades and colours. They go together.'

58 Law and Mol, 'Situating Technoscience: An Inquiry into Spatialities'.

59 This is how Law and Mol put it: 'We have suggested that shape constancy may be understood as a stable pattern of conjoined alterity in which continuity depends upon discontinuity, or presence upon absence, the movement or displacement between here and there. This spatial metaphor does not explain or even articulate globalization. Unlike networks and fluids, it does is not talk about transport through regional space. What it does, instead, is to turn universality inside out. Here, then, and paradoxically, the global is already included in the local.'

60 Law and Mol, 'Situating Technoscience: An Inquiry into Spatialities,' 617.

61 Allen, 'Three Spaces of Power: Territory, Networks, Plus a Topological Twist in the Tale of Domination and Authority,' 206.

62 Allen, 'Powerful Geographies: Spatial Shifts in the Architecture of Globalization'; Allen, 'Three Spaces of Power: Territory, Networks, Plus a Topological Twist in the Tale of Domination and Authority'; J. Allen and A. Cochrane, 'Assemblages of State Power: Topological Shifts in the Organization of Government and Politics,' *Antipode* 42 (2010).

63 Allen, 'Three Spaces of Power: Territory, Networks, Plus a Topological Twist in the Tale of Domination and Authority,' 207.

64 The image of the internet as an ungoverned and ungovernable space while it persisted for some time has been effectively discredited by R. J. Deibert and R. Rohozinski, 'Under Cover of the Net: This Hidden Governance Mechanisms of Cyberspace,' in *Ungoverned Spaces: Alternatives to State Authority in an Era of Softened Sovereignty*, ed. A. L. Clunan and H. A. Trinkunas (Stanford, CA: Stanford Security Studies, 2010).

65 That I use the term 'how' indicates a 'method'. This should be qualified. The series of principles that emerged with the idea of 'acts of citizenship' is less a method and more an 'after method' in the sense John Law has argued. See J. Law, *After Method: Mess in Social Science Research* (London: Routledge, 2004). This chapter is also as method close in spirit to what Bruno Latour says about his book: 'In some ways this book resembles a travel guide through a terrain that is at once completely banal – it's nothing but the social world we are used to – and completely exotic – we will have to learn how to slow down at each step. If earnest scholars do not find it dignifying to compare an introduction of a science to a travel guide, be they kindly reminded that "where to travel" and "what is worth seeing there" is nothing but a way of saying in plain English what is usually said under the pompous Greek name of "method" or, even worse, "methodology".' See Latour, *Reassembling the Social: An Introduction to Actor-Network-Theory*, 17.

66 J. Preston. 2011. Movement Began with Outrage and a Facebook Page that Gave It an Outlet. *The New York Times*, 5 February 2011 [cited 30 July 2011]. Source: http://goo.gl/9d7Q6

67 S. Krishnappa. 2011. Google Man Wael Ghonim Emerges as the Face of Egypt Protests. *International Business Times*, 9 February 2011 [cited 30 July 2011]. Source: http://goo.gl/LsGYs

68 Channel 4 News. 2011. Egypt: Behind the Online 'Hero' Who Galvanised Protests. Channel 4 News, 9 February 2011 [cited 30 July 2011]. Source: http://goo.gl/xRNJq

69 Preston. 2011. Movement Began with Outrage and a Facebook Page that Gave It an Outlet [cited 30 July 2011]. Source: http://goo.gl/9d7Q6

70 We are all Khaled Said. 2010. One Message in Many Languages Campaign. We are all Khaled Said, 31 July 2010 [cited 30 July 2011]. Source: http://goo.gl/LocoZ

71 BBC. 2011. Egypt: 'We Are All Khaled Said'. BBC, 17 February 2011 [cited 30 July 2011]. Source: http://goo.gl/Zp9Zj

72 Z. Harb, 'Arab Revolutions and the Social Media Effect,' *M/C* 14, 2 (2011).

73 M. Martin. 2011. Police from Khaled Said's Egypt Still Terrorize Egyptian Activists. *International Business News*, 30 June 2011 [cited 30 July 2011]. Source: http://goo.gl/GZqXb

74 Channel 4 News. 2011. Google Executive Optimistic About Egypt's Revolution. Channel 4 News, 17 May 2011 [cited 30 July 2011]. Source: http://goo.gl/1943R

75 BBC. 2011. Profile: Egypt's Wael Ghonim. BBC, 9 February 2011 [cited 30 July 2011]. Source: http://goo.gl/FrbiP

76 Ibid.

77   Channel 4 News, Egypt: Behind the Online 'Hero' Who Galvanised Protests [cited 30 July 2011]. Source: http://goo.gl/xRNJq

78   M. L. Sifry. 2011. Did Facebook Bring Down Mubarak? CNN, 11 February 2011 [cited 30 July 2011]. Source: http://goo.gl/1SHpH

79   Krishnappa. Google Man Wael Ghonim Emerges as the Face of Egypt Protests [cited 30 July 2011]. Source: http://goo.gl/LsGYs

80   A. M. Attia et al., 'Commentary: The Impact of Social Networking Tools on Political Change in Egypt's "Revolution 2.0",' *Electronic Commerce Research and Applications* 10, 4 (2011): 369–74.

81   Ibid.

82   LA Times. 2011. Wael Ghonim, Google Exec, Says Egypt's Revolution Is 'Like Wikipedia'. *LA Times*, 14 February 2011 [cited 30 July 2011]. Source: http://goo.gl/pj3jA

83   LA Times. 2011. Google Exec Wael Ghonim in Egypt Says Long Live the Revolution 2.0, 11 February 2011 [cited 30 July 2011]. Source: http://goo.gl/e8kD0

84   U. Mejias, 'The Twitter Revolution Must Die,' *International Journal of Learning and Media* 4, 2 (2011).

85   LA Times, Google Exec Wael Ghonim in Egypt Says Long Live the Revolution 2.0 [cited 30 July 2011]. Source: http://goo.gl/e8kD0.

86   Mejias, 'The Twitter Revolution Must Die,' 4.

87   S. J. Vaughan-Nichols. 2011. The Internet Goes Dark in Egypt. ZDNet, 27 January 2011 [cited 30 July 2011]. Source: http://goo.gl/5XmHz

88   As 2011 came to a close, connectivity or 'we, the connected' became *the* dominant narrative in the media; it was celebrated as the year of the networked revolutions. C. Doctorow. 2012. The Internet Is the Best Place for Dissent to Start: Ethan Zuckerman's Compelling 'Cute Cats Theory' Has Changed My Mind about the Internet's Role in the Struggle for Global Justice. *The Guardian*, 3 January 2012 [cited 5 January 2012]. Source: http://goo.gl/OgOie; J. Harris. 2011. The Year of the Networked Revolution: From the Occupy Movement to the Middle East, Calls for Political and Personal Freedom Were Aided by Social Media. *The Guardian*, 13 December 2011 [cited 5 January 2012]. Source: http://goo.gl/0fOTs; B. Wasik. 2011. #Riot: Self-Organized, Hyper-Networked Revolts – Coming to a City near You. Wired, 16 December 2011 [cited 5 January 2012]. Source: http://goo.gl/IyoZ7.

89   *The Guardian* maintains a site dedicated to LulzSec at http://goo.gl/JkVTV.

90   J. Halliday et al. 2011. LulzSec Hacking Suspect 'Topiary' Arrested. *The Guardian*, 27 July 2011 [cited 7 August 2011]. Source: http://goo.gl/ODkFw

91   C. Arthur. 2011. Alleged LulzSec Hacker Released on Bail. *The Guardian*, 1 August 2011 [cited 7 August 2011]. Source: http://goo.gl/zrKVR

92   J. Menn. 2011. Anonymous Is the Best Known 'Hacktivist' Group, a Virtual Mob that Makes it Easy for People to Participate in Protests. *Financial Times*, 2011 [cited 23 September 2011]. Source: http://on.ft.com/ncyxtE

93   Halliday, Arthur and Ball, LulzSec Hacking Suspect 'Topiary' Arrested [cited 7 August 2011]. Source: http://goo.gl/ODkFw

94   N. Allen. 2011. LulzSec Hacker Group Disbands. *The Telegraph*, 26 June 2011 [cited 26 June 2011]. Source: http://goo.gl/3Of8j

95   R. Gallagher. 2011. Why Hacker Group LulzSec Went on the Attack. *The Guardian* 2011 [cited 14 July 2011]. Source: http://goo.gl/VRkrQ

96   BBC. 2011. Data of Sun Website Users Stolen. BBC, 2 August 2011 [cited 7 August 2011]. Source: http://goo.gl/bUhxy

97   Arthur, Alleged LulzSec Hacker Released on Bail [cited 7 August 2011]. Source: http://goo.gl/zrKVR

98   Gallagher. Why Hacker Group LulzSec Went on the Attack [cited 14 July 2011]. Source: http://goo.gl/VRkrQ

99   C. Arthur and J. Ball. 2011. LulzSec Leader Denies Links to Extremist Groups. *The Guardian*, 29 July 2011 [cited 7 August 2011]. Source: http://goo.gl/JBfRQ

100   Gallagher, Why Hacker Group LulzSec Went on the Attack [cited 14 July 2011]. Source: http://goo.gl/VRkrQ

101   M. Milone, 'Hacktivism: Securing the National Infrastructure,' *Knowledge, Technology & Policy* 16, 1 (2003): 76.

102   Ibid., 77.

103   Ibid.

104   S. Watts. 2011. Newsnight Online 'Chat' with Lulz Security Hacking Group. BBC, 24 June 2011 [cited 7 August 2011]. Source: http://goo.gl/twj4g

105   BBC, Data of Sun Website Users Stolen [cited 7 August 2011]. Source: http://goo.gl/bUhxy

106   C. Nye. 2011. The Art of the Pithy Hashtag. BBC, 4 August 2011 [cited 7 August 2011]. Source: http://goo.gl/nHccN

107   P. Krapp, 'Terror and Play, or What Was Hacktivism?' *Grey Room* 21, Fall (2005): 88.

108   Ibid.

109   Arthur, Charles, Dan Sabbagh and Sandra Laville. 2012. Lulzsec Leader Sabu Was Working for Us, Says FBI. *The Guardian*, 7 March 2012 [cited 18 June 2012]. Source: http://goo.gl/eOTR8

110   No One Is Illegal. 2003. No One Is Illegal Manifesto. No One Is Illegal, 6 September 2003 [cited 19 September 2011]. Source: http://goo.gl/MliJw

111   T. Hayter, 'Open Borders: The Case against Immigration Controls,' in *The Cultures of Economic Migration: International Perspectives*, ed. S. Gupta and T. Omoniyi (Aldershot: Ashgate, 2007), 24.

112   No One Is Illegal. No One Is Illegal Manifesto [cited 19 September 2011]. Source: http://goo.gl/MliJw

113   S. Cohen, *No One Is Illegal: Asylum and Immigration Control, Past and Present* (Stoke on Trent: Trentham Books, 2003).

114   Ibid., 244.

115   Ibid.

116   No One Is Illegal. 2011. No One Is Illegal. No One Is Illegal, 9 June 2011 [cited 19 September 2011]. Source: http://goo.gl/2x0Mh

117   No One Is Illegal. 2011. Solidarity with Dale Farm. No One Is Illegal, 11 April 2011 [cited 19 September 2011]. Source: http://goo.gl/GoAjW

118   No One Is Illegal. 2011. What You Can Do. No One Is Illegal 2011 [cited 19 September 2011]. Source: http://goo.gl/zvyKH

119   No One Is Illegal. 2011. Fight for the Rights of Migrant Workers. No One Is Illegal 2011 [cited 19 September 2011]. Source: http://goo.gl/svytn

120   No One Is Illegal. 2011. UK Retailer Backs National Campaign to End Controls. No One Is Illegal, 19 May 2011 [cited 19 September 2011]. Source: http://goo.gl/llxjG

121 Cohen, *No One Is Illegal: Asylum and Immigration Control, Past and Present*, 3.

122 P. Nyers, 'No One Is Illegal between City and Nation,' *Studies in Social Justice* 4, 2 (2010): 141.

123 No One Is Illegal. 2011. World Passport. No One Is Illegal, 2011 [cited 19 September 2011]. Source: http://goo.gl/aP95y

124 BBC. 2007. Heathrow Protesters Set up Camp. BBC, 12 August 2007 [cited 12 July 2011]. Source: http://goo.gl/9tPnl

125 S. Gray. 2007. Climate Change Protesters Set up Heathrow Camp. *The Independent*, 13 August 2007 [cited 12 July 2011]. Source: http://goo.gl/zzsxi

126 BBC, Heathrow Protesters Set up Camp [cited 12 July 2011]. Source: http://goo.gl/9tPnl

127 B. v. d. Zee. 2011. Climate Camp Disbanded. *The Guardian*, 2 March 2011 [cited 12 July 2011]. Source: http://goo.gl/OAMJ6

128 M. Hickman and N. Morris. 2011. Battle of Heathrow: Opposition to Baa's Injunction Grows. *The Independent*, 27 July 2011 [cited 12 July 2011]. Source: http://goo.gl/MD8PD

129 Ibid.

130 D. Millward and B. Malkin. 2007. Heathrow Climate Protest Grows by the Hour. *The Telegraph*, 14 August 2007 [cited 12 July 2011]. Source: http://goo.gl/NRWC1

131 N. Paris. 2007. Heathrow Campers Glued to Transport Office. *The Telegraph*, 17 August 2007 [cited 12 July 2011]. Source: http://goo.gl/a3sgv

132 M. Smit. 2007. Climate Camp Protestors Skirmish with Police. *The Telegraph*, 19 August 2007 [cited 12 July 2011]. Source: http://goo.gl/BrTYg

133 F. Attewill. 2007. Last Climate Activists Quit Heathrow Camp. *The Guardian*, 20 August 2007 [cited 12 July 2011]. Source: http://goo.gl/kaQJv

134 H. Mulholland. 2007. Heathrow Protesters Clash with Riot Police. *The Guardian*, 19 August 2007 [cited 12 July 2011]. Source: http://goo.gl/b7ngQ

135 Gray, Climate Change Protesters Set up Heathrow Camp [cited 12 July 2011]. Source: http://goo.gl/zzsxi

136 G. Monbiot. 2007. Beneath Heathrow's Pall of Misery, a New Political Movement Is Born. *The Guardian*, 21 August 2007 [cited 12 July 2011]. Source: http://goo.gl/BZPgN

137 Ibid.

138 Climate Camp. 2011. About Us. Camp for Climate Action 2011 [cited 12 July 2011]. Source: http://goo.gl/TUPby

139 Zee, Climate Camp Disbanded [cited 12 July 2011]. Source: http://goo.gl/OAMJ6

140 Climate Camp. 2009. Workshops Programme. Climate Camp 2009 [cited 12 July 2011]. Source: http://goo.gl/hu0Y7

141 UN. United Nations Framework Convention on Climate Change. 2009. The United Nations Climate Change Conference in Copenhagen, 7–19 December 2009. United Nations 2009 [cited 12 July 2011]. Source: http://goo.gl/PRSZh

142 Climate Camp. 2009. Copenhagen 2009: A Call to Action. Climate Camp 2009 [cited 12 July 2011]. Source: http://goo.gl/IuSm8

143 Olivier. 2009. Analysis of Victories in Copenhagen. Climate Camp, 29 December 2009 [cited 12 July 2011]. Source: http://goo.gl/0dexG

144 Ibid.

CHAPTER FOUR

Enacting Citizenship

Chapters 2 and 3 have considered two grand narratives that shape modern political subjectivities. These two are not the only, let alone dominant, narratives. But what makes them 'grand' is their ubiquitous character. Through various rituals, practices, routines, protocols, institutions, declarations, proclamations and statements, each narrative has become the form through which subjects come into being through invitations, interpellations, enforcement, law, norms, rules and regulations that make up heterogeneous and complex fields of political identification.[1] Through citations, repetitions and iterations of those elements that constitute these narratives as fields, subjectivities are performatively taken up. It is often recognized that sovereignty understood as 'we, the people' has performed such a function; it is much less so in the case of connectivity as 'we, the connected'. As we have seen, each narrative has a significant bearing on citizenship understood as political subjectivity.

But what does 'citizenship as political subjectivity' mean? The phrase appeared early in this book and it never quite disappeared or lost its evocative force. Yet, so far I have not explained it either. We focused on the idea of subjectivation in Chapter 3 and political subjectivation would probably have been a better term for continuing our discussion in Chapter 4. But here and now we will depart from a problem that exercised Foucault, Deleuze and Bourdieu. The insistence on the immanent character of the fold (Deleuze), habitus (Bourdieu) or subjectivation (Foucault) leads to an emphasis on how subjects come into being as ethical or moral subjects. But I am interested in political subjectivity as creative, inventive and autonomous ways of becoming political through relating to oneself and others. It may sound surprising but Deleuze, Foucault or Bourdieu were rarely, if at all, interested in political subjectivity as a performative force that breaks habits or ways of doing things and throws the subject into uncertainty, indeterminacy and the unknown. On two occasions that I quoted in Chapter 1,

Foucault reflected on the subject that acts but otherwise he focused on technologies of power and technologies of the self and the relation between the two, which he called governmentality. We will see below during a discussion of Austin that Bourdieu also focused on the subject who conducts himself or herself rather than the subject who acts. I used the phrase 'creative, inventive and autonomous' in Chapter 1, but it is in this chapter that I will develop it. Still, I shall argue, what makes subjectivity political is not only that it is creative, inventive and autonomous but that it also articulates an injustice and demands or claims its redress. It is this demand or claim that gives birth to political subjectivity and its expression to rights. This is what the concept 'enacting citizenship' signifies. It places emphasis on the transformation of practices that lead to the emergence of creative, inventive and autonomous acts of becoming political subjects. Unless we develop a dynamic understanding of citizenship that is performative, it would be impossible to develop the idea of citizens without frontiers as those whose acts traverse frontiers and interrogate and transgress both sovereignty and connectivity narratives.

Citizenship as political subjectivity

Let us start with citizenship and then return to political subjectivity. I find it useful to describe citizenship as the right to claim rights.[2] This phrase highlights the idea that before there are any rights, there is the right to be political and that the right to be political can only exist by exercising it. This may sound like a circular argument but the idea here is that the existence of rights presupposes political subjectivity and rights are effective only in practice. Without practising that right (to have or claim rights), we cannot even claim to be human. If we think that we have rights by virtue of being human, then this phrase reminds us that we have gained the right to say so only because we have struggled *for it* as political subjects. To put it in another way, and perhaps counter-intuitive way, we become political subjects before we become bearers of human rights. Without struggling as political subjects, we cannot have dignity, justice, peace, freedom, speech let alone economic, social, cultural or sexual rights. The source of the right to claim rights is more dynamic than if we assume it is God, humanity or the state. It is social and political struggles that connect and combine demands and claims and articulate them through available sources (legal, illegal, social, cultural, religious or other).[3]

There are basically three ways that we can approach citizenship: status, habitus and acts. If we were to approach citizenship as status, our concern would be things such as rules, regulations and laws that govern who can and cannot be a citizen in a given state. We would want to know who qualifies for citizenship and the laws of acquisition and deprivation of citizenship. We would learn about things such as *jus sanguinis* (whereby a child inherits citizenship via a parent), *jus soli* (whereby a child inherits citizenship via birth regardless of parentage) or *jus domicili* (whereby an adult acquires citizenship by naturalization in a state other than that of his birth). These three principles (*jus sanguinis*, *jus soli* and *jus domicili*) attach statuses to individual or collective bodies. Migration (and immigration) scholars, especially in law but also in sociology and politics, focus on citizenship as status because it affects who can or cannot hold rights in a given state.[4] Approaching citizenship as status also includes consideration of the legal rights and responsibilities of citizens in a given state. This is probably the most dominant way of approaching citizenship. National and comparative rights in modern states itself is a rapidly changing field as these rights and responsibilities in turn change rapidly.[5] We would be interested in knowing what social rights (e.g. welfare benefits, housing subsidies, unemployment insurance) and civil liberties such as privacy, due process in courts and rights to assembly pertain in a given state.

If we were to approach citizenship as habitus, we would be interested in how citizens and perhaps non-citizens practice the rights that they do have.[6] Just because citizens have the right to vote, participate, claim benefits, move and so on, this should not imply that they practice these rights and we would be interested to know why they do and why they do not. Quite understandably, sociologists and anthropologists have most contributed to this approach to citizenship through studies of citizenship practices.[7] Rather than attaching statuses to bodies, approaching citizenship as habitus asks how those bodies come into being and how those statuses get attached to them. That is why they have also been interested in things such as multicultural, sexual, global and environmental forms of citizenship as these indicate different and perhaps sometimes novel ways of practising citizenship.[8]

If we were to approach citizenship as acts, we would be interested in how people constitute themselves as political subjects by the things they do, their deeds. Just notice already the change in approach. It is not so much that we are interested in people but in how the various things that they do – deeds – actually make them who they are or, rather, how they make themselves through the things they do. But, we may ask, this sounds a lot like approaching citizenship as practices just as sociologists and anthropologists have done. Not quite. If we approach citizenship as acts, we would be interested not only what people do but also how the things they do break away from norms, expectations, routines, rituals, in short, their habitus. This is because if we approach citizenship as status and practices, we focus on already constituted orders, as it were, under which those with status practise their citizenship or those without are denied from practising. By contrast, if we approach citizenship as acts, we are interested in how those whose status is not citizenship may act as if they are and claim rights that they may not have. This brings an element of disruption or rupture into the order and may call for the subject to break his or her habitus. If we recall our discussion of Rancière and Laclau, then approaching citizenship as acts clearly shares strong affinities with their approach to political subjectivity. I raised issues with their commitment to people as a whole and admitted that 'politics without people' does indeed sound strange if not dangerous. Yet, pursuing citizenship as political subjectivity requires maintaining this critical distance from the need to identify people as the foundation of political identification for the reasons that I encapsulated in the term 'the sovereign beast' that makes itself present in both narratives of 'we, the people' and 'we, the connected'. This chapter then is not only about citizenship as political subjectivity but also how we might conceive it without the category 'people'. And ultimately it is this possibility that lies at the heart of the concept of 'citizens without frontiers'.

Disobedience as enacting citizenship

It is 19 December 2008. An auction is being held by the US Government's Bureau of Land Management (BLM) of drilling rights for oil and gas development on parcels of national park land primarily in the western states, including wilderness areas in Utah national parks. There are protests outside the federal building in Salt Lake City where the auction is taking place. Among the protesters is Tim DeChristopher, a 27-year-old activist and an economics student at the University of Utah. He decides to enter the federal building rather than protest outside. Asked later about his 'intention', he recounts: 'I went into the auction with the idea of creating a little disruption, maybe making a speech and getting myself arrested.'[9] This so far sounds like he was 'intending' to stage a direct action used widely by activists. When he enters the building, remarkably, the person at the desk asks 'Are you here to bid?' It is a question. But is also an interpellation, that is, an invitation to occupy or inhabit a position, a subject position. Apparently in a spontaneous and unpremeditated manner, he says yes. He receives an auction sign marked Bidder 70. By the time a federal official finally stops him, Bidder 70 will have made successful bids for more than 22,000 acres of land worth $1.8 million. The question arises: Was he a genuine or authentic bidder?

The court decides he was not. But DeChristopher disagrees and asks: What does a genuine bidder mean? This is a good question but the court does not answer it. Instead, it sentences him to 2 years in prison and fines him $10,000 for disrupting a federal auction.[10] Although the sentence could have been harsher for an 'act of civil disobedience', it was still a significant punishment given that in his statement DeChristopher asked the judge to consider various possibilities of community service as punishment. It was widely believed that 'The U.S. Attorney's office went after DeChristopher because they wanted to make an example out of him, to show other activists what happens when you mess with the system.'[11] Calling this a 'Rosa Parks' moment for environmental activism, it is suggested that DeChristopher's act revealed how the US legal system favoured corporate interests.

This act illustrates almost all of the qualities (perhaps save one) of what enacting citizenship involves despite the insistence of both the activist himself and other interpreters to call it an 'act of civil disobedience' rather than an 'act of citizenship'. One quality that it does not perhaps feature is the traversing of frontiers in any obvious way but we will see if that is the case in due course. Throughout this chapter, we will discuss in more detail elements that constitute enacting citizenship and will return to this act, among others, to illustrate conceptual issues. We will also discuss why it is important to call it an act of citizenship and insist on keeping disobedience within the idea of citizenship rather than considering it an exception. But we will make two observations on this act before we start our discussion on enacting citizenship and its relation to the concept 'citizens without frontiers'.

To return to the issue of civil disobedience, quoting the prosecutor's claim that 'The rule of law is the bedrock of our civilized society, not acts of "civil disobedience" committed in the name of the cause of the day,' DeChristopher argues instead that the birth of the United States of America and the rule of law were creations of acts of civil disobedience.[12] Moreover, 'DeChristopher's defence was complicated from the start when the judge refused to hear arguments that he had been compelled to act, to prevent a greater evil.'[13] Here is an intended direct action that turns into a purposive but non-intentional and creative act. DeChristopher is 'compelled' to act against his responsibilities to observe and obey the rules of the auction and instead to act answerably for his understanding of the common good. After all, he thinks, 'the rule of law is dependent upon a government that is willing to abide by the law. Disrespect for the rule of law begins when the government believes itself and its corporate sponsors to be above the law.'[14]

This act reveals the complex qualities that constitute an act: paradoxes of legality and illegality, responsibility and answerability, intentionality and purposiveness, acts and actions, and rupture and change. We are interested in it because it is creative (deliberate yet spontaneous, mischievous yet serious, courageous yet not heroic), inventive (surprising yet predictable, illegal yet acceptable, outrageous yet reasonable) and autonomous (individual yet collective, scripted yet experimental, unauthorized yet meaningful). It also shows why it is important to insist on calling it an act of citizenship and introduce that phrase into our political vocabulary and analytics. That, at least, is the argument we will pursue. I mentioned above that we will depart from the insistence on the immanent character of the fold (Deleuze), habitus (Bourdieu) or subjectivation (Foucault) to describe our relations with ourselves and others. What I propose in the following is to first focus on Hannah Arendt's theory of action as it is relevant both to consider civil disobedience and to interpret action as beginning something new rather than repeating or reiterating behaviour or practice. Then I will broaden the discussion from Arendt to theories of performativity and enactment before I return to the question of citizenship as political subjectivity.

Beginning something new

Arendt starts from the position that action – as distinguished from not only contemplation but also work and labour – enables human beings to perform their agency, which involves bringing something new into the world whose outcomes are unpredictable. For her, if humans were reproducible repetitions of the same whose essence was predictable, we would not need the concept of action.[15] Unlike Deleuze, Foucault or Bourdieu then Arendt differentiates action from conduct and makes action the beginning of something new as her sustained focus. Unfortunately, Arendt relates this capacity to begin something new to natality. For Arendt, each human shares the condition of natality, which gives us the capacity to initiate something new because each human being is born with the inherent capacity to come into the world as new.[16] I am unconvinced about the usefulness of associating this capacity with natality rather than seeing it as a capacity that we historically develop. At any rate, what is significant here is that both speech and action, or more accurately, speech as action reveals this capacity and discloses each human being in the presence of and in relation to others.[17] I like the idea of action as the disclosure of ourselves that we neither anticipate nor determine. Arendt reserves the term 'action' for the actualization of this capacity. To act then means to take initiative, to begin and to set something new into motion. Because humans are newcomers and beginners by virtue of birth, they are always prompted into action, into disclosing themselves to others. Arendt calls this capacity, or what it enables human beings to initiate, a 'miracle'. However, that newcomers bring something new into being is a miracle not because it is mystical but because it is unexpected and unpredicted. As Arendt puts it, 'not because we superstitiously believe in miracles, but because human beings, whether or not they know it, as long as they can act, are capable of achieving, and constantly do achieve, the improbable and unpredictable'.[18] Each human is capable of performing the unexpected and it is only through this performance that each human being is able to disclose himself or herself as human.

> The fact that man is capable of action means that the unexpected can be expected from him, that he is able to perform what is infinitely improbable. And this again is possible only because each man is unique, so that with each birth something uniquely new comes into the world.[19]

What an action reveals or discloses is not a being that already exists but a being that becomes through this disclosure or revelation. From this brief description, we may conclude that Arendt holds a subjectivist view of the agent but that is wrong. That she starts with this capacity does not mean that it expresses a sovereign subject capable of commanding a will and controlling the outcomes of its actions. We shall see shortly how Arendt addresses this but now let us take a step back and consider why it is important to hold a view of the agent that places emphasis on this capacity to bring something new into the world.

Theorizing action became so fundamental to Arendt that it pretty much preoccupied her throughout the 1950s and 1960s, after the publication of *The Origins of Totalitarianism* (1951). In fact, it makes its first appearance at the very end of that book with a section on ideology and terror as key aspects of totalitarianism as a novel form of government. Arguably, we can trace the origins of Arendt's theorizing of action to the end of *Totalitarianism*. There, having traced the conditions that led to the rise of totalitarian regimes, she concludes that totalitarianism is a distinct form of government and should not be equated with despotism, tyranny or dictatorship. What is both important and poignant here is that she ends her genealogical investigations with reflections on isolation, solitude and loneliness. Now, it may appear odd to end a treatise on the origins of totalitarianism with existential themes of solitude and loneliness but this is precisely her point: that totalitarianism both produced and was made possible by a figure of a human being who could not act, or rather whose capacity to act was negated. Totalitarian authorities were dependent upon developing a coercive logic by which individuals became isolated and were unable to act together. What totalitarianism achieved, if that is the word, was to make people invest in its logic by withdrawing from what Arendt already calls 'the great capacity of men to start something new'.[20] Totalitarianism disciplines individuals to invest in its logic, thus convincing them to surrender their freedom rather than invest in their capacity to begin something new. Arendt says 'freedom as an inner capacity of man is identical with the capacity to begin, just as freedom as a political reality is identical with a space of movement between men'.[21] Since power always comes from human beings acting together, Arendt says isolated human beings become powerless. Totalitarianism renders this capacity to act into isolation. When human beings are isolated, they are caught in a situation where they cannot act because nobody will act with them.[22] Arendt insists that isolation and loneliness are not the same. One can be lonely but can still be in the company of others and in fact can act with others. By contrast, isolation is an '. . . impasse into which men are driven when the political sphere of their lives, where they act together in the pursuit of common concern, is destroyed.'[23] But Arendt argues that although totalitarianism exacerbated loneliness and isolation, these were already present realities since the eighteenth and nineteenth centuries and are arguably also present in liberalism of the twentieth century, and, we can add, in neo-liberalism of the twenty-first century. If totalitarianism isolates individuals by coercing them to surrender their capacity to act, liberalism interpellates them to surrender it by individualism. Thus ends *Origins of Totalitarianism*: 'beginning, before it becomes a historical event, is the supreme capacity of man; politically, it is identical with man's freedom.'[24] Moreover, 'this beginning is guaranteed by each new birth; it is indeed every man.'[25]

Arendt expands this notion of beginning as disclosure in *The Human Condition* (1958). The disclosure of a human being happens through words and deeds. For Arendt

> Without the accompaniment of speech, at any rate, action would not only lose its revelatory character, but, and by the same token, it would lose its subject, as it were; not acting men but performing robots would achieve what, humanly speaking, would remain incomprehensible.[26]

Similarly, 'Speechless action would no longer be action because there would no longer be an actor, and the actor, the doer of deeds, is possible only if he is at the same time the speaker of words.'[27] As I just mentioned above, for Arendt, the doer of deeds is not a sovereign subject with intentions and motives. She rejects the automaton conception of the agent who comes under the sway of either inner motives (subjectivism) or outer causes (objectivism).[28] She accepts that

> although everybody started his life by inserting himself into the human world through action and speech, nobody is the author or producer of his own life story. In other words, the stories, the results of action and speech, reveal an agent, but this agent is not an author or producer.[29]

To be blunt, Arendt admits, nobody knows whom she reveals when she discloses herself in deeds and words. This is why accounts given by actors in statements about their intentions, aims and motives can rarely, if ever, be useful material for interpreting the significance and truthfulness of their acts.[30] Since actions are inherently unpredictable and since actors are not reliable sources of interpretation, the full meaning of an act can be seen only when the fleeting moment of the deed is past.[31] The full meaning of an act can only be produced when it has ended. We can already see many of the themes that dominate the way I use the term 'act' to define forms, repertoires, or descriptions of social action. However, Arendt does not distinguish between 'acts' and 'action' and is ambiguous about the difference between ethical and political acts (and action). I will return to both of these issues later but for now we will see how she describes specifically political action.

For Arendt, all action seems political since it is through action that we disclose ourselves to the world. The political arises from acting together since we always disclose ourselves in the presence of others. We share our words and deeds.[32] Actions create publics as spaces of appearance as we appear through them by disclosing ourselves in actions. But if we can only understand the full meaning of actions only when the deeds end, what guarantees their endurance? Arendt only answers this question insofar as she recognizes the need for their endurance and states that deeds have enormous capacity for endurance.[33] She identifies two things that guarantee the endurance of action by making it possible for humans to act. These two faculties are forgiving and promising.[34] Forgiveness ensures that humans are able to take risks in the face of the unpredictability of their actions by trusting those in whose presence they disclose themselves and in whose trust they place their disclosure. This requires courage *and* trust.[35] It is this trust in the forgiveness of others that enables humans to introduce themselves to the world. Thus, forgiveness itself is an act that '. . . does not merely re-act but acts anew and unexpectedly, unconditioned by the act which provoked it and therefore freeing from its consequences both the one who forgives and the one who is forgiven'.[36] Similarly, what protects us when taking risks is that we make and keep promises. This capacity guards us against the unpredictability and uncertainty of our actions.[37] Arendt emphatically states that forgiveness and promising enable the building of trust that is much stronger than any contract or treaty as the foundation of a body politic. The sovereignty of such a body politic, unlike that of 'we, the people', is not based on an identical will that inspires all its members but an agreed purpose for which the promises are binding.[38] The point for Arendt is that the disclosure of ourselves through unpredictable and uncertain actions becomes our way of exercising freedom not as a choice or sovereign will but as a capacity to call something new into being whose outcome is unpredictable.[39] Arendt differentiates '. . . a freedom of choice that arbitrates and decides between two given things, one good and one evil, and whose choice is predetermined by motive which has only to be argued to start its operation . . .' from '. . . the freedom to call something into being which did not exist before, which was not given, not even as an object of cognition or imagination, and which therefore, strictly speaking, could not be known'.[40] Thus, for Arendt, 'men *are* free as distinguished from their possessing the gift for freedom as long as they act, neither before nor after; for to *be* free and to act are the same'.[41] For this reason, 'every act, seen from the perspective not of the agent but of the process in whose framework it occurs and whose automatism it interrupts, is a "miracle" that is, something which could not be expected'.[42] This is why Arendt actually does not speak much about the freedom of the actor but of the action itself. She says

> action, to be free, must be free from motive on one side, from its intended goal as a predictable effect on the other. This is not to say that motives and aims are not important factors in every single act, but they are its determining factors, and action is free to the extent that it is able to transcend them.[43]

The important point about actions is that their goals, ends and meanings

> '. . . have so little in common that in the course of one and the same action they can end up at such loggerheads that the actors stumble into the gravest conflicts and the historians who follow after, whose task it is to accurately relate what in fact happened, can find themselves in endless debates over interpretation.[44]

This is not a regrettable aspect of action for it is an inevitable aspect of political affairs.

If we were to sketch an outline of Arendt's theorizing of action, then we would probably begin with three elements: that the end that an action pursues cannot follow from the means it employs (actions exceed end–means calculability); that its goals cannot be attributed to either internal motives (subjectivism) or external causes (objectivism) and, that the meaning of an action is always contained within itself and when an action ceases, that meaning ceases with the action itself. Arendt says that

> in addition to these three elements of every political action – the end that it pursues, the goal which it has in mind and by which it orients itself, and the meaning that reveals itself in the course of the action – there is a fourth element, which, although it is never the direct cause of action, is nevertheless what first sets it into motion.[45]

Arendt calls this fourth element the principle of action and describes it in 'psychological terms' as 'the fundamental conviction that a group of people share'.[46] For Arendt, action ultimately springs from its principles. These principles do not operate from within but inspire from without. They are too broad to have specific actions with goals anchored to them, although specific aims can be judged against them. 'For, unlike the judgment of the intellect which precedes action, and unlike the command of the will which initiates it, the inspiring principle becomes fully manifest only in the performing act itself . . .'[47] Unlike goals, motives and aims,

> . . . the principle of an action can be repeated time and again, it is inexhaustible, and in distinction from its motive, the validity of a principle is universal, it is not bound to any particular person or to any particular group.[48]

Yet, principles become manifest only through action and '. . . they are manifest in the world as long as the action lasts, but no longer'.[49]

Arendt develops further the idea that the spirit of the laws is the principle of action in an essay on civil disobedience. Her core argument arises from a distinction that she borrows from Montesquieu and maintains throughout her writings on authority, freedom, action and revolution: that there is a difference between the spirit of the laws and their letter. She says ' "The spirit of the laws," as Montesquieu understood it, is the principle by which people living under a particular system act and inspired to act.'[50] When the letter and the spirit of the law come into conflict, the law must give way since the spirit of the law is an expression of negotiation and struggle over a long period of time and provide, as Arendt says, principles that inspire people to act. The right to dissent arises from upholding this distinction. Thus, civil disobedience is compatible with the *spirit* of American laws though it has proved difficult to recognize it.[51] For this reason, Arendt differentiates conscientious objection from civil disobedience since the latter is political whereas the former is ethical.[52]

Again, we can recognize the affinities between how we differentiate responsibility and answerability and how Arendt sees a difference between the spirit and letter of the law. I already mentioned that Arendt does not distinguish acts and action. Nor does she clearly distinguish ethical and political acts. Moreover, her emphasis on natality, the 'supreme' capacity to bring something new into the world whose outcomes are unpredictable, despite her efforts, appears too essentialist or at least mystical. I would rather see the capacity to dissent and rupture a given order of things as a historical capacity. It is historical rather than 'inherent' in the sense that humans have developed this capacity as a result of thousands of years of struggles, negotiations, enactments, performances and institutions. So rather than depending on natality and assuming that this capacity comes with newcomers to the world as a result of their birth, I see it as a historically developed capacity that is worth identifying, maintaining and enhancing. Why? The answer has to do with another term that I use to distinguish ethical or social acts from those that are political. It is justice. Following Derrida, I understand justice very much like Arendt understands the spirit of the law: principles by which people living under a particular system act and are inspired to act as opposed to laws which they must obey. As Derrida states

> . . . justice is not the law. Justice is what gives us the impulse, the drive, or the movement to improve the law, that is, to deconstruct

the law. Without a call for justice we would not have any interest in deconstructing the law.[53]

Going back to Arendt, her overlooking of the difference between acts and action led her to believe that the meaning of action lasted as long as the action itself. We must distinguish between acts as relatively lasting forms, repertoires or descriptions and the relatively short-lived actions that actualize these acts. That is why we can speak about such things as 'acts of forgiveness' or 'acts of violence' because we have developed common understandings of them over long periods of time by acting under those forms or descriptions.

To register these disagreements with Arendt does not mean to reject her theorizing of action. But it does mean to note its shortcomings and seek ways of overcoming them because her insistence on our capacity to act is too important to forget. Given that Arendt provides a powerful and effective theorizing of action, especially with her emphasis on speech and action, or rather, speech as action, it is surprising that she played a relatively minor, if any, role in the development of performativity and speech acts over the last several decades. It is all the more perplexing as her theory of action draws upon, elaborates and stretches reflections on human capacity to act found in Søren Kierkegaard, Friedrich Nietzsche and Martin Heidegger whose works inspire subsequent political thought in the twentieth century.[54]

Subjectivity, performativity, enactment

Thinking about citizenship as performance or enactment enjoins, follows and departs from recent developments in social and political thought towards understanding subjectivity as a performative process.[55] These developments do not have singular but multiple origins and trajectories. As I mentioned, Arendt's theorizing of action is mostly absent from these developments but it figures rather prominently in the way in which I will discuss them.

Genealogies of performativity and enactment

To begin with, it has to be acknowledged that performativity and enactment have had conterminous and entwined developments in diverse fields such as philosophy (in phenomenology with Edmund Husserl, Adolf Reinach, Martin Heidegger and Jacques Derrida and in linguistics with J. L. Austin, John Searle, Stanley Cavell), psychoanalysis (Sigmund Freud, Jacques Lacan, Alain Badiou), sociology and anthropology (Ervin Goffman, Victor Turner), history (Charles Tilly), literature (Mikhail Bakhtin) and drama

(Richard Schechner). It was Reinach who took up 'mental acts' from Husserl and developed the idea of 'social acts' and it was Heidegger who embraced it. Similarly, it was Austin who articulated the importance of performative utterances as acts in the sense of doing things with words. It was Searle who took up Austin and developed intentionality as the essence of speech acts. It was Lacan who first built upon Freud to identify the psychic aspects of acting and it was Badiou who took up Lacan's idea of the act. Goffman studied interaction rituals and performance of the self and it was Turner who drew upon theatre studies to deepen such interaction rituals. Tilly was especially interested in demonstrations and protests within social movements and how they developed repertoires of contentious acts. Bakhtin was concerned with both dramaturgical and speech acts and investigated the significance of acts as genres of speech and writing. Schechner too was focused on the dramaturgical aspects of performance and the formation of subjectivity.[56]

It is probably fair to say that despite their differences in origin and aims, these diverse theorists were all concerned with understanding how we become subjects in a way that rejects both objectivist and subjectivist accounts of social action. How do we give an account of ourselves as capable of creative (deliberate yet spontaneous, mischievous yet serious, courageous yet not heroic), inventive (surprising yet predictable, illegal yet acceptable, outrageous yet reasonable) and autonomous (individual yet collective, scripted yet experimental, unauthorized yet meaningful) acts? Or, thinking with Arendt, how do we give an account of our capacity to bring something new into the world whose outcomes are unpredictable? Arguably, it is this question that drew more recent theorists such as Shoshana Felman, Judith Butler, Eve Kosofsky Sedgwick and Annemarie Mol to various strands of performativity and enactment. Arguably too, this was the question that exercised Deleuze, Foucault and Bourdieu albeit with a focus on conduct rather than action.

All of this is to give you a sense of the complex genealogies of performativity and enactment in theory.[57] Although performance and performativity as concepts may have related origins, performativity has a specific genealogy that begins with John Austin's influential, if ambiguous, *How to Do Things with Words* (1962).[58] This beginning has been both positive and negative in the sense that although his focus on acts as objects of investigation proved innovative and creative, the specific focus on speech as linguistic expression distracted from investigating speech acts as assemblages of bodies and events.[59] As much as thinking about citizenship as enactment enjoins and follows performativity, therefore, there are differences between performativity and enactment.[60] These will become clear as we proceed but it would be useful here to provide a brief consideration of those aspects of Austin's work that bequeathed legacies for later appropriation.

The fascinating thing about Austin is that every distinction he introduced remained unstable and ambiguous and yet continued to stir imaginations and discussions. Take, for example, his key distinction between constative and performative utterances. While he thought that constative utterances describe (or at least attempt to describe) a state of affairs, performative utterances produce the state of affairs. Although nobody finds this distinction actually tenable (ironically, beginning with Austin himself), it continues to stir analytic discussion. As an utterance itself perhaps it embodies an ambiguity about whether it merely describes a state of affairs or brings about or performs it. But what is at stake with this distinction, and why did it prove so contentious and hence fruitful? Perhaps, it states what is obvious for us: that a statement gathers meaning only through the effects of what it produces.

This applies equally to the distinctions Austin introduced later. The differences between locutionary acts that involve saying something, illocutionary acts that involve urging something and perlocutionary acts that involve bringing about further and separate actions. Similarly, the distinctions between originary and secondary acts, between felicitous and infelicitous acts, between conventional and unconventional acts and between serious and non-serious acts were regularly expressed. Again, Austin himself found these distinctions 'troubling'.[61] Still, the most creative aspects of doing things with words, as Austin envisaged (performed?), is the performative force of speech as acts. If we broaden the concept of speech from utterance to expressions (through gestures, gatherings, assemblies, placements) and movements that also involve multiple bodies, then we have the makings of quite distinct objects of investigation – acts.

Clearly, there were early takers, Bourdieu among them. As one can imagine, Bourdieu's main criticism was precisely Austin's exclusive focus on linguistic utterances as speech acts. Bourdieu argues that social acts can succeed only when someone or something endowed with a specific status or property is backed by a group or institution. Acts as diverse as marriage or circumcision or conferment or attribution would never acquire their performative force without social conditions that make such acts recognizable and legitimate. This is the case even when an act is accomplished by a sole agent who still acts within recognized forms and according to certain conventions. Following Austin, those who interpret such acts as though the words used in them possess the performative force to accomplish them fail to appreciate that they are fundamentally social acts in the sense of being instituted and instituting social rituals. There is no illocutionary force without the words themselves. For Bourdieu, social acts are rites of institution and draw their force, illocutionary force if you like, not from linguistic forms that govern them but from social conditions that make them possible. What renders an actor capable of accomplishing an act is precisely the collective belief that guarantees its institution.[62] For Bourdieu, this is not to deny the power of words. But such power is nothing other than the delegated power of the speaker as a social subject.[63]

The illocutionary force of words cannot be found within those words themselves. The authority that gives words their performative force comes from outside of those words themselves. For Bourdieu, what language does is to represent this authority, manifest and symbolize it. Furthermore, the use of language depends on the social position of the speaker that governs the rules of legitimate speech.[64] What makes a speech legitimate is the symbolic power accumulated by the social group or institution that delegates the speaker. That is why the success of a performative utterance depends on the appropriateness of the speaker or his social function as a delegate. A performative utterance would fail if the speaker lacks such capacity or delegation to invest words with the power of his social function. In that sense, all speech acts are social acts and all social acts are acts of authority.[65] For a speech act to accomplish its performative force, it does not need to be understood at all; it only needs to be recognized.[66] For such a recognition to register, the speaker must show that he does not act in his own name and on his own authority but in his capacity as a delegate.[67]

Although Bourdieu's intervention is powerful here in highlighting the fact that performative force is not inherent in words, he does not acknowledge that the success of a performative utterance can also depend on the *inappropriateness* of the speaker or his *lack* of social function as a delegate. Perhaps here the difference between focusing on conduct and on action becomes most clear. Bourdieu's concern is to give an account of the conduct of agents. But a subject who acts is often, if not always, in breach of the conventions that govern conduct. What theorizing acts concerns is giving an account or at least developing a vocabulary or analytics for understanding acts when subjects *fail* to follow conventions. Bourdieu's reminder that the illocutionary force of words cannot be found within those words themselves is important. However, his insistence that the authority that gives words their performative force comes from outside of those words themselves is not very useful principally because it seeks to identify the conditions of the possibility of conduct. Instead, we want to understand the conditions of the *impossibility* of conducting oneself properly. This leads to another related but distinct issue about originary versus mimetic acts.

The most significant aspect of discussion on performativity concerns whether the essence of a speech act is originary or citational or iterative. The issue here is to determine whether an act merely repeats an already existing repertoire albeit under different conditions or brings something 'creative, inventive and autonomous' into the world (or as Arendt would say brings something new into the world with surprising effects). If the former is the case, then what is the point of calling something an act rather than a performance or practice? What is at stake here is more than speech as language. It concerns one of the most vexing matters in social and political thought: as subjects to what extent do we act creatively, inventively and autonomously rather than imitatively, routinely and dependently. If you are a student, what is the promise of enacting yourself as a creative, inventive and autonomous subject by doing exactly what millions of students have always done before? What are you bringing that is new to the world? If you are a mother, what is the possibility of being a creative and inventive caregiver who cultivates autonomy in a child, if billions of mothers have gone through it all before? What are you bringing that is new to the world? If we become subjects by taking up scripts, routines and conventions in life as given, inhabiting ways of being that have been scripted for us then what is the promise of being creative, inventive and autonomous? What are we bringing that is new to the world? These are essentially the questions that Auden's poem 'Unknown Citizen' provokes. By going through various scripts that a citizen is supposed to follow from the point of view of authorities, Auden then asks whether this unknown citizen is free, or Arendt would say whether she practises her capacity to act. Then with a twist of irony, Auden says the question is absurd. This is because if the citizen acted, or she brought something new to the world, we would have heard. What Auden provokes is exactly the question we should be asking about the political subjectivity of the citizen.[68] Why creativity, inventiveness and autonomy? Why insist on our capacity to bring something new to the world with a surprising outcome? For *political* subjectivity, it is essential to have these attributes for without them we cannot imagine subjects capable of enacting themselves as equal, critical and activist subjects who will discriminate between justice and injustice, between equal and unequal and between fair and unfair. Admittedly, if we understand citizenship as political subjectivity, it is because we already hold an idea of subjectivity involving creativity, inventiveness and autonomy. If that subject we call a citizen always acts within given scripts, how do we account for the change in our understanding of rights and responsibilities of citizenship, and traversing frontiers?

This discussion leads me to outline five theoretical propositions as guidelines for investigating acts: (1) ruptures are not citations, repetitions or iterations and they create events; (2) acts and actions are different things. Acts are forms, repertoires or descriptions and actions are *actual* bodily movements; (3) bodies and subjects perform different functions; (4) intentionality and purposiveness are different registers and (5) answerability is a condition of the possibility of acts. We now shall turn our attention to each proposition.

Ruptures are not citations, repetitions or iterations. They create events

When speech act theorists such as Austin and Searle and their critics such as Derrida address issues of citation, iteration and repetition, in a way they are struggling over the vexing issue of subjectivity as action and acts. When we do things with words to what extent are we citing, iterating and repeating them (action) and to what extent are we creating and inventing them (acts)? Unlike Austin and Searle, Derrida believes that for an act to be a speech act proper, it has to be a rupture in the sense of an interruption between the sender and receiver of speech. If it were not a rupture, it would not be an act. So successful performatives always involve infelicity, misfires and mis-understandings and they are not ideal speech situations. Note that this is contrary to Bourdieu's thinking about speech as appropriate conduct versus speech as inappropriate act. Without such a distinction, we would assume a machinic citation, iteration and repetition of speech and thus assume all communication to be ideal communication, all acting as ideal acting.[69] As Loxley says 'Derrida's interventions repeatedly suggested that iterability was both the condition of the possibility of a proper speech act, and at the same time – in the same move – the condition of its impossibility.'[70]

Butler though goes further. She insists that we need a term to describe what happens when citationality and iterability exceed their possibilities, reveal their vulnerabilities and open up opportunities for subversion – act-ing otherwise. Butler names this 'resignification'. Acts can cite, iterate and repeat but they can also do so differently and not necessarily as more of the same.[71] But how do we know when an act is resignification rather than iteration? Again, we would need to return to the idea of rupture.

We had earlier encountered the idea of rupture when discussing 'we, the people'. Both Rancière and Laclau described the moment when politics arises as a rupture. For Rancière, politics is an interruption of the dominant order.[72] Similarly, Laclau believes that the moment that we inhabit is one that will require ruptures through acts that will have aggregating effects on politics.[73] But what is meant by rupture? Laclau uses derivative versus constitutive to define rupture. He says, for example, the birth of a people as a historical actor creates a configuration that is not derivative but constitutive.[74] But in what sense can we delineate derivative from constitutive? The birth of a peo-ple 'constitutes an *act* in the strict sense, for it does not have its source in any-thing external to itself'.[75] Laclau also uses words such as transgressive and subversive to define rupture. This transgression is an act that does not simply replace existing order but introduces a different order.[76] This is

> because the act, on the one hand, brings about a new (ontic) order, but, on the other, has an ordering (ontological) function, it is the locus of a

complex game by which a concrete content actualizes, through its very concreteness, something that is entirely different from itself . . .[77]

Yet, this is not a revolutionary or spectacular act, or rather an act is never revolutionary or spectacular, precisely because it cannot define itself in advance. For a rupture to be transgression or subversion, it cannot name in advance its own effects.[78]

Still, for both Rancière and Laclau, the concept of rupture (and its relation to acts) remains ambiguous and certainly undertheorized. Laclau identifies his concept of the act with that of Lacan's 'passage to the act' but this is problematic, as we shall see later. Similarly, we find the idea of rupture as the essence of politics in Badiou. For him 'all resistance is a rupture with what is. And every rupture begins, for those engaged in it, through a rupture with oneself.'[79] Badiou insists that 'the essence of politics is not the plurality of opinions. It is the prescription of a possibility in rupture with what exists.'[80] He suggests that what accomplishes these ruptures are declarations, interventions and organizations. Yet, Badiou does not relate rupture to acts let alone considering rupture as the essence of acts. Instead, Badiou considers something an act only if it is revolutionary in the sense of bringing about a radical transformation.

Derrida too struggles with the idea of rupture. He increasingly identifies the force of performativity with rupture. In many ways, he is critical of speech acts as exemplified especially by Austin and Searle primarily on this point.[81] For Derrida

> . . . . the originary performativity that does not conform to preexisting conventions, unlike all the performatives analyzed by the theoreticians of speech acts, but whose force of rupture produces the institution or the constitution, the law itself, which is to say also the meaning that appears to, that ought to, or that appears to have to guarantee it in return.[82]

Contrasting performativity with performance (citational, repetitive, iterative), Derrida thinks that if an iterative event intervenes in performativity, it is always accidental and not intrinsic.[83]

For Butler what is politically significant about rupture is '. . . the moment in which a subject – a person, a collective – asserts a right or entitlement to a liveable life when no such prior authorization exists, when no clearly enabling convention is in place.[84] To put it in other words, for Butler, the force of performativity is its creativity insofar as an act is 'not inherited from prior usage, but issues forth precisely from its break with any and all prior usage. That break, that force of rupture, is the force of the performative'.[85] Still, what exactly does it mean to say or do something that will not inherit its force from prior usage but break with it? This is where a rupture and an event become conflated. We can provisionally suggest that what reveals an act as a rupture is the event that the act produces. As Derrida says

> . . . that wherever there is some performative, that is, in the strict and Austinian sense of the term, the mastery in the first person present of an 'I can,' 'I may' guaranteed and legitimated by conventions, well, then, all pure eventness is neutralized, muffled, suspended.[86]

If indeed a performative utterance produces the event of which it speaks, it is this aspect that transforms a performative utterance into an act without prior convention. The difference between performativity and enactment is slight and nuanced but important. We shall use performativity to indicate citation, repetition and iteration of forms, repertoires and descriptions under which political subjectivity is produced. We shall use enactment to shift the focus on actions that bring about events as rupture in the order of things in a given site where political subjectivity is constituted.

We have seen that the idea of rupture has troubled theorists for whom the essence of politics is the interruption or disruption of an existing order of domination. What is evocative about using rupture is its ambiguity: it gains meaning only when it is demonstrated or illustrated. We cannot address these issues further here, but to get a better grip on the uses of 'enacting citizenship', we can consider rupture as an event that acts produce. It turns out that the capacity to bring something new into the world is a lot more complex than it appears.

Acts and actions are different things. Acts are forms, repertoires and descriptions; actions are bodily movements

Acts are not actions. This is among the most counter-intuitive propositions of enacting citizenship. To follow Hacking, although he does not make an explicit distinction between acts and actions, we can say that acts are descriptions.[87] As Hacking says 'What is curious about human action is that by and large what I am deliberately doing depends on the possibilities of description.'[88] All acts are acts under a description and as descriptions change so do the possibilities of acting. These descriptions are not merely constative but also performative descriptions precisely because '. . . numerous kinds of human beings and human acts come into being hand in hand with our invention of the ways to name them'.[89] As I write this, for example, a newspaper reports that a couple has been arrested and charged with 'preparing acts of terrorism'.[90] At first, that phrasing sounds odd. How does one prepare for an act if an act is said to be a rupture? But rupture, to repeat, does not necessarily imply spontaneity although an act can also occur 'without preparation'. The issue here is that we can conceive others and ourselves acting only under certain descriptions and these descriptions are open to interpretation, contestation and classification with or without our or their intervention or awareness. The police have clearly identified various actions that they allege the couple engaged in, and interpreted or classified these under the description 'acts of terrorism'. What constitutes an act of terrorism is contested and it arises from various practices of naming, analyzing and interpreting actions through legal, ethical and social norms and rules. It also changes as actions that come under that description or are done in its name are constantly added or removed from its repertoires. This example illustrates the difference between acts (as descriptions) and actions. That the police clearly interpreted certain actions under this description does not mean that its classification will remain stable. Acts always involve interpretation. Which actions should come under which forms, repertoires and descriptions always remains contested.

We can think about 'acts of generosity', 'acts of hospitality', 'acts of hostility', 'acts of war' and so on in these ways. These descriptions always change and include or exclude a range of actions to constitute them. What about 'acts of citizenship'? The repertoire of actions that can come under the description 'acts of citizenship' is vast. It can include such actions as voting, serving in the military, paying taxes, fulfilling jury duty, volunteering for non-profit organizations, donating for charitable purposes and perhaps running for political office. How do we reconcile these actions with the requirement that acts produce events and that these events are ruptures? Would these actions come under the description 'acts of citizenship' if it is required that they produce ruptures? To answer that question, we need to further specify the meaning of acts of citizenship. As discussed earlier, regarding the essence of political subjectivity, what renders the emergence of a political subject is the demand (Laclau) or claim (Rancière) that an action has articulated. Moreover, the demand or claim involves the articulation of a wrong; it is a demand for and claim to justice (Derrida). Finally, such claims or demands institute equality in the sense that their articulation does not necessarily issue from a previous convention (Butler).

So identifying certain actions in order to consider whether they should come under the description 'acts of citizenship' is not about classifying those actions in the abstract but about investigating the grounds on which they involve claims or demands and their consequences.

Bodies and subjects perform different functions

We have distinguished bodies and subjects on several occasions without dwelling on its significance. Considering citizenship as political subjectivity then entails understanding the conditions under which bodies are implicated in those claims and demands that constitute them as subjects.

Becoming political subjects does not mean becoming singular in the sense of becoming only 'political' subjects. Both the ways in which a body becomes political and bodies themselves are multiple. It would not come as a surprise that our bodies inhabit various subject positions such as Canadian, teacher, brother, swimmer, consumer, Muslim, theorist and so on. These subject positions are themselves descriptions under which we act and the ways in which we take up these positions involves processes of subjectivity or sub-jectivation. It is also not surprising to say that no two bodies will occupy or take up the exact same combination of subject positions. So when we say 'subjects', these are the positions that bodies occupy or inhabit. Sometimes when we attribute action to a subject, we do not mean to indicate that a subject position is acting but we are referring to body that is acting under a description, a subject position.

Yet, it is not only subject positions (and the ways in which bodies are subjectivated into them) that are multiple. Our bodies are sites of contesta-tion of multiple forces arising from and giving rise to subjectivation. To say this is to accept that a body contains tensions of conflicting desires and drives. Taking up a subject position of being a Muslim may come to conflict with becoming secular. Similarly, becoming a Canadian can come into conflict with becoming European. But then again these descriptions can change. Can one act under the description of secular Muslim? Can one become both Canadian and European? It was not that long ago, for example, that nation-states did not allow dual nationality as it was seen as a conflict to hold dual national identities and to perform one without threat to the other. Yet, that description is changing. Now some (though not many) nation-states are allowing for dual nationalities.

The aim of this discussion is to highlight the fact that we need to be pre-cise in using terms bodies and subjects when describing acts under which actions are performed. But, more importantly, it is also to illustrate that 'subjects' do not already exist prior to acts; the performance of acts through actions bring them into being. A secular Muslim, if there is such a thing, will not come into being unless a subject comes into being under that description that produces it. Conversely, unless there is a performative utterance that produces the event through which a subject 'secular Muslim' comes about, that description will not have an effective existence. This is a good moment to return to the force of the performative as rupture. What may constitute rupture here is precisely that there may not be a previously existing conven-tion that authorizes to act under the description of secular Muslim.

Intentionality and purposiveness are different registers

Again, Hacking is relevant here. He says performing an action always requires an intention, that is, an intention to act under some description.

But does this intention express deliberation, calculation and planning? Does it indicate that the subject is conscious of its effects and in control of its unfolding? Clearly, acting under a description is not adequate to address the issues of intentionality. The question is how that description is taken up and whether it is performed (citation, iteration and repetition) or enacted (rupture). If we understand intentionality to mean an ends–means calculation that motivates the subject, and that the subject exists prior to the act that it intends to bring about, then we are thinking at a different register. As we have seen, earlier bodies caught in an act often do not have the possibility for such calculations but orient themselves towards a scene. This orientation is purposive because bodies sense the subject position they are taking up but are neither able to calculate nor predict its outcomes. If we understand intentionality as action directed towards an outcome under a recognized and recognizable description, we are underestimating non-intentional but purposive ways in which bodies uptake subject positions. Becoming subjects and acting under descriptions, and the question of what happens when bodies occupy or inhabit these positions, all involve registers of intentionality and purposiveness.

Answerability is the condition of possibility of acts

If all acts are acts under descriptions, what compels us to act under one description rather than another? Again, this perhaps cannot be answered in the abstract as it will depend on the grounds on which an act is performed and its consequences. But often what gives direction, guidance or orientation to acts or acting under description are those responsibilities that implicate or interpellate certain bodies. Here I could exemplify this by returning to the example of conscientious objection (Act 3) mentioned in Chapter 1. Instead, let me try again with a more mundane example to illustrate that an act may require nerve at the same time as not being heroic. I am writing this sentence in a library whose reading room, for example, states various user rules and requirements in a booklet that sprawls into six pages. I am told that I must show my library card for inspection, that I should use only pencils, that my hands should be clean when handling books and documents, that I should turn the sound of my laptop off, and that my phone should be on silent mode. In addition, I should not bring bags or umbrellas, pens, highlighters, sharp implements, food, drink or gum and certainly not cameras into the reading room. These are the responsibilities that I agree to when I am performing under the description of 'reader' at this library. These responsibilities ensure that all readers enjoy the privileges of the library as equal readers. These responsibilities are enforced by the library staff but also are observed and corrected by readers themselves. I am justified to ask the reader sitting next to me to decrease the volume on her earphones precisely because of our equal responsibilities but I am not entitled to do so in the square outside as it is governed by different responsibilities. Such responsibilities then govern how we perform ourselves. But is this acting? That such responsibilities are already codified means that they have become citational, repetitive and iterational and that performing as a reader requires creatively and actively but nonetheless routinely following these rules.

What if I break them? What if I become irresponsible? That would be a rupture and it would be acting under a certain description and it would have consequences of legality and illegality. But what if I act under a description I feel is justified given the circumstances? What if I cite a different rule, repeat a different norm, iterate a different regulation that, collectively, constitute an unauthorized convention? As Rancière might say, my act becomes *improper* to its immediate grounds but grounded in a different – and perhaps an equally if not more effectively justifiable – reason. This is where the concept of answerability becomes essential. Our acts may contravene our responsibilities but are answerable to the principles for their enactment. In fact, as emphasized, answerability is basic to understanding acts. Yet, there is nothing mystical about answerability. Just consider a Bradley Manning (Act 3) or Rachel Corrie (Act 2) or Daniel Barenboim (Act 20) here. Each acts against a wrong (injustice) and under a convention that does not authorize them to occupy or inhabit the description each chooses.

Acts of citizenship

The foregoing is merely an outline of the basic qualities of acts and specifically acts of citizenship where the concepts performativity and enactment are its key aspects. Citation, repetition and iterability are the qualities of performativity, whereas rupture and answerability are fundamental to enactment. Taken together, familiar concepts such as action, events, bodies, subject positions, intentionality, purposiveness and responsibility acquire new inflections and nuances. But how then do we go about investigating acts? Beyond the theoretical propositions we have discussed, are there methodological propositions? We have already focused on some basic qualities and principles for investigating acts. We have identified creativity, inventiveness and autonomy as the basic qualities of acts. We then made a distinction between performativity and enactment focusing on rupture as a key distinguishing quality. We then distinguished between acts and actions, subjects and bodies, intentionality and purposiveness, and responsibility and answerability. Taken together, these propositions enable us to identify acts as objects of investigation and the acts featured in this book illustrate these propositions. Still, we need to discuss four methodological propositions concerning acts: (1) events; (2) sites; (3) scales and (4) durations. We will then have a vocabulary or analytics for investigating acts.

Investigating acts

The beginning point of investigating an act is always an event. As you may have already noticed when reading the acts in this book, I usually begin with an event. It is the event that reveals or discloses an act and it is the event that embodies its rupture effect. But what is an event? As innocuous as it sounds that question is incredibly complex but I will keep my answer tightly connected to acts so that we can get a reasonably stable grip on it. Similarly, 'where' an event happens and its 'reach' and 'duration' are complex issues. I will introduce these propositions for investigating acts with illustrations not to give you a sense that they neatly resolve all problems but to convince you that we are better off with this vocabulary and analytics than not.

Events happen but not all that happen are events

Actions happen all the time. They have the character of being routine, ordinary and occur at a certain time and place. Sometimes, actions condense or accelerate the experiences of those who either witness or commit them. But such actions are repetitions or citations. By contrast, events are actions that become recognizable (visible, articulable) only when the site, scale and duration of these actions produce a rupture in the given order. But by an order I not only mean grand things such as social, political or economic orders but any assemblage of relatively lasting and enduring ways of doing things. You may remember the example of the library that I used to introduce the difference between responsibility and answerability. Well, I am still there and things are happening. People are carrying books and some are even reading them, some people are looking at their screens and are so enchanted that I am tempted to ask what makes them smile like that. The staff is shelving books. There is an announcement about the closing time. All this is happening around me. But none of it constitutes (so far) an event. A given state of affairs or an order of things is held together and creating a setting or situation. What must happen for this order not to continue its relative stability? Some thing happens and changes the state of affairs or the order of things. This is often expressed as 'things will never be the same' or 'things were never the same after.'

As I write these sentences, 'street riots' are occurring in London.[91] I am still in the library but now I am following reports on the internet. On

Friday, 4 August 2011, Mark Duggan, 29, is shot dead by police at Ferry Lane, Tottenham.[92] This death occurs during an arrest by police officers dealing with gun crime in 'the African and Caribbean communities.' On 6 August, about 300 people gather outside Tottenham police station asking questions about the circumstances of Duggan's death. The confirmation of his death has not communicated to the family after 48 hours. The group chooses Broadwater Farm estate, the site of a riot in 1985 against another shooting, thus linking their questions to a longer grievance about shootings associated with murderous police repression of blacks in the city. Following the march, riots and violence break out. Police cars and a bus are burned, several buildings set alight and considerable looting is perpetrated often but not in all cases by masked youths.[93]

Of course, the details, reasons and effects of these riots are extraordinarily complex and there will be much discussion for years to come. But because this is unfolding at the moment, it helps me think through some of the theoretical issues that I am trying to articulate here. Is this an event? If so, what is the event? Is there an act here that produces the event? When and how do we exactly settle these questions? We can begin with those actions that produced the event that we want to identify: the shooting, the gathering, the burning and the looting create an event in the sense that they interrupt or rupture the given state of affairs. Without the gathering outside the police station serving as a symbolic starting point for the march, would the action of shooting have become an event? It is the gathering and questioning that turned it into an event about demanding justice. Without further actions, it could have been interpreted as an act of citizenship demanding an explanation and justice for yet another shooting of a black man under questionable circumstances. But since the original event was followed by further actions such as burning and looting, the event escalated into another scale to include 'acts of violence' and 'acts of rage'. Descriptions of the acts as well as the subjects that they produced are contested and confusing. Media interpretations range between 'demonstrators' and 'protesters' before they settle on 'rioters'. Clearly, the ground is shifting rapidly and the classification of actions, acts and actors are becoming a stake in the struggle over meaning. Similarly, the interpretations of acts range from 'disturbances' to 'riots'. The important thing to note here is that these acts and their subjects, as we have stressed before, do not exist as such but are interpretations or descriptions that constitute acts.[94] To put it differently, acts (or actions interpreted as acts) become contestations about events and how to interpret them. Surely, there is a huge difference between interpreting the events that unfolded in London as 'acts of citizenship' demanding justice or as 'acts of violence' expressing rage, fury and feral conduct?

These events also produce sites (as various actions spread from Tottenham to Enfield, and Brixton).[95] They shift the scale of acts in the sense of their reverberations and spheres of influence. If these riots remain confined within the sites currently identified, the events that they produced and the rupture in the given that they have created will have different effects than if they 'spread' to other sites especially outside London to other British cities. Moreover, for how long these events will remain linked to a series of events in the past such as the symbolic link made between the gathering outside the police station and the 1985 shooting at the Broadwater Farm estate remains to be seen. So the sites, scales and duration of an act are related and affect the rupture that it produces. This brief discussion on an event I hope gives you a sense of how we can begin investigating acts by deducing them as contested interpretations of actions and events. And let us not forget that we are always interested in citizenship as political subjectivity so we are not interested in all actions and events but those that constitute subject as claimants of rights and justice and thus a political.

Sites are not places or spaces

Tottenham High Road, Broadwater Estate farm and Brixton are places but Tottenham Riots, Brixton Riots and Broadwater Estate Riots are sites: They are ephemeral actual events that become enduring virtual remembrances. These are sites of contestation or struggle around which certain issues, interests, stakes as well as themes, concepts and objects assemble. While sites are spatial, they are not merely locations or places. To put it another way, sites are places or locations only insofar as social or political struggles invested in these places or locations with strategic values express them symbolically or materially. All locations or places will have values or meanings associated with them but what renders a location or place as a site is the strategic value for the struggle for rights that is the basis of enacting citizenship. Thus sites are both temporal and temporary. But this is the case only if we think of them as merely physical places. They also become imaginary spaces to which actors in the future will orient. So 'Tottenham' is not only a physical place but also an imaginary space that evokes resonant images.

Scales are not nested and hierarchical levels

As mentioned earlier, sites and scales are not mutually exclusive and discrete but overlapping and connected elements of acts. So when investigating an act, it is always important to consider the overlapping and connected aspects of sites and scales through which various actions enact acts. Sometimes it is necessary to use site-scales together and sometimes as separate attributes, depending on the specific situation under investigation. As also noted earlier, sites and scales are central categories because when we use already existing categories such as states, nations, cities, sexualities, ethnicities and so on, we inevitably deploy them as 'containers' with fixed and given boundaries. These are jurisdictions: territorialized authority. By contrast, when we begin with 'sites' and 'scales' with fluid and dynamic elements formed through contests and struggles, their boundaries become a question of empirical determination.

We have seen that sites are places that are invested with strategic value for struggles that claim rights. Scale is a significant concept to investigate acts as it indicates the reach and scope of various actions assembled and interpreted as acts. Especially when considered in conjunction with the phrase 'staging an act', the reach and scope of the act staged determines its effects. When we often say that certain actions *exceed* their intentions, we mean that the reach of their effect is exceeding the boundaries convention that authorizes them. Thus, the scale of an act – its reach and scope – becomes a crucial element for understanding its effects.

Duration is not fixed and given

How long does an act last? The question is not about the actual time it takes for an event to happen. For, as we have seen, sites of actions last as long as the actions themselves. By contrast, acts last much longer than actions or events. To produce events and acts, descriptions must retain a certain intensity. Otherwise, they lose their performative force. The time it takes for a description to gain and lose its performative force through which subjects become political is a matter of empirical investigation and cannot be determined theoretically. We can illustrate this again by returning to the London 'riots'.

On the first night of the riots, a journalist recorded a speech act by a woman who confronted and berated youths for looting shops.[96] Later named as the 'heroine of Hackney', a video clip shows Pauline Pearce passionately and angrily telling youths that if they have a cause, then they should riot for it rather than destroy the businesses of ordinary people who worked hard to build them.[97] So far, this speech act lacks the performative force and rupture that constitutes an act. Why? Watching the clip, the viewer realizes that Pearce is not only being ignored by everyone present but also seemingly lacks addressees – an audience to receive the speech and its performative force. It seems that this speech act is greeted with indifference at the moment of its actual performance. Yet, its recording and subsequent transmission through both YouTube and other media, begins to transform her action into an 'act of reason', 'act of heroism' and 'act of bravery'. Various video artists picked up the footage and turned it into a speech act with subtitles and music (some featuring Bob Marley). Thus, an action that could have disappeared as soon as it was performed became an act with performative force. But did it transform anything? Did it interrupt a state of affairs or the order of things and thus constitute an act, let alone an act of citizenship? If we consider the moment of its performance as the only criterion, the answer would have to be negative. But its interpretation (and thus actualization) as an act occurs later and it takes time. Thus, the duration of the act cannot be reduced to the moment of its performance, it must include its subsequent interpretation and description.

Activism as traversal citizenship

So far, this chapter focused on elaborating on how to think about and investigate citizenship as political subjectivity. There is no need to repeat the whole vocabulary and analytics now. Instead, the idea here is to show that investigating citizenship as political subjectivity, approaching citizenship as acts rather than status or habitus involve quite difficult tasks. I think it has rewards and so we need to persevere as there is one more piece to this jigsaw puzzle. How do we distinguish those acts of citizenship that traverse frontiers from those that do not? How and when can we claim that an act remains 'within' frontiers? Does traversing concern only bodies and subjects or does it also involve the sites, scales and durations of acts? Earlier we discussed that 'frontiers' are not merely a metaphor for 'limits' but are actual spaces through which subjectivities are formed. We also discussed topological ways of thinking about spaces and identified, with Mol, Law and Allen, regions, networks, fluids and fires as kinds of spaces through which subjectivities are formed. Frontiers encompass regions, networks, fluids and fires to create dynamic spaces of doable, sayable and visible. Frontiers are interstitial spaces that traverse these four kinds of spaces. This is a key aspect of the figure of citizens without frontiers. To think of frontiers as interstitial spaces requires imagining them as dynamic zones that traverse these four kinds of spaces. Traversing these spaces involves reaching out, extending and conducting ourselves as if we are others. It now remains to show that citizens without frontiers are traversal subjects. That is what the next chapter considers.

ACT 14. OF SPEECH: WAGING PEACE

In 2007, a box containing 30,000 testimonials from refugees on the border of war-stricken Darfur was sent to the charity, Waging Peace.[98] A couple of months later, another 30,000 testimonials had been collected from those living in the camps. In April 2008, Downing Street received a petition bearing 60,000 signatures.[99] This was the largest petition ever sent by African citizens to the United Kingdom. This act of petition poses a simple but a powerful question: How will you exercise your responsibility despite borders? Of those who signed 70 per cent were women, making it the largest expression from women in Africa.[100] Amidst their personal stories of hardship and violence, collective demands were clear. Anna Schmitt, the aid worker who suggested the petition, thought the petitions expressed a straightforward intention: 'They want a UN peacekeeping force and they want an end to the violence.'[101] Yet, every act exceeds the intentions of those who enact it. The petition had other consequences than those intended.

Admittedly, Darfur does not occupy the prime-time imagination.[102] When attention is drawn to the atrocities, victims of Darfur are spoken for. This was reflected in a strong correlation between a surge in celebrity advocacy and heightened coverage of Darfur and when polls showed little public interest otherwise.[103] Little of this activity went beyond rhetoric and sporadic charity. It is then understandable that when in 2007 Anna Schmitt was collecting evidence of the crimes committed against refugees living in the camps on the border, village elders expressed their pessimism about the effectiveness of representing the Darfuri through traditional advocacy.[104]

Schmitt wanted to break away from the routine of others representing Darfuris. She came up with an alternative means through which Darfuris could speak for themselves: a petition. This act of petition was unique. It partly revived an older tradition of usage in situations when constitutional arrangements were absent. An oft-cited example is that of 1770s' Connecticut when the majority of government legislation was based on petition recommendations.[105] Although the petition has lost this function of affirmation, it has become a tool of appeal (when it is recognized by the state) through which citizens can directly raise grievances and question policy as a matter of political debate, and if successful a matter of legislation.[106] In fact, it is worth remembering that what gained the internet its initial democratic credential was precisely the proliferation of online petitions with collected emails standing for signatures. The act of petition occupies a special space in democratic claim making.

Yet, what makes this act of petition by mostly Darfuri women outstanding is the authority of the appeal. Why the UK government? There is no direct link between the 60,000 petitioners and the UK state, except for the intermediary bodies of aid agencies and peacekeepers (or absence thereof), which, in this instance, was bypassed. The petition by the 60,000 refugees was not addressed to an already established authority obligated to hear it. Rather, it vests that authority at the same time that it appeals to it.

This absence of authority was embodied in its very form: 'the camp elders had absorbed the concept of a petition and elaborated it into a human tapestry of personal testimony.'[107] The petition was an assortment of both demands and stories, or rather demands within stories. Although it was not a traditional 'sign below' to an agreed set of grievances, consensus surfaced through qualitative similarity. For example, Hanna narrates a harrowing tale of how the Janjawid killed and raped villagers. Thirteen-year-old Sumaiya describes similar events, in defiance finishing with: 'I am Darfurian, I am Sudanese. I will not fear anything, not even death. It is my right to go back to my home.' Mothers stated: 'we the mothers want them to enter Darfur immediately. They have displaced us, and killed us and raped us in front of our children and husbands. They killed our children and burnt our houses. This was all done by the Janjaweed in our homeland.' Others voiced these demands by arguing that '[w]e support resolution 1706. We want the Janjaweed disarmed and the war criminals brought to trial; they have committed serious crimes: crimes against humanity.'[108] This was as much an act of petition as it was an act of testimony.

The petition was not accepted in the House of Commons debates. It was unheard. The act of a petition by citizens without frontiers transgressed the relationship between state and citizen as bounded entities. The only petition on Darfur discussed in the 2008 Commons session was in response to one submitted by West Oxfordshire students. On this matter, Hansard documented that 'The Petitioners therefore request that the House of Commons urges the Government to move the issue of the Darfur genocide to the top of the political agenda and media spotlight, and to keep it there.'[109] The House agreed with it. The performative force of the 2008 Darfuri petition was that it did not reach its destination.

ACT 15. OF FURY: MARIYAM MANIKE

I was never political until the death of my son, Hassan Evan Naseem. I became political at that moment. Now, the reform movement in the Maldives is everything to me. The day we voted in a new government in our first democratic election – on October 28 – was the greatest of my life, but it still couldn't bring my son back.[110]

How does one become a political subject? What does such a moment produce? These are extraordinarily complex questions. Yet, those moments are poignantly simple when told by those who experience them. Can we hear them? Can we listen to their voices as irreducibly singular yet recognizably traversal enactments?

'Your son died last night.' Those are the words Mariyam Manike heard in the early hours of 20 September 2003 at her home in Malé, Maldives.[111] She received the news from a prison guard and was advised to go to the hospital.[112] Mariyam saw the body of her 19-year-old son, who had been incarcerated in the Maafushi Jail for drug possession at the age of 17 years.[113] Upon noticing that his body was covered in bruises, Mariyam knew that he had been tortured.[114] For Mariyam, this moment sparked a transformation: 'I was never political until the death of my son, Hassan Evan Naseem. I became political at that moment.'[115] The hospital staff attempted to contain her subsequent outburst, but she resisted and shouted to 'everyone who came there to go on the streets and say someone has been killed in jail'.[116]

Soon after the hospital released the body, the authorities sent it to the cemetery. Yet Mariyam told them to postpone the burial. She felt this would have prematurely buried the evidence before anyone could see what Hassan experienced during the last moments of his life and what caused his death.[117] Mariyam showed the body to those who gathered in the cemetery. She wanted everyone to see and share in the sense of injustice. Eventually, the president came to the cemetery, stating that he would 'look into it'.[118] What followed was a contrived inquiry, which located primary responsibility with the Maafushi Jail Security Unit, finding them to have acted contrary to Maldivian law.[119] The expression of formal rights did not guarantee their substantive implementation. In terms of the sentencing that followed, Fusfaru, the individual who gave the order that Evan should be transferred to the notorious 'Range' section of the prison (where he suffered the fatal injuries), was sentenced to 6 months in prison.[120]

After Evan's death, Mariyam joined the 'reform movement' and became actively involved in the Maldivian Democratic Party.[121] With Mariyam's call for mobilization and justice, she helped transform what was bound to remain yet another concealed case of torture leading to death, into an event. Her act prepared the grounds for mobilizing people against a regime. This contextualization of a particular incident to a wider call for justice and democracy was one of the central acts that instigated the riots following his death.[122] 'Evan Hassan,' was translated from the name of a victim to a call for reform. From 20 to 21 September 2003, crowds gathered outside government buildings and set fire to armoured cars and jeeps, in a show of protest against the death of Evan and another inmate. Relatives and friends of the deceased displayed an 'unusual show of protest against the government of President Maumoon Abdul Gayoom, who has been in power for 25 years'.[123] After 5 years of struggle and intermittent but effective mobilizations, the president stepped down in 2008 after losing the country's first-ever democratic election to Mohamed Nasheed.[124] While ushering in a new constitution, elections and a democratic regime were due to numerous factors, torture and the lack of civil liberties were implied as the major instigating grounds for outrage.[125] The importance of Mariyam's act can be surmised in her own words: 'my son's murder helped bring down a dictatorship.'[126]

The subsequent remembrance of Evan also became a political act, irrevocably tethered to justice and democracy. Idhikeeli, a pro-democracy group, held a vigil in 2007 to remember Evan Hassan. The police treated this as a threatening act while for participants it was a rallying call for justice.[127] This further reflects how various actors conceive of the symbolic status of Evan, which Mariyam carved through her act of disseminating her grief and political opposition.

Mariyam now continues to fight even after the institution of a democratic government. Unsatisfied that justice had been delivered by either the sentence of Fusfaru or the subsequent prosecution of the eight police officers who were charged with murder but only placed under house arrest, Mariyam sought to pursue the case further.[128] In 2009, Mariyam aimed to hold Maumoon Abdul Gayoom and 'senior officials of the defence ministry' as culpable in Evan's death.[129] In particular, the struggle to convict Adam Zahir, the chief of police who was allegedly in command of those tortures, continues for Mariyam Manike.[130]

Mariyam's act of becoming political is at once so particular and traversal. It is particular as it intensifies the tragic pain of a mother realizing that her son was tortured to death. But her act of becoming political traverses frontiers and joins acts of fury against injustice enacted by mothers from Argentina to Turkey.

Notes

1 É. Balibar, 'Culture and Identity,' in *The Identity in Question*, ed. J. Rajchman (New York: Routledge, 1995).

2 Note that this phrase is different from 'the right to have rights' as is commonly attributed to Hannah Arendt. See A. Schaap, 'Enacting the Right to Have Rights: Jacques Rancière's Critique of Hannah Arendt,' *European Journal of Political Theory* 10 (2010); M. R. Somers, *Genealogies of Citizenship: Markets, Statelessness, and the Right to Have Rights* (Cambridge: Cambridge University Press, 2008). The phrase was also used by a United States Supreme Court Chief Justice Earl Warren in 1958 in a dissenting decision when he said 'Citizenship is man's basic right, because it is nothing less than the right to have rights.' See M. M. Ngai, *Impossible Subjects: Illegal Aliens and the Making of Modern America, Politics and Society in Twentieth-Century America* (Princeton, NJ: Princeton University Press, 2004), 127.

3 The relationship between human rights and citizenship is very complex and we cannot discuss it here. A. Brysk and G. Shafir, 'Globalization and the Citizenship Gap,' in *People Out of Place: Globalization, Human Rights, and the Citizenship Gap*, ed. A. Brysk and G. Shafir (London: Routledge, 2004); See K. Nash, 'Between Citizenship and Human Rights,' *Sociology* 43, 1067–84 (2009); M. R. Somers and C. N. J. Roberts, 'Toward a New Sociology of Rights: A Genealogy of "Buried Bodies" of Citizenship and Human Rights,' *Annual Review of Law and Social Science* 4 (2008).

4 This is by far the most dominant approach to citizenship and the literature has grown phenomenally. When my colleague Bryan Turner and I surveyed the field, we were rather shocked by its rapid development since Bryan founded the journal in 1997, which we have been editing jointly since 1999. See E. F. Isin and B. S. Turner, eds, *Handbook of Citizenship Studies* (London: Sage, 2002). Since then, the field of citizenship studies continued to grow and there is no volume that can capture even that part of the literature whose approach I designate as 'status'. See E. Guild, 'Security and Migration in the 21st Century,' *Security and Migration in the 21st Century* (Cambridge: Polity Press, 2009); C. Joppke, *Citizenship and Immigration* (Cambridge: Polity Press, 2010).

5 Perhaps the best contribution – at least it is most cited – to approaching citizenship as status through perspective of rights is T. H. Marshall, *Citizenship and Social Class*, ed. T. B. Bottomore, *Pluto Perspectives* (London: Pluto Press, 1949). Also see Somers, *Genealogies of Citizenship: Markets, Statelessness, and the Right to Have Rights*.

6 The term habitus used analytically by Pierre Bourdieu to indicate those habits that we learn by doing over relatively long periods of time so much so that it becomes our habitus, that is, embedded in our bodies that we take it for granted and repeat without much thinking or questioning. He was interested in things such as the learned 'feel for the game' (whether it is a political or sports game) and dispositions. See P. Bourdieu, *The Logic of Practice* (Stanford, CA: Stanford University Press, 1990). His *Distinction: A Social Critique of the Judgement of Taste* (Cambridge, MA: Harvard University Press, 1987) is a classic deployment of his idea on how we acquire taste as habitus. This idea

is especially useful to designate how people learn to conduct themselves and expect others to do the same.

7 See R. Barnes et al., 'Citizenship in Practice,' *British Journal of Social Psychology* 43 (2004); Schattle, *The Practices of Global Citizenship*.

8 D. T. Evans, *Sexual Citizenship: The Material Construction of Sexualities* (London: Routledge, 1993); W. Kymlicka, *Multicultural Citizenship: A Liberal Theory of Minority Rights*, *Oxford Political Theory* (Oxford: Clarendon Press, 1995); A. Latta, 'Environmental Citizenship,' *Alternatives Journal* 33, 1 (2007); A. Linklater, 'Cosmopolitan Citizenship,' *Citizenship Studies* 2, 1 (1998).

9 Jeff Goodell, 'Meet America's Most Creative Climate Criminal,' *The Rolling Stones*, 7 July 2011 [cited 24 February 2012]. Source: http://goo.gl/WRCu5

10 Suzanne Goldenberg, *The Guardian,* 'US eco-activist jailed for two years,' *Wednesday*, 27 July 2011 [cited 24 February 2012]. Source: http://goo.gl/YsWEK

11 Jeff Goodell, 'Rosa Parks Moment: Climate Activist Tim DeChristopher Sentenced to Prison,' 27 July 2011 [cited 24 February 2012]. Source: http://goo.gl/ZPq2P

12 Tim DeChristopher, 'I Do Not Want Mercy, I Want You to Join Me,' Statement to Court, 27 July 2011 [cited 24 February 2012]. Source: http://goo.gl/9Tegx.

13 Suzanne Goldenberg, *The Guardian*, 'US Eco-activist Jailed for Two Years,' *Wednesday*, 27 July 2011 [cited 24 February 2012]. Source: http://goo.gl/YsWEK

14 Tim DeChristopher, 'I Do Not Want Mercy, I Want You to Join Me,' Statement to Court, 27 July 2011 [cited 24 February 2012]. Source: http://goo.gl/9Tegx

15 H. Arendt, *The Human Condition* (Chicago: University of Chicago Press, 1958), 8.

16 Ibid., 9.

17 Ibid., 176.

18 H. Arendt, 'Introduction into Politics,' in *The Promise of Politics*, ed. J. Kohn (New York, NY: Schocken Books, 2005), 114.

19 Arendt, *The Human Condition*, 177–8.

20 H. Arendt, *The Origins of Totalitarianism*, new with added prefaces 1973 edn (New York: Harcourt Publishers, 1951), 473.

21 Ibid.

22 Ibid., 474.

23 Ibid.

24 Ibid., 479.

25 Ibid.

26 Arendt, *The Human Condition*, 178.

27 Ibid., 178–9.

28 H. Arendt, 'What Is Freedom?' in *Between Past and Future: Six Exercises in Political Thought* (New York: Viking Press, 1961), 144.

29 Arendt, *The Human Condition*, 184.

30 Ibid., 192.

31 Ibid., 191–2.

32 Ibid., 197.

33 Ibid., 233.

34 Ibid., 237.

35 Arendt, 'What Is Freedom?' 156.
36 Arendt, *The Human Condition*, 241.
37 Ibid., 237.
38 Ibid., 245.
39 H. Arendt, 'Concern with Politics in Recent European Political Thought,' in *Essays in Understanding, 1930–1954: Formation, Exile, and Totalitarianism*, ed. J. Kohn (New York: Schocken Books, 2005), 429.
40 Arendt, 'What Is Freedom?' 151.
41 Ibid., 153.
42 Ibid., 169.
43 Ibid., 151.
44 Arendt, 'Introduction into Politics,' 198.
45 Ibid., 194.
46 Arendt, *The Human Condition*, 152; Arendt, 'Introduction into Politics,' 194. Arendt says that she is using the term principle following Montesquieu's argument on forms of government: 'Therefore what the definition of governments always needed was what Montesquieu called a "principle of action" which, different in each form of government, would inspire government and citizens alike in their public activity and serve as a criterion, beyond the merely negative yardstick of lawfulness, for judging all action in public affairs. Such guiding principles and criteria of action are, according to Montesquieu, honour in a monarchy, virtue in a republic and fear in a tyranny.' Arendt, *The Origins of Totalitarianism*, 467.
47 Arendt, *The Human Condition*, 152.
48 Ibid.
49 Ibid.
50 H. Arendt, *Crises of the Republic: Lying in Politics, Civil Disobedience, on Violence, Thoughts on Politics and Revolution* (New York: Harcourt Brace Jovanovich, 1972), 94.
51 Ibid., 99.
52 Ibid., 98.
53 J. D. Caputo, ed., *Deconstruction in a Nutshell: A Conversation with Jacques Derrida, Perspectives in Continental Philosophy*, No. 1 (New York: Fordham University Press, 1996), 16–17.
54 See D. R. Villa, *Arendt and Heidegger: The Fate of the Political* (Princeton, NJ: Princeton University Press, 1996); D. Walsh, *The Modern Philosophical Revolution: The Luminosity of Existence* (Cambridge: Cambridge University Press, 2008).
55 V. Bell, *Culture and Performance: The Challenge of Ethics, Politics, and Feminist Theory* (Oxford: Berg, 2007); J. Loxley, *Performativity* (London: Routledge, 2007).
56 T. C. Davis, *The Cambridge Companion to Performance Studies* (Cambridge: Cambridge University Press, 2008); D. S. Madison and J. Hamera, eds, *The Sage Handbook of Performance Studies* (London: Sage, 2006); R. Schechner, *Performance Studies: An Introduction* (London: Routledge, 2002); R. Schechner, *Performance Theory*, rev. and expanded edn (London: Routledge, 1988). Sociologists such as E. Goffman, *The Presentation of Self in Everyday Life* (Garden City, NY: Doubleday, 1959); E. Goffman, *Strategic Interaction*,

vol. 1, *Series in Conduct and Communication* (Philadelphia: University of Pennsylvania Press, 1969) and anthropologists such as V. W. Turner, *The Anthropology of Performance* (New York: PAJ Publications, 1987), and historians such as C. Tilly, *Contentious Performances* (Cambridge: Cambridge University Press, 2008), made significant contributions to understanding action as performance.

57 An excellent introduction to these genealogies is Loxley, *Performativity*. But Loxley limits his focus to linguistics and speech acts.

58 The debate continued with disagreements on 'speech acts'. See J. R. Searle, *Speech Acts: An Essay in the Philosophy of Language* (Cambridge: Cambridge University Press, 1970) and J. Derrida, *Limited Inc*, trans. G. Graff (Evanston, IL: Northwestern University Press, 1988), especially on the question of intentionality, and with interventions by S. Felman, *The Scandal of the Speaking Body: Don Juan with J.L. Austin, or Seduction in Two Languages* (Stanford, CA: Stanford University Press, 2003). Also see J. Butler, 'Burning Acts: Injurious Speech,' *U. Chi. L. Sch. Roundtable* 3 (1996); J. Butler, 'Performative Acts and Gender Constitution an Essay in Phenomenology and Feminist Theory,' *Theatre Journal* 40 (1988), with their focus on how bodies are performed. Yet another distinct, albeit related, history of performativity can be traced back to M. Bakhtin, *Toward a Philosophy of Act*, ed. M. Holquist (Austin: University of Texas Press, 1993). See A. Reinach, 'The Apriori Foundations of the Civil Law,' *Aletheia: An International Journal of Philosophy 3 (1983): 1–142*. B. Smith and A. Burkhardt, 'Towards a History of Speech Act Theory,' in *Speech Acts, Meaning, and Intentions: Critical Approaches to the Philosophy of John R. Searle* (1990).

59 Overall, it must be said that performativity responds to an impasse of dualisms that vexed social and political thought for decades: subjectivism versus objectivism, structure versus agency, idealism versus materialism, and essentialism versus constructivism. Thus, performativity includes not only prominent theorists such as those mentioned above but also Foucault, 'Technologies of the Self'. P. Bourdieu, *Language & Symbolic Power* (Cambridge, MA: Harvard University Press, 1993). G. Deleuze and F. Guattari, *What Is Philosophy?* (New York: Columbia University Press, 1994). Rancière, *Disagreement: Politics and Philosophy*; Rancière, *On the Shores of Politics* and J. Derrida, *Without Alibi*, ed. P. Kamuf (Stanford, CA: Stanford University Press, 2002).

60 Clearly, the ways in which the concept performativity has been deployed in social and political thought and social sciences are complex and intricate as much as influential. Here I briefly highlight the most productive aspect of performativity and how performativity and enactment are complementary and yet distinct concepts for studying citizenship not only as a given status but also how that status is creatively transformed by its performance and enactment.

61 J. L. Austin, *How to Do Things with Words* (Oxford: Oxford University Press, 1962), 109.

62 Bourdieu, *Language & Symbolic Power*, 125–6.

63 Ibid., 107.

64 Ibid., 109.

65 Ibid., 111.

66 Ibid., 113.

67 Ibid., 115.

68 Obviously, I want to limit my comments on Auden's poem sincc I feel it provokes these questions better than any words at my command. On Auden and citizenship with some comments on 'The Unknown Citizen', see R. L. Caserio, 'Auden's New Citizenship,' *Raritan* 17, 2 (1997); J. Lucas, 'Auden's Politics: Power, Authority, and the Individual,' in *The Cambridge Companion to W.H. Auden*, ed. S. Smith (Cambridge: Cambridge University Press, 2004).

69 Loxley, *Performativity*, 97.

70 Ibid., 102.

71 J. Butler, *Subjects of Desire: Hegelian Reflections in Twentieth-Century France* (New York: Columbia University Press, 1999), 189.

72 Rancière says 'Politics does not happen just because the poor oppose the rich. It is the other way around: politics (that is, the interruption of the simple effects of domination by the rich) causes the poor to exist as an entity.' Rancière, *Disagreement: Politics and Philosophy*, 11.

73 Laclau says that we 'inhabit a historical terrain where the proliferation of heterogeneous points of rupture and antagonisms require increasingly political forms of social reaggregation – that is to say, that the latter depend less on underlying social logics and more on acts. . . .' Laclau, *On Populist Reason*, 230.

74 Ibid., 228.

75 Ibid.

76 Ibid., 229.

77 Ibid.

78 Ibid., 237.

79 A. Badiou, *Metapolitics*, trans. J. Barker (London: Verso, 2006), 24.

80 Ibid.

81 Austin, *How to Do Things with Words*; Searle, *Speech Acts: An Essay in the Philosophy of Language*.

82 J. Derrida, *Specters of Marx: State of the Debt, the Work of Mourning and the New International* (London: Routledge, 1994), 36–7.

83 Derrida, *Without Alibi*, 114.

84 J. Butler, *Undoing Gender* (London: Routledge, 2004), 224.

85 J. Butler, 'Sovereign Performatives in the Contemporary Scene of Utterance,' *Critical Inquiry* 23, 2 (1997): 148.

86 Derrida, *Without Alibi*, 239.

87 Hacking, *Historical Ontology*; I. Hacking, *Rewriting the Soul: Multiple Personality and the Sciences of Memory* (Princeton, NJ: Princeton University Press, 1995).

88 Hacking, *Historical Ontology*, 108.

89 Ibid., 113.

90 *The Guardian*. 2011. Reading the Riots. The Guardian in Partnership with the London School of Economics. Supported by the Joseph Rowntree Foundation and the Open Society Foundations 2011 [cited 6 January 2012]. Source: http://goo.gl/EqxH6

91 It is 10:49 AM on Monday, 8 August 2011.

92 BBC, 'London Riots: Timeline of Violence,' 8 August 2011, http://goo.gl/YbUZ6

93   Paul Lewis, 'Tottenham Riots: A Peaceful Protest, Then Suddenly All Hell Broke Loose,' *The Guardian* [cited 24 February 2012]. Source: http://goo.gl/YM9wC

94   BBC has already asked: 'Was Tottenham's Riot a Cry of Rage?' in a report by Matt Prodger on 8 August [cited 24 February 2012]. Source: http://goo.gl/rYhZ9

95   *The Guardian*, 'London Riots Spread South of Thames,' 8 August 2011 [cited 24 February 2012]. Source: http://goo.gl/eLDWh

96   D. Gardham. 2011. 'Hackney Speech Woman' Revealed to be Local Jazz Singer. *The Telegraph* 2011 [cited 16 August 2011]. Source: http://goo.gl/OyJeU

97   Ibid.

98   D. Aitkenhead. 2008. From Darfur with Love. *The Guardian*, 24 April 2008 [cited 16 September 2011]. Source: http://goo.gl/d1mkE

99   Waging Peace. 2008. 25 April 2008: Petition Containing the Voices of over 60,000 Darfuris Delivered to Downing Street. Waging Peace 2008 [cited 16 September 2011]. Source: http://goo.gl/fG1RM

100   L. Roland-Gosselin, 'Petition: Summary' (Waging Peace, 2008).

101   Aitkenhead, From Darfur with Love [cited 16 September 2011]. Source: http://goo.gl/d1mkE

102   C. Eke, 'Darfur: Coverage of a Genocide by Three Major Us Tv Networks on Their Evening News,' *International Journal of Media and Cultural Politics* 4, 3 (2008): 284.

103   L. Tsaliki et al., *Transnational Celebrity Activism in Global Politics: Changing the World?* (Chicago: Intellect Books, 2011), 93, 94.

104   Aitkenhead, From Darfur with Love [cited 16 September 2011]. Source: http://goo.gl/d1mkE

105   S. A. Higginson, 'A Short History of the Right to Petition Government for the Redress of Grievances,' *The Yale Law Journal* 96, 1 (1986): 146.

106   Ibid.

107   Aitkenhead, From Darfur with Love [cited 16 September 2011]. Source: http://goo.gl/d1mkE

108   Darfuri Refugees, 'Selected Testimonials from Darfuri Refugees in Chad' (Waging Peace, 2007).

109   Hansard. 13p Parl. Deb. H.C. 14 May 2008 (House of Commons, 2008).

110   M. Manike. 2008. 'My Son's Murder Helped Bring Down a Dictatorship'. *Financial Times*, 13 December 2008 [cited 9 July 2011]. Source: http://goo.gl/bCWpS

111   Ibid.

112   Ibid.

113   Minivan News. 2008. Torture in the Jails Is Not Finished: Mariyam Manike. Minivan News, 20 September 2008 [cited 9 July 2011]. Source: http://goo.gl/QcM5M

114   Ibid.

115   Ibid.

116   Ibid.

117   Ibid.

118 Manike, 'My Son's Murder Helped Bring Down a Dictatorship' [cited 9 July 2011]. Source: http://goo.gl/bCWpS

119 Republic of Maldives. 2004. Investigative Findings on the Death of Hassan Evan Naseem. Presidential Commission, The President's Office, 27 January 2004 [cited 12 December 2011]. Source: http://goo.gl/GSLk7

120 Minivan News. 2005. 15 Minutes with Evan Naseem's Mother Mariyam Manike. Minivan News, 13 March 2005 [cited 9 July 2011]. Source: http://goo.gl/8rmBU

121 Minivan News, Torture in the Jails Is Not Finished: Mariyam Manike [cited 9 July 2011]. Source: http://goo.gl/QcM5M

122 F. Harrison. 2003. Maldives Capital Tense after Riot. BBC, 22 September 2003 [cited 9 July 2011]. Source: http://goo.gl/xqtZv

123 Ibid.

124 BBC. 2008. Profile: Maumoon Gayoom of the Maldives. BBC, 29 October 2008 [cited 10 July 2011]. Source: http://goo.gl/Dtk0q

125 Ibid.

126 Manike, 'My Son's Murder Helped Bring Down a Dictatorship' [cited 9 July 2011]. Source: http://goo.gl/bCWpS

127 Idhikeeli. 2007. Vigil Held to Remember Torture Victim and Stand up against Torture. Idhikeeli, 22 September 2007 [cited 9 July 2011]. Source: http://goo.gl/vszdZ

128 A. Naish. 2009. Defence Ministry Taken to Court. *Dhivehi Observer*, 3 February 2009 [cited 9 July 2011]. Source: http://goo.gl/Wa1aJ

129 Ibid.

130 P. Burnell. 2009. 'Torture' Chief's Two UK Homes. BBC, 24 March 2009 [cited 10 July 2011]. Source: http://goo.gl/6ZALi

CHAPTER FIVE

Citizens without Frontiers

In 2010, the UK government introduced the International Student Service (ISS), or 'international service', for providing global volunteering experience to young people.[1] Ostensibly, it is a service that will provide thousands of students aged 18–22 years with the funds to fight against global poverty. The government addresses potential youth in the following manner: 'ISS has been designed to increase your understanding and experience of the world, and to help you learn how you can help the world's poorest people as a global citizen.'[2] Volunteers are given training before they depart for their destinations and receive orientation training when they arrive. Once they return, they also become part of a network of volunteers that contributes experiences and skills to a growing number of international citizens. Volunteers spend about 3 months in situ and are told that this will 'make a real difference to the lives of some of the world's poorest people'.[3] ISS ensures that 'Volunteers will work in small groups on projects designed to protect and promote the rights of women, children, and people living with disability or HIV/AIDS.' It promises that

> working with a team leader and a local community organization, you will help local people transform their communities by taking part in activities such as running awareness campaigns, helping small businesses reach more customers and developing inclusive activities for young people.

It is of course encouraging that the UK government is helping youths to become active international citizens and investing in them and in the people and places to which they are contributing. In effect, the UK government is acting as an international citizen by cultivating citizens without frontiers. A commentator called this programme 'big society without borders' to signal its connection to the government's domestic ideological programme akin to the earlier government's 'the third way'. The 'big society without borders' is ostensibly enabling young people to traverse frontiers, develop actual and effective relations with people in other places and contribute their passions and skills in making the world a better place to live.

Yet, there are problems with this script. And it is not necessary that ISS will potentially lead to practices of new colonialism, as was reported in the media in reference to a think-tank report.[4] Although ISS can lead to such consequences, 'the big society without borders' has subtler and far more troubling consequences.[5] It illustrates well one of the concepts of enacting citizenship and the distinction it advocates between active citizenship and activist citizenship.

We have already discussed the key concept of rupture as a transformation in the existing state of affairs or order of things. We have also seen how an act always presupposes a description under and through which we enact ourselves as political subjects. There are numerous ways through which such descriptions become recognizable (sayable and doable) repertoires expressed through performances and enactments. One way is the articulation or elaboration of a prescription by authorities that constitute themselves as a legitimate force. Often such prescriptions are translated into scripts as programmes, norms, rules and regulations of conduct that govern accepted and acceptable modes of action. These scripts are not necessarily written codes of conduct but an assemblage of positive conduct that is encouraged, cultivated, rewarded and embodied. They serve as technologies of government that resonate with strategies of government that articulate various aims. Since scripts are technologies and strategies of government that aim to calibrate conduct, they also aim to capture, tame and if necessary, stultify creativity, inventiveness and autonomy. Technologies of government are not interested in encouraging creativity, inventiveness and autonomy; rather they are interested in creativity, inventiveness and autonomy only insofar as they can be harnessed for calibrating conduct.[6]

Governing authorities are always intent on developing the scripts of 'active citizenship'. Since governing subjects through their liberties means engaging them, active citizenship becomes a programme of political subjectivation. Authorities in modern societies govern subjects through activating and also shaping, conditioning and influencing their aspirations, desires and wills. Producing scripts for active citizenship is among the most prominent businesses of government. That is why a distinction between active and activist citizens becomes crucial. Active citizens are those political subjects that become activated through scripts, which aim to cultivate conducts that are conducive to strategies articulated by governing authorities. Activist citizens are those political subjects who struggle against injustice (wrong), for equality and for identification. Activist citizens relentlessly pursue possibilities for writing new scripts with creativity, inventiveness and autonomy.

So, then, is the UK government's laudable aim to create global citizens by creating an international service for volunteering in poor countries the production of a script of active citizenship? It aims to produce conduct that is consistent with the broader aims of government and to harness the creativity, inventiveness and autonomy of young people. It also aims to ensure that their conduct does not lead to consequences that illustrate, demonstrate or reveal, for example, contradictions between the ICS programme for helping poor countries and how that poverty is produced through a Foreign Policy that facilitates trade in arms or pharmaceuticals.

Traversing frontiers

This chapter deals with the apparent paradox of calling activists who traverse frontiers 'citizens without frontiers'. Why call them citizens? When we discussed various movements under the name 'without frontiers' in Chapter 1, I noted that 'citizens without frontiers' would be a paradox. We can imagine academics, doctors and lawyers without frontiers but 'citizens without frontiers' just does not sound right precisely because citizens are confined within the borders of their states. But this paradox arises only if we fail to make a crucial distinction between active and activist citizens. Simply put, it is paradoxical only if we limit the possibilities of international citizenship to the authoritative scripts of governments. But if we consider the creative, inventive and autonomous acts that rewrite the scripts of international citizenship as traversing frontiers, then 'citizens without frontiers' becomes a possibility. This is a move that involves differentiating the active and activist citizen and, I suggest, investigating acts becomes a political responsibility.

This chapter focuses on this traversal political subjectivity that I call 'citizenship without frontiers'. It distinguishes traversal citizenship from universal citizenship. While the latter takes its scope from the state or even the nation-state, traversal citizenship recognizes (or institutes) the right to act across or against frontiers. Traversal citizenship is also different from human rights because it is based on the exercise of the political capacity to act for justice or against injustice. Traversal citizenship is not about asserting the right of every resident on this earth to exercise his or her freedom but it is about maintaining and developing the capacity to act across frontiers and with answerability. We are thus compelled to investigate actors who exercise this capacity not because it is universal or it is a right that belongs to every human. Rather, it is because they exercise a right that does not exist. This argument does in fact resonate with those who argue for activists without borders and justice without borders but in this chapter I make a case for retaining the vocabulary of citizenship to describe their activism and to distinguish it from universalism, globalism or cosmopolitanism.[7]

But this chapter also presents a second and more figurative image of traversing frontiers. So far the focus has been on traversing boundaries or borders of nation-states but we can also demonstrate that political subjects traverse other boundaries such as identities, interests and affiliations and acts across them. So traversing frontiers can literally mean to act across geographic boundaries but also figuratively indicate acting across social and cultural boundaries.

Why political subjectivity without frontiers?

Over the last two decades, we have learned a few quintessential things about citizenship. Two among them have proved to be the most valuable for me. First, no matter what political and social theorists may say about citizenship, people have proved themselves as flexible, intelligent, if not, ingenious, practitioners of the art of performing or enacting their rights and the rights of others. Second, the performing and enacting of rights often interrogate and challenge and thus traverse not only geographic but also social and cultural frontiers. Citizenship is often portrayed or represented as though boundaries manage to contain the performances and enactments of rights. However, when people are enacting rights, they mostly do what is workable and practicable for achieving their claims. The boundaries between different kinds of rights such as human, social, economic and sexual rights and kinds of jurisdictions such as states, and international and supranational legal bodies may be the means through which people negotiate and enact rights, but often people do not treat these as given or immutable. Neither of these points is inconsequential for debates that place these various rights in hermetically sealed and ostensibly pure categories while people just simply get on with performing and enacting them. Instead, we can condense these two lessons into a heuristic definition of citizenship that does not attempt to encompass and explain all instances of this multifarious institution but serves as a beginning point of investigation. In Chapter 4, I argued that citizenship is studied as status, habitus or act and I provided examples from various interdisciplinary and disciplinary fields to illustrate how this is often done. Now, I will provide a 'definition' of citizenship that takes into account its complex layers as an institution that neither presupposes a given body politic that authorizes it nor a given subject that is already authorized by it. On the contrary, both bodies, political and subjects, are produced through the institution of citizenship.

> Citizenship is a dynamic institution of domination *and* empowerment that governs *who* are citizens (insiders) and non-citizens as their others (strangers, outsiders) and abjects (aliens) and *how* these actors are to govern themselves and each other through a body politic. Citizenship is

not membership. It is a relation that governs the conduct and action of the (subject) positions that constitute it. The essential difference between citizenship and membership is that while the latter governs conduct *within* social groups, citizenship is about conduct and action *traversing* all of the social groups that constitute a body politic. Being a citizen almost always means being more than an insider. It also means being one who has mastered modes and forms of conduct that are appropriate to being an insider. This creates an actor both in the sense of a *person* (law) but also a *persona* (norm). For non-citizens, to become citizens means either adopting modes and forms of conduct of being an insider (assimilation, integration, incorporation) or challenging these modes and forms and thereby transforming them (identification, differentiation, recognition) through actions. What constitutes citizenship and its appropriate modes and forms of conduct are always objects of struggle among citizens, subjects and abjects through claims to citizenship as justice. It is through these claims to citizenship as justice that citizenship becomes a site of rights (and obligations). These claims and the combination of rights and obligations that define citizenship also traverse different sites and scales and produce different subjects. Thus, *rights* (civil, political, social, sexual, cultural, ecological), *sites* (e.g. bodies, courts, borders, networks, media), scales (e.g. cities, empires, nations, states, federations, leagues), *subjects* (e.g. citizens, non-citizens, abjects), and *acts* (e.g. dissenting, voting, volunteering, blogging, protesting, resisting, and organizing) are the elements that constitute a body politic.[8]

This relational definition of citizenship attempts to capture it as a contested field through which rights and responsibilities are articulated in the constitution of a body politic. This does not mean that when citizenship is not contested, it ceases to be an object of investigation. Clearly, laws and norms that constitute a body politic and the configurations of political subjectivities within it are matters of considerable interest. That is why studying citizenship as status and habitus is indispensable. Of equal interest is, however, how acts transform these laws, norms and habits and how they affect the configurations of political subjectivities. The emphasis on enacting citizenship is meant precisely to draw attention to these issues of transformation and change that we discussed with a focus on the concept of 'rupture' in Chapter 4.

Why acts of citizenship?

We have been using the term 'acts of citizenship' to describe how people perform rights to justice and constitute themselves as claimant subjects. If that is the meaning we have given to the phrase, then what does it aim to accomplish it? There are various ways to answer that question or at least to begin to address it. We discussed in Chapter 4 literatures on performativity and enactment as well as five theoretical propositions (ruptures versus citations, repetitions or iterations; actions versus acts; bodies versus subjects; intentionality versus purposiveness and responsibility versus answerability) and four methodological propositions (events, sites, scales and duration) for investigating acts. But now and in relation to the discussion of the importance of studying acts of citizenship, I want to focus on the difference between the doer and the deed. This is especially important for understanding traversing social and cultural frontiers. As will become clear very quickly, the difference between the doer and the deed is perhaps among the most vexed questions in social and political thought. But, again, I will keep the focus firmly on illustrating its importance rather than providing an account. Simply put, societies like ours are obsessed with the doer. Let us just think about this for a moment. Something happens. A deed is done. Say, a soldier named Bradley Manning leaks classified information that he has acquired by virtue of the position he holds. A frenzy ensues about *him*. Who is he? Where did he grow up? How did *he* grow up? What kind of person is he? All these questions are asked about the doer. Socially, it seems, we get fixated on giving an account of the doer. Meanwhile, at least at first, it seems that the court of law prepares to give a very different account. It gathers material to establish the legality or illegality of the deed. The law does not seem interested in the doer. It appears that it is interested in the deed. Furthermore, it does not appear to be interested in giving an account of the deed either. It appears that it is *only* interested in establishing the legality or illegality of the deed. But appearances are misleading. Arguably, the law is interested in the doer insofar as it can connect the deed to him or her. It establishes the legality or illegality of the deed in order to assign the appropriate punishment to the doer. Yet, all the same, the law is not interested in the deed unless there is a doer that can be made accountable for the deed. This becomes most apparent in courts where if the law cannot connect the deed to the doer, it is inevitably drawn into making a social deduction from the doer to the deed: Is the accused the kind of doer that is capable of this deed? What that often involves is asking questions about the 'character' of the doer. The assumption is that if the doer can be classified as possessing a certain kind of character, it is more likely that the doer can be linked to a deed. We can only surmise how many court cases must be decided by that logic. Arguably, then, both socially and legally, our societies cannot separate a deed from the doer and always assume that there is a doer behind the deed and that the doer always precedes the deed. As many scholars have argued, this has its origins in a specific concept of responsibility based on the law, especially criminal law and punishment regimes.[9]

It is not necessary to discuss this issue further. I am interested in how it affects political thought *about* citizenship. In political thought, the doer is called the subject; the deed is often called the act. Interestingly, and indeed regrettably, political thought inherits that assumption of the relationship between the deed and the doer when it investigates the relationship between acts and subjects. This is perhaps why we have so many books on the subject: the ticklish subject, the sexual subject, the colonial subject, the postmodern subject, the birth of the subject and so on and only a handful of scattered contributions on acts as such. To put it simply, acts are vastly neglected. There are further reasons and consequences for this neglect but my aim is not to discuss them. I just want to say that 'acts of citizenship' is about reversing two basic assumptions: that the doer comes before the deed and that there is a doer behind the deed. As regards citizenship, the emphasis on the subject is easy to illustrate. Since citizenship is primarily concerned with and functions as a legal status, we are often concerned with establishing who are the subjects of citizenship. Just think for a moment about words such as 'integration', 'cohesion' or 'assimilation'. Are these not policies about establishing who are the subjects of citizenship? In fact, the entire citizenship regime is about dividing subjects into citizens and non-citizens. Citizenship thus becomes assignment or ascription.

What if we think about citizenship first as acts and then its subjects? What if we focus first on the deeds and then doers of citizenship? What do people do when they act like (or as if they were) citizens? How do people perform their rights and the rights of others? How do we recognize those acts that are of citizenship and those that are not? Over the past few years, the consequences of some scholars asking these kinds of questions have been remarkable. In fact, so remarkable that some may think that these questions do not constitute citizenship studies at all. It seems as if scholars are now split into three ways of studying citizenship as described earlier: those who focus on status (law), those who focus on habitus (sociology and anthropology) and those who focus on acts, their genealogies and their topologies. This split is unhelpful. If there is something new about investigating citizenship as acts, it is that it combines insights from law, sociology, anthropology, history and, of course, politics. If we are concerned with how political subjectivity is performed and enacted, in other words brought into being, then is not asking whether this constitutes citizenship a vital question? But we cannot answer that question in the abstract. The investigations that this question gives rise to should demonstrate its practicality. I shall come back to this thought but now I need to turn to a discussion of frontiers.

Why without frontiers?

It is perhaps obvious that the currently dominant uses of the term culture are national (whether ethnic or civic) and civilizational. The national and civilizational usage of culture is inherited from the nineteenth century. But thinking about acts and subjects perhaps provides a different perspective on how we can use culture. To continue with the terms doers and deeds for a moment, we can use culture in a limited and limiting sense to designate 'ways of doing'. There are ways of doing things that emerge from the tasks that people set for themselves. We academics have our ways of writing, for example; and so do print journalists, novelists and so on. We have ways of doing writing and each of these ways can be described as a culture of writing. Our ways of doing things have histories. We do certain things in certain ways because it proved useful to the task we set ourselves. Of course, culture is never without tension or conflict because there are always those who will attempt to press their ways of doing things on others. And there will be those who will resist. Perhaps that is why cultures are dynamic entities: because they embody this *agon* about ways of doing things. If we think of culture as ways of doing things, then it is more important to focus on doers than on ways. Or, to still follow the logic mentioned earlier, it is more interesting to focus first on deeds then second on doers. This has implications for understanding the question of otherness. When we think about otherness, we are immediately led to think about the other as the doer. But if we thought about culture as ways of doing things, we would be less interested in the other than the otherness of ways of doing things. We would be much less interested in whether the other as doer is this or that than what he or she does and whether we are drawn into or away from her ways of doing things. This may have led us down a rather obscure path. But hopefully it will all come together when we return to meanings of traversing frontiers.

Why traversing frontiers?

On 25 May 2009, the then Governor of Canada Michaelle Jean when visiting Nunavut 'used a traditional Inuit knife to help gut [a seal] then ate a slice of raw heart'.[10] The BBC reported this event as 'Canada's governor general, Michaelle Jean, has helped to butcher and eat a seal [heart] in an apparent act of solidarity with hunters'.[11] This act was reported with a bit more flair in *Huffington Post*'s Green section, Huffpost Green. It recounts

> Hundreds of Inuit at a community festival gathered Monday as Jean knelt above a pair of seal carcasses and used a traditional ulu blade to slice the meat off the skin. After cutting through the flesh, Jean turned to the woman beside her and asked: 'could I try the heart?' She swallowed a piece whole and deemed it tasty, saying: 'It's like sushi . . . And it's very rich in protein.'[12]

Admittedly, there are a number of remarkable things about this act. That a Haitian refugee became the Queen's Representative in Canada and came to enact solidarity with Inuit hunters might be one of them. That she enacted this solidarity in response to the European Union's (EU) ban of seal products from Canada could be another. When asked later if her actions were a message to the EU, she apparently said: 'Take from it what you will.' But perhaps the most telling response came from an EU spokeswoman for the Environment Commissioner who said the act was 'too bizarre to acknowledge'. What was actually bizarre about this act? That a governor general enacted it? That it was a barbaric way of doing things? Or that it was a non-Inuit person who enacted it?

Whatever the EU spokeswoman may have found bizarre about the act, her reaction helps illustrate a point I was making earlier on the question of otherness. That if we think about culture as ways of doing things, we would be less interested in the other as doer than the otherness of her ways of doing things. We would be much less interested in whether the other as doer is this or that than what she does and whether we are drawn into or away from her ways of doing things. That the EU spokeswoman considered it bizarre I think is evidence enough that she was drawn away. Then the question may become why she is drawn away from it.

But there is something else in this act that is of interest as we reflect on the idea of 'traversing'. This act interrogates and transgresses various boundaries between the doable and sayable. But one that it transgresses most symbolically is an opening to another way of doing things. That is what it symbolizes: an opening to another way of doing things. We often think of cultures (and identities they precipitate) as closed memberships. What this act does is to rupture that closeness. By doing as the other, even if only once, it traverses the frontiers of culture and society. Michaelle Jean acted as if she were Inuit. Clearly, this does not make her an Inuit but she acted as if she were one, if only for a moment. This captures the deeper notion of traversing that I want to bring to your attention. We not only often think of cultures and societies as closed membership, as I mentioned already, but also assume that its members behave in ways that enhance and further its (i.e. culture or society) and their (i.e. its members) interests. This hermetically sealed and purist view of culture and its membership makes it almost impossible to think how people act across their ways of doing things. I submit that our obsession with the doer leads us to see culture as hermetically sealed since we derive deeds from doers and we limit our imagination, just as if we are in a court of law, by the ostensible and given capabilities of the doer. Yet, who would have thought that a governor general of Canada, a refugee from Haiti, would have eaten the heart of a seal in Nunavut? It is just not written in the script. (To avoid misunderstanding, I am not saying that this act was right or wrong. We can have a discussion about that. I am pointing out the fact that we often traverse other ways of doing things and we are not necessarily imprisoned in our *habitus* – understood as relatively enduring dispositions. On the contrary, our *habitude* – that our disposition to act certain ways can produce unexpected outcomes – is changeable.) This is really the main reason why I describe the basic qualities of acts as creative (deliberate yet spontaneous, mischievous yet serious, courageous yet not heroic), inventive (surprising yet predictable, illegal yet acceptable, outrageous yet reasonable) and autonomous (individual yet collective, scripted yet experimental, unauthorized yet meaningful).

Let me provide another example that happens in three acts. Act one: Two men are kissing in a pub in Soho, London. Act two: The publican asks the two men to stop kissing. But she does not stop there. She then asks them to leave the pub all together. This was reported by the BBC on 14 April 2011 as 'Gay couple removed from Soho pub for kissing'.[13] The British papers around that time provided details of these two acts. For one, they reported that the two men widely publicized their ejection from the pub, which the media reported with incredulity. What interests me is a third act. The following day on 15 April 2011, hundreds of people gathered in an act of protest against the ejection in front of the central London pub.[14] Protesters enacted a mass kiss-in. As might be expected, the doers could be classified as 'gays'. But among the protesters, there were men who were neither gay, nor considered themselves as gay, and yet were kissing each other. Why would they do that?

Here is where I am heading with this. After discussing a Haitian refugee who as a governor general eats a seal's heart, we moved to 'straight' men kissing each other in an act of solidarity with gay men. What both illustrate is, again, that when we shift our focus from doers to deeds and from subjects to acts, things no longer appear as they had seemed. People traverse frontiers of ways of doing things for protest, solidarity, defiance, resistance or whatever and they cannot be reduced to their assumed or ascribed identities.

In describing these acts, I am not using the notion of boundaries as a metaphor to replace the actual borders that contain a given body politic. But these things are related. These two acts do not only traverse actual boundaries but also symbolic boundaries. This is what I mean by traversing frontiers. Once enacted, they become 'memorized' as repertoires of performativity that we may 'remember'. Being a citizen means being a traversal political subject.

Not convinced? Well then shall we consider a final example? This comes in three acts too. On 24 January 2011, a police officer in Toronto enters Osgoode Hall Law School to advise female students specifically on how to stay safe.[15] 'You know, I think we're beating around the bush here,' the officer says and adds: 'I've been told I'm not supposed to say this – however, women should avoid dressing like sluts in order not to be victimized.'[16] As a reporter later would say, '. . . little did he know that he would unwittingly inspire a movement that has caught fire across Canada and the US'. It is not any wonder really. Often acts exceed the intentions of their actors and make them unknowing and unwitting subjects in the act. I could not think of a better act to convey this aspect of enacting citizenship. What makes this an act of citizenship, following our earlier discussion, is that a police officer is giving advice (technologies of government) to young women (subjectivation) on how to avoid trouble in public spaces (calibrations) for their own good or freedom (strategies of government). The trouble is the addressees of this speech act are creative, inventive and autonomous subjects. They beg to differ.

Two Toronto feminists decide to publicize this. So on 3 April, they organize the first SlutWalk. Thousands of women walk through Toronto with provocative clothing. Their manifesto states:

> we are tired of being oppressed by slut-shaming; of being judged by our sexuality and feeling unsafe as a result. Being in charge of our sexual lives should not mean that we are opening ourselves to an expectation of violence, regardless if we participate in sex for pleasure or work. No one should equate enjoying sex with attracting sexual assault.[17]

Now, that was the second act, which turned the first inside out – a reversal. The third act was a series of enactments in several cities that became a movement called SlutWalk and involved people protesting with clothing that ironically traverses the inner logic of the police officer's thought. Over the next few months, the movement spreads to Europe and further and it becomes an international phenomenon. On 4 June 2011, SlutWalking enters the United Kingdom with marches in Cardiff, London, Edinburgh and Glasgow.[18]

Now, there are fascinating aspects of this phenomenon that captured the imagination of many women and men. On the one hand, it revives some of the earliest feminist resistances while, on the other, it invents a new defiant vocabulary and uses new social media technologies that perhaps befit a new generation at a time when it has become a sort of sport to declare feminism dead.

Much more can be said about how an act inspires a mobilization (if indeed inspire is the word to use given the unwitting and unintentional act that gave rise to it). Nonetheless, what I want to call a fourth act of this scene illustrates again my point about traversing frontiers. On 1 June 2011, a Minneapolis blogger wrote 'On Being a Male SlutWalker'.[19] Organizing other men to join the walk, he says

> I want people to understand that rape is a violent act and not a sexual one, and I want them to understand that it is the rapists that should be punished when it happens. Judging from the SlutWalk Minneapolis Facebook page, there are over 1,400 other people who would agree with me.

He gives other reasons for his solidarity with women such as the rape of his girlfriend before he met her. But what this illustrates, again, is the capability to act without frontiers.

All these acts are ruptures not because they are spectacular or momentous but because they are *ruptures in the given order of things* and people both act across and in unscripted ways.

Now, if we put all these three meanings together, what are we left with? We can, of course, debate some of my illustrations or how I interpret them. We can say, yes, but there is also another way of seeing that act. And so on. But the point here is not to investigate these acts in all their tensions, paradoxes and undecidability. It is to illustrate how we overlook the fact that what separates or divides people is not who they ostensibly are; it is what they – we – perform and enact. And since we do different things at different times and in different spaces, what separates us from others is always dynamic and changing. That is at least what we have learned from studying acts of citizenship. The difference between the doer and the deed has significant consequences on how we theorize citizenship especially if that citizenship is said to traverse frontiers for social justice. How people enact constituting themselves and others as a claimant of social justice by traversing social and cultural frontiers is also a question of geographic frontiers.

Why not global activists?

Through the examples, I have given are we not witnessing 'a full-blown global civil society or an integrated transnational polity, at least a trend toward new forms and new levels of transnational contention'?[20] That is how Sidney Tarrow sees it. For Tarrow, although new actors are emerging in this global civil society, states remain essential for what he calls 'contentious politics'. What Tarrow sees is a kind of cosmopolitanism that is anchored in the life of states. What happens through contentious politics with a cosmopolitan bend is that we see people operating within and beyond their societies 'both in other countries and in the ambit of international regimes, institutions, and practices'. It is these people Tarrow defines as rooted cosmopolitans: *'individuals and groups who mobilize domestic and international resources and opportunities to advance claims on behalf of external actors, against external opponents, or in favor of goals they hold in common with transnational allies'.*[21] For Tarrow, transnational activists are a subgroup of rooted cosmopolitans and they are *'people and groups who are rooted in specific national contexts, but who engage in contentious political activities that involve them in transnational networks of contacts and conflicts'.* What makes transnational activists different from domestic activists is 'their ability to shift their activities among levels, taking advantage of the expanded nodes of opportunity of a complex international society'. We are then increasingly witnessing 'a fluid, cosmopolitan, but rooted layer of activists and advocates . . . that uses domestic resources, expertise, and opportunities to advance the collective goals of the people it claims to represent'.[22] Tarrow recognizes that some activists make these claims in the name of globalization and others against its ravages. It is also the case that some advance more concrete and practical aims and others purport ideological commitments. For Tarrow, what unites these movements is their grounded claims in specific situations.[23] 'Its activists are the connective tissue of the global and the local, working as activators, brokers, and advocates for claims both domestic and international.' Tarrow sees this multifarious phenomenon and its connective tissues against the image of a world 'neatly divided into a camp of statists and globalizers on one side opposed by a composite movement for "global justice" on the other. Such condensation makes for exciting politics and popular journalism, but it is reductionist on both counts.'[24]

Although this view of transnational activism seems to capture the essential aspects of the contentious politics of citizens without frontiers, it is a very different view. Even Tarrow's first point is at odds with the image of this book. He defines rooted cosmopolitanism as the politics of states as though states exist as already defined and definable containers. Once we take a defined polity as the basis of politics through which some actors located in this polity engage in contentious politics across its boundaries, it begins to give an image of neatly defined actors and boundaries. The idea that there is rootedness imagines a politics of autochthonous (indigenous) identification that re-enacts the ideas of sovereignty, territory and people. That the concerns of these rooted people extend beyond the boundaries that contain them makes them cosmopolitans in the sense of care and concern. That there is also a generational aspect of this rootedness where 'the vast majority of citizens identify primarily with their localities and their national states, [and] younger citizens are more likely to feel attachments to the continental or global levels than their elders' becomes a questionable claim.[25] So then it seems we have two containers in this understanding of a new contentious politics. Although state and global 'levels' are not diametrically opposed, there is on the one hand, a global civil society (as an integrated and integrating whole), and on the other, domestic civil societies (parts). In this view, transnational actors are rooted cosmopolitans who connect these parts to the whole through their networks. I have been critical of this whole-parts politics throughout the book.

Yet, it would not be an exaggeration to say that this view pervades the literature on global activism. Like Tarrow, recognizing that transnational movements are multifarious, Ruth Reitan insists that there is a confluence of slogans, issues, campaigns and alternative visions and that this confluence is so remarkable that many participants and observers have begun referring to these vast mobilizations as one single movement or network, calling it differently depending on their vantage point: anti-corporate globalization, anti-capitalist, anti-imperialist, globalization from below, global justice and solidarity, global social justice, or simply a movement of movements or a network of networks.[26]

She sees the intellectual task as 'theorizing the relationship between the globalization of neoliberalism and resistance to it, by asking both why and how activists are shifting from the local and national to include the transnational level of contention'.[27] Reitan argues that this confluence is resulting in new roles for transnational actors. She suggests, for example, that 'NGOs, especially those acting across borders, have traditionally assumed a position of distance from those directly suffering, and thus an independent vantage point from which to judge who is worthy of their sympathy and altruistic advocacy.'[28] By contrast, new global activism is developing two kinds of solidarity, based on reciprocity and identification, that are replacing altruism. Reciprocal solidarity emerges when activists 'draw a *connection* between the suffering of others and their own plight and claims'.[29] The solidarity that mobilizes them also invokes empathy rather than sympathy towards the suffering of others. Thus, 'this perceived *connection* invokes *empathy with*, rather than sympathy for, others' struggles, leading to a solidarity among them based on reciprocity and a sense of ultimately interconnected fates'.[30] But then why such disparate yet related activities should be called a movement named 'global activism' is not clear.

It is appropriate to end this chapter by returning to the UK government's laudable initiative, the ISS, and the intention to create international citizens. I left the discussion rather abruptly by saying that ISS aims to produce conduct that is consistent with narrower aims of government. It aims to limit young people's imagination to a narrow compass of what it means to traverse frontiers and what it means to relate to others in other places. It frames 'being an international citizen' as a question of aid, assistance and giving rather than intervention, which is presumably the prerogative of the state. Its training activities and placements also frame 'being an international citizen' narrowly by erasing other activities of the state, corporations and professions whose practices traverse frontiers and often produce some disastrous effects. All this may be considered rather harsh if unfair for the good intentions of the government and youths who are involved in becoming international citizens through such governmental programmes. There may well be some youths who come away from these activities with experiences that do not quite conform to the intentions of governmental programmes and that produce different subject effects. In such cases, the creativity, inventiveness and autonomy of some of its subjects would contravene its intended purposes.

ACT 16. OF DECLARATION: 'WE, THE ROMA NATION'

On 1 January 2001, the International Romani Union (IRU) signed a declaration, 'We, the Roma Nation'.[31] The declaration announces that the union does not want a state. This is a declaration of 'we, the people' without a state. Is that possible? Is a 'we, the people' without a state, without sovereignty, without territory possible? Perhaps it is not. This brutal answer renders this declaration a rupture, a break from the given order. What constitutes its performative force, certainly without intention, is to request, to claim, in fact, to affirm, the impossible. The order under which we live cannot say yes to this request and its enactment. 'We, the people' without a state, without sovereignty, without territory cannot come into being; it can only be a minority. 'We, the Roma Nation' is possible only if it demands, claims and requests to become a nation with a state, with sovereignty, with territory. So the declaration, certainly without intention, by demanding the impossible points out the arbitrariness of our order. Must a demand to become 'we, the nation' always be trapped in territory and sovereignty? That is a fundamental question that shapes the order in which we live.

Yet, this act of declaration both confounds and simplifies that post-national citizenship called 'European citizenship'. Doesn't it guarantee freedom of movement across states at least throughout Europe? No, it does not. Doesn't the declaration of European citizenship ask for that freedom? Yes, it does. It illustrates that European Union citizenship still remains firmly rooted with the identification of 'we, the people'. Without that identification, without nationality, enacting European citizenship becomes impossible.

But why was the IRU compelled to declare 'we, the Roma nation'? Yes, this declaration has the performative force of pointing out the trap of 'we, the people' but doesn't it also fall into it?⋅ The Roma constitute between 10 to 12 million people and as such comprise the largest minoritized population in Europe, with inhabitants in every European state.[32] The Roma diaspora is scattered throughout communities within these member states, and often live a disparate and diffused existence.[33] The Roma is as invented, or made up, as any people. Although its origins are traced to the waves of migration from Northern India to Europe between the ninth and fourteenth centuries, who exactly settled in Central and Eastern Europe is complicated.[34]

This is because the Roma is an invented group of various ethnicities (more explicitly than other ethnic groups). It is a generic term that refers to East European 'gypsies' or the Vlax Roma, but has been applied to refer to Sinti, Manouches, Romanichals, Kalo and others.[35] The term Roma gained this more expansive claim from 1971 onwards, after the first World Romani Conference in London, where a flag and national anthem were adopted. Given the plurality of the ethnic groupings and their interaction within host communities, they do not actually have common traditions.[36] Cultural expressions are just as disparate as the differences within Europe as a whole.[37] Thus, the ability to speak Romani or any other common language is not fundamental to the ethnic identity of the Roma, with some abandoning bilingualism but maintaining other markers of ethnic difference.[38] The act of naming these disparate people as the Roma is already an act of symbolic violence. What the Roma, or more precisely, their genealogies, demonstrate is how each nation has been invented and founded on violence. Once invented, nations become intolerant of those who do not fit into their narratives of invention. That is perhaps why the Roma experience political, legal and economic marginalization, including within Hungary and Romania where they form a significant entrenched minority.[39] As the Council of Europe Assembly remarks: 'The Romani community is still not regarded as an ethnic or national minority group in every member state, and thus it does not enjoy the rights pertaining to this status in all the countries concerned.'[40]

While intended to be helpful, this statement also betrays the people who have come to be classified as the Roma and are asked to live under its description despite their differences. Why can't people enjoy rights without becoming 'we, the people'? Many Roma fail to conform to sociolegal norms such as registering the birth of a child and 'do not hold official property titles'.[41] Imbued with a history of persecution (with many still experiencing deep-seated prejudice)[42] and an impossibility of political representation,[43] the Roma have taken steps to address the fact that they have had no role to play in constructing the rules under which they live. Although some measures have been taken by national governments in an attempt to ensure Romani representation, the IRU has pursued other means of political representation.[44] The IRU is of the opinion that the voices of the Romani people need to be globally heard and they therefore seek the best possible method for achieving recognition.[45] Consequently, they have circumvented the nation-state and appealed directly to international forums and, at the Fifth Romani World Congress held in Prague in 2000, produced a 'Declaration of Nation', which does not seek resolution in a state.[46] The significance of this act becomes apparent in light of the situation facing the Roma:

> While the territorial focus of the international system encourages those seeking self-determination to claim territorial autonomy, dispersed ethno-national communities are left without a satisfactory and fair remedy to their grievances because the practice of self-determination through territorial independence or autonomy is not suited to them.[47]

Whether the Roma have addressed this in a creative, inventive and autonomous manner by claiming non-territorial national status through their 'Declaration of Nation' is questionable.[48] The declaration states that:

> We are aware that the main characteristic of the Roma Nation, the one of being a Nation without searching for the establishment of a State, is today a great, adequate resource of freedom and legality for each individual, and of the successful functioning for the world community.[49]

Although they do not attempt to speak for all Roma, the idea that the Roma denounce belonging to a conventional territorial nation-state is widely articulated. The Roma claim themselves as a nation on a par with territorial nation-states but without asserting claims of sovereignty.[50] The particular nature of non-territoriality, and how it is to be achieved under the current international system, is left problematic.[51]

How do the Roma, or their intermediaries and advocates, respond to this problem? One solution advocated by the Roma, upon which this act draws its strength, has been outlined by academics writing in the field of Romani studies. They argue that the Romani Movement uses the 'Renner–Bauer non-territorial cultural autonomy model'.[52] The model would offer the Roma 'self-determination through participation and non-territorial autonomy for ethno-national communities without disrupting the territorial continuity of current states and, thus, the stability of the world order'.[53] Both Klímová-Alexander and McGarry argue that this model represents the best possible outcome for the Romani people in terms of achieving political representation on the international stage in a manner true to the act of framing a non-territorial people. But it also falls into the trap of sovereignty and territory by reworking the question into a multicultural discourse of 'polyethnic rights'.[54] This renders the question intelligible to current state accommodation and recognition practices. This translation of the 'Declaration of Nation', and the ease with which it slips into a demand for minority rights, becomes a multiculturalist demand once the act is received by the structures it addresses.

Arguably, *The Strasbourg Declaration on Roma* issued by the Council of Europe in 2010 disrupted this. The recommendations of *The Strasbourg Declaration on Roma* appeared to fill the void produced by the seemingly paradoxical non-territorial claims to nationhood by addressing the Roma issue in terms of a 'pan-European response', constituting the Roma as European citizens entitled to the same rights as national citizens, without enforcing a model of assimilation. The framework of the declaration gave policy backing to the 'Declaration of Nation' in terms intelligible to (liberal) multicultural citizenship. This becomes clear through recommendations (19) to (29) which extend and advocate a liberal approach to the Roma which includes protecting against abuse of citizens, as well as recommendations for empowerment such as access to services and opportunities citizens are entitled to.[55] It is then supplemented by (32)–(40), which presuppose, but do not explicitly state, differentiated and targeted delivery through multiculturalist sensitivities.[56]

The Czech Republic, a state previously criticized for its treatment of the Roma, has also directly welcomed both the Romani act of bypassing the nation-state and their constituting of themselves as European and Human at the Fifth Romani World Congress. The Ministry of Foreign Affairs supported the 'Europeanization of Romani identity' and concurred that the problems they face are international in scope.[57] A document titled 'the Ministry of Foreign Affairs conception of the Roma issue' highlights this position:

> We understand Europeanization here as to grasp the Romani issue as an affair which concerns every European state where a Romani lives today. From this it also follows the will to seek a solution to the Romani issue at an international/ European level.[58]

There is a genuine possibility of a shift in the scale of the Roma question from member states to Europe. But which Europe? Neither the Europe of human rights (through the European Court of Human Rights) nor the Europe of citizenship rights (the European Union) is able to protect the rights of Roma to mobility. The question remains. Could the claims to nationhood without statist or territorial aspirations become an act for citizenship without frontiers? Can the Roma challenge the European Union to live up to its promises of protecting what Mesfin Gedlu has called 'the most European nation'?[59]

ACT 17. OF RESISTANCE: INTERNATIONAL SOLIDARITY MOVEMENT

On 28 December 2000, during a march into an Israeli base near Beit Sahour, protestors walked into the compound. They met with little resistance from a confused military who eventually stated that they wanted the base evacuated. Then, as the protestors left, a French protestor 'climbed up a watchtower and planted a Palestinian flag. Palestinians wanted to do that but they couldn't [since] they would have been shot, but this international managed to do it'.[60] The images soon circulated on national television causing embarrassment to the Israeli military. The resistance won a minor victory, with the military moving the base some 200 yards away from its previous position.[61] But the most effective consequence of this act of raising a flag was the foundation of a movement – a new script through which citizens without frontiers could be enacted. This was the moment when resistant foreign bodies proved more worthy and thus effective than those indigenous or autochthonous to the site of struggle.

Founded by mostly Palestinian and Israeli activists in 2001, the International Solidarity Movement (ISM) provides 'the Palestinian people with international solidarity and an international voice with which to nonviolently resist an overwhelming military occupation force'. The movement not only signifies resistance to the Israeli state and its sponsorship of violent nationalism but it is also a counterpoint to the sponsorship of a violent Palestinian nationalism.[62] It was co-founded by Huwaida Arraf, a 25-year-old Palestinian bearing dual American and Israeli citizenship.[63] Prior to establishing ISM, she campaigned for non-violent resistance with the involvement of internationals (Westerners) as a contributory force that can help resist Israeli occupation in ways not open to Palestinians. She also saw them as a moderating force, which could help steer resistance away from the more virulent forms, breaking the circle of violence.[64] Arraf argued that since Palestinian life is worthless to the Israeli military than that of foreign bodies whose presence could prevent violence, 'the death of an International could cause a PR disaster . . . Internationals were therefore protecting Palestinians from lethal violence'.[65] As we have seen above, the potential of international foreign bodies for the Palestinian cause had become clear almost a year before ISM was founded.

Over the last decade, the ISM has aimed 'to support and strengthen the Palestinian popular resistance by providing the Palestinian people with two resources, international solidarity and an international voice with which to nonviolently resist an overwhelming military occupation force'.[66] Most of its activists come from the United States or the United Kingdom. The majority of ISM activists are in their 'twenties or beyond the years of raising a family'.[67] They join the movement through informal networks such as internet newsgroups and student lobbies. After paying their own way to Palestine, they receive training in non-violent direct action methods.[68] Aside from providing 'protection to Palestinians or documenting army actions', they provide food and medicine to Palestinian homes.[69] They enact the

> nonviolent politics of habitational resistance: witnessing, documenting, standing with Palestinians in their homes and at checkpoints, assisting with

the harvesting of olives under the threat of settler violence, and, perhaps most visibly, working in communities that are most directly affected by the construction of the Wall.[70]

The ISM also works outside Palestine to put pressure on the activists' respective nations. It aims to provide a voice for Palestinians while its members also speak as citizens against their state's relationship with Israel. These aims are carried out through everyday actions as part of the Boycott, Divestments and Sanctions (BDS) agenda, supplemented by protests in their respective countries. The ISM then becomes an effective means through which various repertoires or scripts are prepared, and produced and bodies are trained. The ISM may be a single movement but it is at the forefront of what Omer calls the 'global Palestine solidarity movement'.[71] Omer finds that groups like the ISM abstract a Palestinian story and place it in terms such as 'indigenous rights' or 'neoliberal imperialism' and thus communicate it to a broader audience and movement. The ISM shifts the scale of the struggle against the Israeli occupation and the reach of its sites. He finds that this levels discordant voices within communities yet it functions effectively as a framing process to build alliances.[72]

The ISM provides greater international legitimacy to the cause and enables better circumvention of Israeli securitization. On 2 May 2002, ISM activists sought to deliver food supplies to over a hundred Palestinians who had taken refuge in the Church of Nativity during the Israeli invasion, which began a month earlier. Bethlehem was under Israeli military occupation and the church was under siege.[73] The 23 activists managed to enter the church and deliver their supplies without being shot at or gassed. Several remained within the church. According to Arraf, the actions by the ISM activist could prevent the Israelis from firing on the church.[74] The Israeli response was to arrest the activists. This act also enabled a *Los Angeles Times* journalist to enter the church. In sum, it fulfilled one of the main functions of the ISM: to expose the day-to-day life of Palestinians to an international audience.

Thus, aside from the measures of direct action taken, documentation has become central to the ISM, 'not just to show that there are illegal and unjust actions going on, but also to provide a real means of evidence for accountability to the police and courts, case by case'.[75] Job flyers call for 'Media Activists' who would '[l]earn to humanize the voice of the struggle by reporting on events ranging from anti-occupation demonstrations to house raising demolitions'.[76] Shaista Aziz exemplifies this further as she documents the intricate lives of paramedics who move from site to site 'patching up' civilians who have been shot. She combines these events with her experience (as someone from the West) in order to enable greater sympathy for their situation.[77] The ISM thus seeks to establish a framing process of the conflict to further a non-violent resolution, while assisting Palestinians in their day-to-day struggles with the Israeli security apparatus. Yet, as the Gaza flotilla enactment has shown, the presence of resistant foreign bodies also provokes its own violence.

ACT 18. OF SHARING: OPEN RIGHTS GROUP

If Austin has shown us how to do things with words, who will show us how to do things without words?[78] In 2010, the Open Rights Group (ORG), an internet rights advocacy organization, staged an act of protest outside the British Houses of Parliament against the Digital Economy Bill.[79] Protesters held 'black wordless placards and black gaffer tape' to produce the effect of showing the 'dark days ahead'.[80] Theirs was an act without words. Of course, words were exchanged later but to express wordlessness is to search for them. Who owns words? (We will leave aside sounds and images for now.) Isn't this the question that the internet radically intensifies? The internet is the site where we cannot do anything without words. (This perhaps even applies to dissemination of sounds and images.) To advocate for open rights on the internet then potentially means that this quite basic yet fundamental question now concerns everyone anywhere. Does ORG live up to its name?

The ORG was established in 2005 in the United Kingdom as a lobbying group with the aims of 'defending freedom of expression, privacy, innovation, consumer rights and creativity on the net'.[81] It is really remarkable how in such a short period of its history all those things that were considered inherent in the internet (freedom, innovation, access, creativity) became things that needed defending. If the Internet has became a site for creative, inventive and autonomous acts, it has also become a site for governing such acts through laws such as the Digital Economy Bill. ORG fought the bill strongly, but ultimately failed to prevent its passing. The Digital Economy Act 2010 legislates against online copyright infringement and lays out penalties for such infringement, among other things.[82] The Act would ensure that 'persistent file-sharers' are permanently barred from accessing the internet. The Act would enable copyright holders to prevent access to sites hosting illegal content.[83] ISPs will be provided with guidelines on how to deal with web piracy; if illegal downloads do not fall by 70 per cent within 12 months, new and more stringent methods of preventing illegal downloading will be introduced.[84]

ORG believes that the Act puts forward 'indiscriminate sanctions' targeting alleged copyright infringers, which would affect a much wider group of people, if not their freedom to create on the internet. ISP addresses are often linked to households and so there can be instances where one 'illegal' file-sharer resides with several other people who do not download illegally, but the whole household would suffer collectively by having their internet access blocked.[85] ORG argues that 'disconnection is an inappropriate sanction': such wide-sweeping powers, when exercised by ISPs, will mean that people's jobs and even entire businesses will likely be affected. The group is also concerned about the potential of the bill to invade the privacy of individuals. If ISPs are allowed to monitor content from users, this could allow them to develop databases of information, which could be linked to individual users.[86]

Francis Davey of ORG insisted that 'the key question of who will be disconnected from the Internet and for what reason is subject to no democratic control and requires no consultation to be made'.[87] ORG claims that 'overzealous' legislation on file sharing has led to 'the marginalization of citizen and consumer rights'.[88] They believe that the government is ignoring the wider 'welfare' benefits that increasing digitization lends to citizens, and they recommend 'a commitment to a broader and deeper understanding of the social and economic impact of digitization'.[89] They 'believe that digital goods in the creative economy have competing roles as both economic and cultural or knowledge "goods", facilitating democratic conversations, economic innovation, and scientific collaboration'.[90] They argue that because the digital realm should be regarded as a public good, the government should tread lightly in this area, for fear of sabotaging the benefits the internet bestows on citizens. Ostensibly, ORG seeks to extend liberal democratic standards into sites previously governed unaccountably. ORG, for example, states on their website that '. . . there needs to be a renewed commitment to copyright exceptions that permits the fair use and reuse of culture and knowledge'. But what is the reason for this commitment to copyright extensions? It is because

> these bring not only softer, social benefits such as rights that create a greater environment for democratic expression . . . [but also] . . . economic benefits when follow-on innovators are encouraged, [and] educational and research benefits where researchers' ability to analyze content in new ways is permitted . . .[91]

As mentioned earlier, the wordless protest shows more than the lack of voice and the impending disconnections that could result from the Digital Economy Act. As James Boyle argues, the protest without words also dramatically and tragically shows the lack of a vocabulary with which to think about the use of the internet as a site for creative acts. Boyle suggests that 'we need not only a semantic reorganization, or a set of conceptual and analytic tools, but a movement of people devoted to bringing a goal to the attention of their fellow citizens'.[92] He argues that the success of this depends on learning from the successful framing process instigated by groups such as environmentalists, as we have seen in the case of Climate Camp. This kind of framing clearly does not exist for ORG. Their wordless placards reflect more than the means of protest but their very manifestation reflects the tragedy of not being able to articulate the 'conceptual and analytical' tools that Boyle finds necessary.

ORG's concern with internet civil liberties and consumer rights is part of a wider liberal movement against what they consider to be an overbearing surveillance state. In a memorandum submitted to the 2008–2009 Select Committee on the Constitution (UK), ORG's concerns were remarkably similar to other liberal and libertarian organizations such as Big Brother Watch and NO2ID. ORG stated how basic civil liberties (the right to privacy) are being eroded through an 'armoury of legislation' and that a 'disciplinary society' is emergent from a 'centralized, faceless, database state'.[93] They later argue that the constitutional guarantees, which prevent the abuse and unaccountability of this mass surveillance, are lacking in enforcement.[94] Returning to the question posed earlier on whether ORG lives up to its name, sadly the response would have to be an emphatic no. This is for two reasons.

On the one hand, ORG's demand for greater internet freedoms is also a demand for the state to increase data flow accountability and transparency. On the other hand, the main argument against the Digital Economy Act was not that it curbs, for example, a copyleft movement (arguably an effective illustration of open rights), but that it was too weak and rushed.[95] Their disagreements with the Bill demonstrate the weakness of their vocabulary: (1) that the Bill enables indiscriminate targeting through disconnection which results in collective punishment instead of punishing individual perpetrators; (2) that more robust evidence would be needed to prosecute; and, that (3) it would stifle innovation in the burgeoning cultural industries. These hardly raise the basic but fundamental question asked earlier on the politics of ownership: Who owns words (and images and sounds) as exemplified in the conflicts between producers and distributors on the internet.[96]

More curiously, the opposition of ORG to the 'centralized, faceless, database state' is not because it has unleashed forms of surveillance where no authority holds the reins of an enforceable system of checks and balances, but because they see it as intruding on peoples' ability to discipline themselves and each other. It seems ORG laments the pervasive disciplinary society weakening and being replaced by an all too visible (yet invisible) surveillance state. We can conclude form this that their protest against the Digital Economy Act 2010 was not so much *for* civil liberties and open rights but, following their critique of the weakness of the Act. Instead, it was about the fact that individuals are not educated in the up-to-date rules of copyright infringement and thus are unable to govern themselves. This makes them vulnerable being the victim of legal practices that are out of touch with online sociality. It is almost as if ORG in its own zealous advocacy of 'we, the connected' becomes a guardian of not open rights but regulating rights without asking fundamental questions. This illustrates the power of the dominant narrative 'we, the connected'. By contrast, an act for open rights proper would question how words are produced, distributed and owned on the internet.

Notes

1 What is considered as a 'gap year' is an industry in Western countries. 'There are as many as 85 specialist "gap year" providers in the UK, which when combined place over 50,000 participants in over 90 countries.' See Birdwell, *Service International*. The problem with private providers is that only affluent youths can afford them. By contrast, the UK government covers all the costs of the programme from its Aid Budget.

2 UK Department for International Development (DFID), International Citizens Service (ICS), http://goo.gl/K56lv.

3 UK Department for International Development (DFID), International Citizens Service (ICS), 'What could you do?' http://goo.gl/dSdDf.

4 The think tank in question is Demos. Its report was widely quoted in the media. See Birdwell, *Service International*. Although the report does raise issues about new colonialism, it appears less an ideological concern than their interpretation of survey results in which some correspondents expressed concerns about the real effectiveness of their volunteering against its stated aims.

5 Among the most ideological reporting was that of *The Guardian*, which jumped on the term 'new colonialism'. D. Boffey. 2011. Students Given Tips to Stop Gap Year Travel Being 'a New Colonialism'. Thinktank Demos Warns Poorly Planned Volunteering Stints in Developing Nations Can Do More Harm than Good. *The Guardian*, 30 July 2011 [cited 24 February 2012]. Source: http://goo.gl/U0P2U

6 Please note that Foucault called such technologies of government as 'disciplines'. That choice of the term evokes images of negative power, whereas 'scripts' are contested and contestable programmes of action regardless of their interest in creativity, inventiveness and autonomy only insofar as calibrating conduct with its strategies. Scripts are different from disciplines (Foucault) and controls (Deleuze) but obviously related to them.

7 E. Balibar, 'Historical Dilemmas of Democracy and Their Contemporary Relevance for Citizenship,' *Rethinking Marxism* 20 (2008).

8 This is a reworked version of a definition used in Isin, Engin F. 'Citizenship in Flux: The Figure of the Activist Citizen.' *Subjectivity*, no. 29 (2009): 371–2.

9 It was Nietzsche who most explicitly articulated this as a problem of method. He said 'For just as the popular mind separates the lightning from its flash and takes the latter for an action, for the operation of a subject called lightning, so popular morality also separates strength from expressions of strength, as if there were a neutral substratum behind the strong man, which was free to express strength or not to do so. But there is no such substratum; there is no "being" behind doing, effecting, becoming; "the doer" is merely a fiction added to the deed – the deed is everything.' F. W. Nietzsche, *On the Genealogy of Morality*, ed. K. Ansell-Pearson, trans. C. Diethe (Cambridge: Cambridge University Press, 1994), I.13. For Nietzsche, this was a central insight with which he credited himself and which argued that sets him apart from other philosophers: 'If I have any advantage over other psychologists, it is that my vision is keener for that most difficult and insidious form of backward

inference with which the most mistakes are made – the inference from the work to the maker, from the deed to the doer, from the ideal to the one who needs it, from every manner of thinking and valuing to the commanding need behind it.' F. W. Nietzsche, *The Anti-Christ, Ecce Homo, Twilight of the Idols, and Other Writings*, ed. A. Ridley and J. Norman, trans. J. Norman (Cambridge: Cambridge University Press, 2005), 272.

10 BBC. 2009. Canada's Governor Eats Seal Heart. BBC, 26 May 2009 [cited 24 February 2012]. Source: http://goo.gl/aIw8B

11 Ibid.

12 Huffpost Green. 2009. Canadian Governor General Eats Raw Seal Heart in Support of Hunters. *Huffington Post*, 26 May 2009 [cited 24 February 2012]. Source: http://goo.gl/Th8TS

13 BBC. 2011. Gay Couple 'Removed from Soho Pub for Kissing'. BBC, 14 April 2011 [cited 24 February 2012]. Source: http://goo.gl/XYHEi

14 BBC. 2011. Gay Kiss Pub Protest at Soho's John Snow. BBC, 15 April 2011 [cited 24 February 2012]. Source: http://goo.gl/M6Ozz

15 A. Topping. 2011. 'Slutwalking' Phenomenon Comes to UK with Demonstrations in Four Cities. British Cities to Host Mass Anti-Rape Demonstrations as Part of Global Movement Sparked by Canadian Policeman's Remarks. *The Guardian*, 9 May 2011 [cited 24 February 2012]. Source: http://goo.gl/DnWjN. Also see the account given on Slutwalk website. http://goo.gl/KFKEf

16 E. Pilkington. 2011. Slutwalking Gets Rolling after Cop's Loose Talk about Provocative Clothing. Lecture to Toronto Students Ignites Protests across Canada and US at Culture of Blaming Rape Victims. *The Guardian*, 6 May 2011 [cited 24 February 2012]. Source: http://goo.gl/3xZPp

17 T. Gold. 2011. Marching with the Slutwalkers. The Slutwalk Movement Has Divided Feminists. Should Women Try to Reclaim the Word? And Is Undressing the Best Way to Protest against Rape? *The Guardian*, 7 June 2011 [cited 24 February 2012]. Source: http://goo.gl/zBFRh

18 Ibid.

19 'On Being a Male SlutWalker', http://goo.gl/wsaeh

20 Tarrow, *The New Transnational Activism*, xiii.

21 Ibid., 29. Italics original.

22 Ibid., 34.

23 'From sturdy port inspectors defending seamen's rights on shore to Greenpeace opposing oil platforms at sea; from well-dressed NGO insiders in New York and Geneva to activists on the ground in Sudan or Afghanistan; from quiet supporters of the "good" NGOs supporting peace, the environment, or human rights to the noisy protesters of Seattle or Genoa, transnational activism is a many-sided phenomenon.' Ibid., 209.

24 Ibid., 207.

25 Ibid., 209.

26 Reitan, *Global Activism*, 10.

27 Ibid., 16.

28 Ibid., 20.

29 Ibid.

30 Ibid., 20–1.
31 International Romani Union. 2001. Declaration of a Roma Nation. International Romani Union, 1 Jan 2001 [cited 15 September 2011]. Source: http://goo.gl/qtPei
32 J. Berényi. 2010. The Situation of Roma in Europe and Relevant Activities of the Council of Europe. Council of Europe, 26 February 2010 [cited 31 August 2011]. Source: http://goo.gl/NaNe4
33 I. Klímová-Alexander, 'Transnational Romani and Indigenous Non-Territorial Self-Determination Claims,' *Ethnopolitics* 6, 3 (2007).
34 D. Ringold et al., *Roma in an Expanding Europe: Breaking the Poverty Cycle* (Washington, DC: World Bank Publications, 2005), xiii.
35 L. Kalaydjieva et al., 'A Newly Discovered Founder Population: The Roma/ Gypsies,' *BioEssays* 27, 10 (2005): 1085.
36 D. Tarnovschi, 'The Construction of a New Roma Ethnic Identity,' in *Interculturalism and Discrimination in Romania: Policies, Practices, Identities and Representations*, ed. F. Rüegg et al. (Berlin: Lit Verlag, 2006), 105.
37 Ibid.
38 Y. Matras, *Romani: A Linguistic Introduction* (Cambridge: Cambridge University Press, 2002), 242.
39 A. McGarry, 'Ambiguous Nationalism? Explaining the Parliamentary Under-representation of Roma in Hungary and Romania,' *Romani Studies* 19, 2 (2009).
40 C. Tabajdi. 2002. Legal Situation of the Roma in Europe. Council of Europe, 19 April 2002 [cited 31 August 2011]. Source: http://goo.gl/KSMcQ
41 Reuters. 2011. Factbox-Stateless Groups around the World. Reuters, 23 August 2011 [cited 31 August 2011]. Source: http://goo.gl/khQDY
42 Berényi, The Situation of Roma in Europe and Relevant Activities of the Council of Europe [cited 31 August 2011]. Source: http://goo.gl/NaNe4
43 Ibid.
44 Klímová-Alexander, 'Transnational Romani and Indigenous Non-Territorial Self-Determination Claims.'
45 E. Sobotka, 'They Have a Dream: The State of Roma Affairs in the Czech Republic,' *Central European Review* 3, 18 (2001).
46 Ibid.
47 McGarry, 'Ambiguous Nationalism? Explaining the Parliamentary Under-representation of Roma in Hungary and Romania,' 396.
48 M. Goodwin. 2004. The Romani Claim to Non-Territorial Nation Status: Recognition from an International Legal Perspective. European Roma Rights Centre, 27 May 2004 [cited 31 August 2011]. Source: http://goo.gl/JCtrs
49 International Romani Union, Declaration of a Roma Nation [cited 15 September 2011]. Source: http://goo.gl/qtPei
50 Ibid.
51 Sobotka, 'They Have a Dream: The State of Roma Affairs in the Czech Republic.'
52 Klímová-Alexander, 'Transnational Romani and Indigenous Non-Territorial Self-Determination Claims.'
53 Ibid., 396.

54 Kymlicka, *Multicultural Citizenship: A Liberal Theory of Minority Rights*.
55 Council of Europe. 2010. The Strasbourg Declaration on Roma. Council of Europe, 20 October 2010 [cited 31 August 2011]. Source: http://goo.gl/UXo0f
56 Ibid.
57 P. Vermeersch, *The Romani Movement: Minority Politics and Ethnic Mobilization in Contemporary Central Europe* (Oxford: Berghahn Books, 2007).
58 Ibid., 177.
59 Ibid.
60 G. Rishmawi and N. Golan, 'Helping to Bring Back Hope,' in *Peace under Fire: Israel/Palestine and the International Solidarity Movement*, ed. J. Sandercock (London: Verso, 2004), 6.
61 Ibid.
62 http://palsolidarity.org/
63 C. Seitz, 'Ism at the Crossroads: The Evolution of the International Solidarity Movement,' *Journal of Palestine Studies* 32, 4 (2003): 54.
64 Ibid.
65 G. Faure, 'The Truth about Occupation,' in *Peace under Fire: Israel/Palestine and the International Solidarity Movement*.
66 International Solidarity Movement. 2011. About Ism. International Solidarity Movement 2011 [cited 19 September 2011]. Source: http://goo.gl/r2ocw
67 Seitz, 'Ism at the Crossroads: The Evolution of the International Solidarity Movement,' 51.
68 Ibid.
69 Ibid., 52.
70 J. Collins, 'Between Acceleration and Occupation: Palestine and the Struggle for Global Justice,' *Studies in Social Justice* 4, 2 (2010): 208.
71 A. Omer, ' "It's Nothing Personal": The Globalisation of Justice, the Transferability of Protest, and the Case of the Palestine Solidarity Movement,' *Studies in Ethnicity and Nationalism* 9, 3 (2009): 498.
72 Ibid., 499.
73 D. B. Warner, 'International Peacemakers Enter Bethlehem Church of Nativity,' in *Peace under Fire: Israel/Palestine and the International Solidarity Movement*.
74 Ibid.
75 International Solidarity Movement, About Ism [cited 19 September 2011]. Source: http://goo.gl/r2ocw
76 International Solidarity Movement. 2011. Media Activists Needed in Palestine. International Solidarity Movement, 7 July 2011 [cited 19 September 2011]. Source: http://goo.gl/EdlCb
77 S. Aziz, 'How I Became a Terror Tourist,' in *Peace under Fire: Israel/Palestine and the International Solidarity Movement*.
78 Austin, *How to Do Things with Words*.
79 B. Hodge, *Barefoot into Cyberspace: Adventures in Search of Techno-Utopia* (Commons Attribution-ShareAlike 2.0, 2011), 73.
80 Ibid.
81 Open Rights Group. 2011. About ORG. Open Rights Group 2011 [cited 10 August 2011]. Source: http://goo.gl/2jgfN

82 *Digital Economy Act*, 2010, c. 24.
83 BBC. 2010. Q&A: The Digital Economy Bill. BBC, 9 April 2010 [cited 10 August 2011]. Source: http://goo.gl/Aur2.
84 Ibid.
85 Open Rights Group. 2010. Digital Economy Bill: Brief to Lords on Second Reading 2010 [cited 9 August 2011]. Source: http://goo.gl/xKlBS
86 Ibid.
87 F. Davey. 2009. The Digital Economy Bill – A First Critical Look. Open Rights Group, 1 December 2009 [cited 9 August 2011]. Source: http://goo.gl/CTkWu
88 Open Rights Group. 2011. Hargreaves Review of Ip and Growth. Open Rights Group, 22 February 2011 [cited 9 August 2011]. Source: http://goo.gl/1JxIY
89 Ibid.
90 Ibid.
91 Ibid.
92 J. Boyle, *The Public Domain: Enclosing the Commons of the Mind* (New Haven, CT: Yale University Press, 2008), 242.
93 House of Lords. *Surveillance: Citizens and the State* (London: Authority of the House of Lords, 2009), 433.
94 Ibid.
95 Open Rights Group, Digital Economy Bill: Brief to Lords on Second Reading [cited 9 August 2011]. Source: http://goo.gl/xKlBS
96 Ibid.

CHAPTER SIX

Emancipating (Acts of) Citizenship

The houses of our City
are real enough but they lie
haphazardly scattered over the earth,
and her vagabond forum
is any space where two of us happen to meet
who can spot a citizen
without papers.
    —W. H. Auden, *Thanksgiving for a Habitat* (1958)

If we have recognized activists who traverse frontiers for justice as activist citizens, then how can we recognize their traversal politics? What shall we call the politics instigated, instantiated and enacted through acts of those who traverse frontiers? How can we understand actors whose political subjectivity exceeds the borders that confine their bodies and acts? Can this politics of traversing frontiers – whose subjects are citizens without frontiers – be called a politics of traversal citizenship?

Taking the state apart – from the nation

For centuries now, we have been living under a regime or order that we have constituted as the sovereign, which authorizes political subjectivity: the nation-state. What we are experiencing now – and the acts featured in this book are a testimony to both its dangers and possibilities – is that the state is being taken apart from the nation.[1] This is the undoing of the event, which Arendt named as 'the conquest of the state by the nation'.

But this taking apart has been prematurely interpreted as the decline of the state or the crisis of sovereignty – failing to distinguish the state from the nation. This taking apart does not put the state where (or how) it was before its conquest by the nation. If I grasp it adequately (and that is a big if), the crisis of the present is *the* taking apart of the state from the nation. If you recall, we drew from Arendt in Chapter 2 to ask: 'what does it exactly mean to say that man is an emancipated and dignified being without an encompassing order?' Arendt's answer was that for a very brief moment in history, man had appeared without belonging to an encompassing order but soon succumbed to 'we, the people' (simply 'the people' for Arendt). This incredibly short-lived emancipation was followed by the conquest of the state by the nation. When she refers to emancipated man without an encompassing order does she mean something like a creative, inventive and autonomous subject that we have argued an act produces? Does she mean that it was the nation-state that denied man the capacity to begin something new whose outcomes were unpredictable? If indeed today the state is being taken apart from the nation, are citizens being emancipated? The acts featured in this book illustrate that this is not the case. I have argued that professionals such as academics, auditors, entrepreneurs, footballers, investors, journalists, lawyers and managers move through distinct but overlapping fields (of expertise, knowledge and competence) that traverse national borders. To put it another way, *sans-frontiérisme* has become the slogan of professions; we may not yet consider them as emancipated but their movements are considered legitimate if not desirable. But when non-professionals enact movements, their *sans-frontiérisme* is considered illegal. We have witnessed a neurotic hyperactivity about blocking movements of those who are considered illegal, precisely they are not professional. The security discourse on rebels, insurgents, traffickers, spies, infiltrators and gangsters whose movements traverse frontiers are consistently illegalized.[2] Clearly, for professionals, frontiers are *no longer* an impediment to their field of action. Yet, if *citizens* move across borders, unless authorized, their acts are treated as trespassing, their bodies are caught in border regimes and their subject positions come to be described as 'migrant', 'refugee' or 'alien'. In many states, *sans-papierisme* has become their slogan to struggle for the right to stay. While the image of the mobile citizen prevails, many bodies are being sequestered within frontiers involving borders, boundaries, fences and walls. This may be the greatest confinement.[3] For some others then, borders have *not yet* disappeared. Indeed, there is a widening gap between bodies that can act across borders and those who remain confined within them. Cosmopolitanism or universalism has proved to be ineffective in closing this gap between the no longer and the not yet citizens because neither corresponds to a field of action in which bodies can act. To put it differently, we may well be in that space (or time) of in-between 'no longer' and 'not yet' that provides opportunities for thinking and acting differently. If 'we, the people' is no longer convincing or effective, 'we the connected' has not yet become so. Rather, the invitations and interpellations for an integrated, coherent and wholesome identification with cosmopolitan, global, multitude or networked identifications are dangerous possibilities. Moreover, to invest in these identifications (to accept the invitation and interpellations) is not only dangerous for participating in the creation of new scripts but also defeatist. By setting ideals of political subjectivity that cannot be fulfilled, such identifications lead to a politics of defeatism. If we are caught between no longer and not yet and between *sans-frontiérisme* and *sans-papierisme*, where do we look for inspiration?

To get an appreciation of this gap, a moment in time between no longer and not yet citizens, perhaps it would be useful to hear a speech addressed to French citizens more than two centuries ago. The speaker was Jeremy Bentham and his address was to the French Assembly and urged citizens to emancipate their colonies in order to emancipate themselves.

Emancipate your colonies!

Jeremy Bentham's speech act, delivered on 7 February 1793, extols the virtues of liberating colonies not for their sake – though it will also help them – but for the sake of French citizens and their government. For Bentham, emancipating distant colonies would mean entering into equal relations with them as trading partners and that way serving the interests of capital by releasing the productive capacities of colonies. Although recognized as a classic argument symbolizing the relationship between liberalism and capitalism, in 1793, it was anything but accepted or acceptable. What makes this speech act of interest to us today is that while currently unimaginable, in two centuries from now, our inheritors may well take for granted a world without internal colonies. That world may not be without borders. But it may have a radically different configuration. Our 1793 moment may or may not have come, but it is conceivable that the sovereign rights of nations to choose their people mostly on blood and biology (rather than people choosing their own government regardless of birth) may come to pass as a rather short moment in history.

For that alone, it is worth dwelling on that moment in 1793. Bentham's starting point is liberty. He says to French citizens 'you choose your own government: why are not other people to choose theirs? Do you seriously mean to govern the world, and do you call that liberty?'[4] Bentham then asks them 'are you the only men who have rights?' He says it is an illusion that France can maintain its colonies because it cannot govern them adequately at a distance. Moreover, 'Think not, that because I mentioned them first, it is for their sake in the first place that I wish to see them free. No: it is the mischief you do yourselves by maintaining this unnatural domination . . .' Just in case the French think that emancipating colonies means giving up dominion over them, Bentham says 'hear a paradox – it is a true one. Give up your colonies, they are yours: keep them, they are ours.' Speaking as an Englishman, he understands that the benefits of entering into relations as equal trade partners outweigh the economic, social and political costs of governing them at a distance as the English had discovered the hard way a decade or so earlier in its American colonies. So 'shake off your splendid incumbrances, the sins of your youth are atoned for, and your character for truth, probity, moderation, and philanthropy built on everlasting ground'. It may be true that

> . . . you have your lights [but the English] have their prejudices, [and] they may find it not so easy as you may think to comprehend the doctrine of forced liberty they may prefer a made constitution which gives tranquillity, to an unmade one under which security is yet to come . . .

It is fascinating to reflect on this idea of emancipation two centuries after it was enacted by a speech act. Clearly, Bentham sees this emancipation as a double: It liberates the dominant and the dominated. There is a sense here – whether rhetorical or effective – that this emancipation benefitting both the dominant and dominated is attested by its expression as a paradox. It is a kind of emancipation that although it shifts the mode of government – from colonial to liberal – it does not change the fact that these colonies will still remain as French. It is not that the fact of domination changes; its mode does. Nevertheless, letting go of colonies so that they can actually better benefit the empire is a powerful argument. And the main issue of the cost of governing is especially poignant. But of course what Bentham has in mind here, particularly as the author of *Panopticon*, is not merely the economic cost of government but the social, political, cultural and symbolic investment required to govern in a direct way.[5] For Bentham, forced liberty was not liberty at all.

What would a speech act say today about emancipating (acts of) citizenship? It is almost as if one can topologically turn Bentham not only upside down but also inside out, as if his argument was laid on a Möbius strip.[6] Can one imagine the emancipation of citizens from the confinement of the nation-state without ever crossing a border? Do citizens choose their governments, as Bentham was so cocksure about? Can emancipation involve not only letting your colonies go but unchaining the last remaining figures of contained politics? When all is said and done, the movement to Occupy everywhere in 2011 may have just accomplished that – at least in our imaginations.

Occupy everywhere: The enjoyment of being political

On 12 March 2011 in Porto and Lisbon, around 200,000 people protested against the Portuguese government's austerity measures under the banner *Geração à Rasca*, 'the desperate generation'. This was followed by protests in several other cities leading to the articulation of several demands among them to stop intergenerational injustice and subservient government.

On 15 May 2011, on a hot day in Madrid, some people began setting up camp in the city's Puerta del Sol Square. It took much work and preparation and it is not accidental that the ongoing financial crisis that began in 2008 and the uprisings that began with the Sidi Bouzid Revolt, Tahrir Square, Benghazi, Daraa and Homs in 2011 with their slogans of outrage and dignity had considerable echoes on the streets in Madrid on that hot May day. So too, perhaps, did a small pamphlet written by a 90-year-old French veteran of war, Stéphane Hessel, entitled *Indignez-vous!* (2010), translated into English as *Time for Outrage!* (2010).[7] Those who enacted the Madrid encampment were named *Indignados* or the 'outraged' after the Spanish translation of Hessel's book. The encampment articulated a series of demands but also instituted creative, inventive and autonomous ways of reaching decisions through assemblies and establishing a culture of openness.[8] By setting itself against violence, the *Indignados* encampment immediately provided an effective repertoire that became rapidly enacted in more than 60 cities in Spain for the rest of May. By the time the occupiers of Puerta del Sol Square decided to end their occupation in June, similar occupations had begun happening in other European cities.

On 25 May 2011, the Syntagma Square in Athens was occupied. Its occupation continued on and off through several months of struggle against brutal police tactics and multiple evictions.[9] On 14 July, 25-year-old Daphne Leef pitched a tent in Habima Square in Tel Aviv in protest of the cost of housing. She then invited others through social media. What began as a housing protest spread into acts of squatting in derelict buildings in Jerusalem and grew into the largest social justice movement in Israel's history involving more than a half million people demonstrating in squares and streets in August and September.[10]

On 13 September, a Canadian subversive anti-advertising group Adbusters proposed occupying Wall Street to protest against injustice and moneyed politics.[11] On 17 September, a group of people began setting up camp in Zucotti Park in New York (eventually 'renamed' as Liberty Park). Anonymous, an amorphous and fluid group of cyber hackers, joined the call and urged people to converge on the park with the slogan 'Occupy

Wall Street'. The choice of the park was strategic since it was privately owned and the owner had to make a request to the police to remove the protesters. This gave the occupiers a foothold on the site. Despite an uncertain start and small numbers, the park soon became a site of national and international focus. By 9 October, it was estimated that some 95 cities in the United States had occupation sites.

On 10 October, a campaign was launched to occupy the London Stock Exchange and Paternoster Square. Both became off-limits quite quickly as the former due to injunction against occupation and the latter being a privately owned square received protection from the police. About 3,000 people gathered outside St Paul's Cathedral and a few hundred began setting up camp. Coverage over the next few days focused on how this occupation led to several resignations from the Cathedral as church leaders wavered and wobbled on how to manage the encampment. However, the site raised various thorny issues that may forever remain hidden from public view such as the relations between the local government of the City government and the financial industry; the function of lobbyists within government; investment practices and unequal distribution of profits and power within the financial services industry itself and between those within the industry and the outside. It was certainly a rupture. Little did I know, for example, that on 12 November, as I stood on the steps of St Paul's – photographing the Lord Mayor's procession against the encampment and its dancers with Anonymous masks – that I was witnessing '. . . a break with tradition lasting more than 800 years, [as] the 684th lord mayor was blessed at the cathedral's south entrance instead of the steps because of the protesters' tents'.[12]

On 15 October, there was a call to occupy squares and streets associated with finance in cities around the world. Some 900 cities became sites of occupations including Auckland, Sydney, Hong Kong, Taipei, Tokyo, São Paulo, Paris, Madrid, Berlin, Hamburg, Leipzig and many others. The fact that the Occupy encampments from Cairo to Madrid and from London to New York are called by street and square names points to another aspect of these as enactments. Each indicates how the city is both literally and metaphorically the battlefield of subjects, bodies and rights. It is the historical constitution of the city. Laying claims against injustice always involves and provokes claiming rights to the city. That is why those voices critical of occupations on grounds of their ineffectiveness or lack of a programme are wide of the mark and (deliberately or otherwise) fail to distinguish the spirit of acts from actions. Maintaining and nourishing the spirit of dissent against unjust government is more important than for achieving political gains (though of course without the latter, it is also questionable how long the spirit can be maintained). The performative force of dissent though is perhaps the most important, and surprising, outcome of Occupy.

The shaking of nations

Although staged in different sites and grounds, there are clearly explicit and implicit connections among the occupations. That said, it would be difficult to call it a global movement let alone the awakening of a multitude or global activism.[13] Of course, these interpretations and proclamations are on offer because, as we have seen throughout this book, it is also partly the interpretations of multifarious actions that render them into acts. At one register, Occupy can be seen as a turning point in the transformation from 'we, the people' to 'we, the connected'. It has a number of significant features in this respect: Many encampments were organized through social media networks; prominent activist groups such as Anonymous and Adbusters were prime mobilizers; the actors, who ranged from democrats to anarchists, were as multifarious as the demands, if any, that followed them. For all these reasons, Occupy could perhaps be seen as the birth of the 'we, the connected' in its actual form. That activists have consistently and persistently avoided articulating singular demands, that they have always rejected a hierarchical organization and leadership structures and that their means have predominantly been peaceful civil disobedience may lead us to think that indeed this was 'we, the connected'.

It is here that I would like to draw a sharp difference between interpreting the possibilities of Occupy as constituting 'citizens without frontiers' and viewing them as global activism or transnational activism. If, and when, Occupy disbands without a singular and dominant narrative, without a singular message or demand, it will still have accomplished a significant political task. It will have created a performative force that can be reassembled and maintained through various actions. If Occupy remains a performative force capable of producing an event, it will have achieved a more radical transformation than those who dream of dismantling a universal enemy whatever it is called. Its enactment will have achieved a rupture in the given and maintained the threat of its assemblage in the future. Through the performative force of enactment, ranging from the carnivalesque to deliberation, Occupy has created sites of not only refusal, resistance and disavowal but also discipline, commitment and deliberation. These will likely have lasting effects for generations to come.

On 14 November 2011, when the Archbishop of Canterbury, Rowan Williams, addressed the Lord Mayor's Banquet at St Paul's Cathedral, steps away from the Occupy encampment, his remarks deliberately drew attention to the legal aspect of the occupation. Identifying a fault line between order and rupture or between responsibility and answerability on the grounds of the Cathedral, he said, 'St Paul's with its environs has become, literally and metaphorically, a theatre in which conflicts are played out.'[14] The choice of 'theatre' to describe the site of a conflict being played out on St Paul's square may sound melodramatic but the Archbishop offered something more sociological. He recognized that city squares have special symbolic value historically and have been sites of such conflicts.

> The defining moments in the history of the last couple of hundred years are so often linked with particular urban landscapes – the Paris of 1789 and the Petersburg of 1917, Tiananmen and Prague, the Bucharest of 1989; and now the Cairo or Athens of 2011.[15]

He said 'The underlying drama played out in these various urban theatres, is one of alarming instability, a drama of the "shaking of nations". Few if any can see the route back to security and stability.' For Williams, that phrase essentially captures the tension between order and rupture and asks us to remove what is shaken and keep what is unshakable. Williams says

> so we have to ask, faced with the drama of our times, what it is that 'cannot be shaken', what it is that we cannot imagine being toppled and shattered like the icons of fallen dictators? Is there anything whose loss would simply make everything else meaningless?

This is a profound question. But can it be answered by those whose lives are contained and confined within the nation? What if what needs to be shaken is the confinement itself? What if the confinement and containment are that which cannot remain?

One of the most provoking aspects of Occupy was its enactment of traversal (rather than universal) citizenship precisely because it asked this question by traversing many frontiers: shifting the sites of politics from organized institutions such as parliaments and courts to squares and streets; traversing repertoires of actions across different sites and articulating specific vocabularies that call into question given assumptions about justice and injustice, equality and inequality, and fairness and cheating.

But is Occupy a movement or an act? To call it a movement would conceal what makes it a promising form or repertoire. It began with and always required acts to instigate it. From the first act of protestors in Porto and Lisbon to the demonstrators in Madrid and Barcelona who took to the streets, occupied squares, wrote pamphlets, pitched tents and issued subversive advertisements, the occupy movement involved numerous creative, inventive and autonomous acts that gradually became a repertoire to follow and eventually coalesced into a movement. Not all acts coalesce into movements but movements are impossible without acts.

Yet, one of the most curious aspects of Occupy despite enacting traversal citizenship was how it also pointed out the difficulty of a politics of those who do not move. It is impossible to gauge this accurately but following Occupy acts as closely as possible, I have not been able to detect much actual traversing of citizens across the different sites. In other words, American remained American, Spanish remained Spanish and Greek remained Greek protests. Nevertheless, there was considerable diffusion and dissemination of repertoires, vocabularies, symbols and slogans but the movements remained insular and contained. You could see activists such as Naomi Klein and authors such as Slavoj Žižek mingling with protesters and proclaiming their desires but arguably these figures were crossing borders under professional protection. While the joy of becoming political by acting across frontiers cannot (any longer) remain within borders, it is not (yet) among the rights that we have. The question of our times is how to institute the right to have rights as a political right without frontiers.

Between no longer and not yet

I emphasized above a widening gap between bodies that can act across borders and those who remain confined within them. I also suggested that cosmopolitanism and universalism have proved to be ineffective in closing this gap between those who are no longer and not yet citizens because neither corresponds to a field of action in which bodies can act. I concluded that, if 'we, the people' is no longer convincing or effective, 'we the connected' has not yet become so.

Quoting Hume's remark that generations do not succeed each other like silkworms transform into butterflies, Arendt once remarked that nonetheless there are times in life when it feels as though such a transformation is indeed taking place.[16] She said

> for the decline of the old, and the birth of the new, is not necessarily an affair in continuity; between the generations, between those who for some reason or other still belong to the old and those who either feel the catastrophe in their very bones or have already grown up with it, the chain is broken and an 'empty space,' a kind of historical no man's land, comes to the surface which can be described only in terms of 'no longer and not yet.'[17]

It is curious that she calls this an 'empty space' while she envelops it with two temporal categories: arguably, 'no longer' and 'not yet' indicate moments or durations in time. How could she have imagined what remains between the two as a space, let alone an empty space? Yet, it is that ambiguity that is most poignant with meaning. Perhaps we should call that space an 'interstitial space' because it is pregnant with possibilities, allowing for the birth of creative, inventive and autonomous acts.

The abiding concern of this book is to recognize the interstitial spaces created by acts that traverse frontiers. It is also to develop a vocabulary or analytics with which to understand these acts and their interstitial spaces. These interstitial spaces are formed by, on the one hand, the 'we, the people' grand narrative *no longer* commanding the credulity it once had and, on the other hand, the 'we, the connected' grand narrative *not yet* commanding credulity. To avoid misunderstanding, that 'we, the people' has lost its credibility does not mean it has lost its drive. So 'no longer' should not be thought of as 'not any more'. On the contrary, as the work of migration and refugee studies has identified, new borders, fences and walls are being relentlessly erected, though rather desperately, to contain and confine citizenship by drawing sharper boundaries around its edges. Many acts featured in this book attest to various reincarnations of the sovereign beast enacted by both states and subjects, which sharpen such boundaries between themselves and others. Similarly, 'not yet' should not be thought of as 'almost there' as if there is a final, let alone guaranteed, end towards which it is developing. In fact, 'almost there' is exactly how those grand narratives seeking to gain our credulity would have us view them. If the not yet 'we, the connected' grand narrative provides grounds for incredulity towards 'we, the people', it also simultaneously inherits dangerous tendencies such as subsuming everything under overarching categories, totalizing manifold movements and homogenizing the multiplicity of events under singular terms.

All this might sound abstract and remote from lived experiences. But let me illustrate the paradox of this interstitial space between no longer and not yet with the example of a campaign network of which I am a member or an 'Avaazer'. The organization is called Avaaz and it defines itself as 'a global web movement to bring people-powered politics to decision-making everywhere'.[18] Avaaz apparently means 'voice' in several European, Middle Eastern and Asian languages and the organization was 'launched in 2007 with a simple democratic mission: organize citizens of all nations to close the gap between the world we have and the world most people everywhere want'.[19] Its slogan is 'the world in action' and it organizes campaigns in 15 languages to take action meaning 'signing petitions, funding media campaigns and direct actions, emailing, calling and lobbying governments, and organizing "offline" protests and events' and this is 'to ensure that the views and values of the world's people inform the decisions that affect us all'.[20] The organization claims that it has more than 10 million members and it has taken more than 60,000 actions since 2007. What are these actions? It claims, for example,

> The proposed Belo Monte dam complex, an environmental catastrophe in the making, has been delayed – thanks in part to the spectacular delivery

led by indigenous tribes-people of more than 600,000 petition signatures from Avaazers in Brazil and around the world.

It reports that

> over a million people, including 200,000 in France, signed an explosive petition to ban pesticides that are mass-killing bees the world over – and, standing with a team of French beekeepers, delivered the petition to the French Agriculture Minister at a major conference. The campaign continues, building pressure for action in France, the EU, and around the globe.

It boasts support from no less than Richard Branson in one of its campaigns:

> The war on drugs has cost billions in tax money, funneled trillions of dollars into organized crime, cost countless lives, and achieved zero results. Then a group of former presidents formed The Global Commission on Drugs to boldly speak out for reform. They faced one problem – politicians claimed they couldn't act because there was no public support for change! So Avaaz joined the fight. We launched the campaign, and in one week, our community proved the politicians wrong, with over 600,000 Avaazers calling for an end to the war on drugs.[21]

Although these campaigns sound as though they deliver petitions to authorities (often prefaced with the slogan 'citizens of the world say'), the organization also claims actions that would require rather strong, if not military-level, logistics. It claims, for example, that

> Avaaz has been at the heart of the struggles for democracy in the Arab world. Funded by $1.5 million in small member donations, we've broken the media blackouts that dictators tried to impose – training a huge number of citizen journalists and equipping them with top flight technology to get information out.[22]

That claim would be difficult to verify. Provided that it is accurate, it raises the question of how Avaaz reached the level of expertise that such an operation requires. Its claim that 'Avaaz is closing the gap between the world we have and the world we want, one campaign at a time' is even harder to substantiate. Nonetheless, it is worth thinking about an organization that is clearly addressing a niche by organizing action worldwide or, rather, across frontiers.

Avaaz is mobilizing two motives that are, taken together, proving effective means of mobilizing people if not action. First, it enjoins the recognition that any political issues today can *no longer* be contained within the confines of states and that they traverse frontiers. Second, there is *not yet* an institutional structure or framework that directly enables political subjects to act as citizens in this way. Thus, by recognizing interstitial spaces through which politics is being played out and by addressing political subjects, Avaaz is interpellating their capacity to act. Yet, it also reproduces inherent dangers in the 'we, the people' grand narrative by enjoining the 'we, the connected' grand narrative as a totalizing and homogenizing device. What is most troubling about Avaaz is that it substitutes our capacity to act with our capacity to react – which is by no means the same thing – and thereby invites us to surrender our capacity by isolating us from each other.[23] Perhaps even more troubling is its use of 'people' for mobilizing action. It assumes that 'we' are a people and that as a people we know what we want before we experiment with becoming political through acting together (rather than merely reacting to events). This is not an idle matter and it would be wrong to think that Avaaz is using such vocabulary for its inspiring rhetorical qualities. Using speech to frame action and action to frame speech, or more accurately, speech as action, is a fundamental aspect of enacting political subjectivity and of enacting our capacity for a political subjectivity that brings something new into the world whose outcomes are yet unknown. How we speak about acts matters. It matters even more when Avaaz increasingly presents itself through a means–end vocabulary where the performance of every action is measured against its tangible effects and quantifiable indicators. It begins to develop a delusional image of political action where rather than revealing ourselves by acting together with and in relation to others with unpredictable and surprising outcomes including our very selves, we count our successes and failures in terms of influence on already existing political institutions. To be sure, we can argue that, in the absence of new forms, campaigns and organizations such as Avaaz are at least showing the space between the no longer and the not yet. I will concede that. But it inherits the danger of the political vocabulary of the sovereign beast by reinvesting in a constituting people as a homogenous bloc with common boundaries.

Theorizing acts, especially those that traverse frontiers, is a response to these tendencies and dangers and is meant to resist their effects by providing a vocabulary or analytics with which to think about acting as political subjects. We discussed earlier how the basic qualities of acts are creative (deliberate yet spontaneous, mischievous yet serious, courageous yet not heroic), inventive (surprising yet predictable, illegal yet acceptable, outrageous yet reasonable) and autonomous (individual yet collective, scripted yet experimental, unauthorized yet meaningful). We discussed performativity and enactment as well as five theoretical propositions (ruptures versus citations, repetitions or iterations; actions versus acts; bodies versus subjects; intentionality versus purposiveness; and responsibility versus answerability) and four methodological propositions (events, sites, scales and duration) for investigating acts. The most important aspect of theorizing acts is the starting point: rather than working with a normative framework, it investigates how people exercise their capacity to act by bringing something new into the world whose outcomes are unpredictable or cause a rupture in their everyday lives and habitus. This capacity of enacting ourselves otherwise than being just ourselves is the capacity for political subjectivity. But expressing this political enactment as subjectivity opens the way to misunderstanding. Theorizing acts begins with the deeds of doers, and so it is doers who receive attention. This accepts the fact that there can be no enactments without doers. To act is a political capacity that developed historically. There can be no parliament of things without historical beings that are making claims. But it does not follow that doers are sovereign or already given subjects. Acting is always social and it always involves acting in the presence of and in relation to other beings such as ourselves. Nor does it follow that there are doers behind deeds as sovereign subjects who are in command of their deeds with motives, intentions and aims. Acts produce subjects who are often just as surprised as everybody else by the outcomes of their acts. Yet, that does not mean that acts are random or irrational. Acts are always purposive or, rather, purpose oriented. The disclosure of oneself as a subject requires a space, or rather, produces a space of appearances through which one becomes a subject of one's own act.

The importance of drawing a distinction between acts and action is to indicate that acts are forms or descriptions that we accumulate over long periods of time. We do this by action. By revealing ourselves in the presence of and in relation to others, we open ourselves to unpredictable and surprising outcomes. Just because these outcomes are unpredictable and surprising does not mean that our actions are random, thoughtless or isolated. On the contrary (and this is another reason why it is important to draw a distinction between actions and acts), we open ourselves through 'principles' or the 'spirit' of acts. We are aware of the existence of such acts as kindness, violence, forgiveness, hospitality and many more. These exist as principles or a spirit that we as social and political beings developed over a long period of time in different spaces. To engage in action means to actualize these acts though we do not know in advance how our actions will turn out. There are numerous acts that we have developed as social and political beings. We have also developed ways of understanding them under categories we invented such as 'ethical', 'aesthetic', 'political', 'cultural', 'social' and so on. Clearly, those acts that come under the description 'political' are the abiding concern of this book especially those acts that traverse frontiers. If each act is defined by a principle, I recognize those acts that make demands or claims against injustice as political acts.

The main argument of the book is that our acts do traverse frontiers. What we have not developed is either the principle or the spirit of laws for traversing frontiers. Some of the acts that I gathered in this book are both attempts and failures to bring the various actions of actual actors engaged in politics under the description of 'citizens without frontiers'. What I hope this book illustrates is that we have not yet developed repertoires that fit the description 'citizens without frontiers'. This would enable acting as citizens across and beyond frontiers without being disguised as professionals. I have also argued that it is more practical and effective to develop these repertoires than to invest in global or cosmopolitan forms of governance as integrating models. Arguably, while among the most developed and sophisticated attempts to develop a supranational or cosmopolitan form of governance, the European Union still does not know how to imagine citizenship except as mobility and as a politics of those who move.

How do we then begin to develop these repertoires of action? This is also one of the underlying arguments of this book: We have already begun developing them but we do not yet know how to recognize or describe them. Therein lies the importance of developing a vocabulary or analytics of acts. I have placed the activist citizen at the centre of such an analytics as opposed to the active citizen partly because the active citizen is already absorbed into nationality and partly because the active citizen is made in the image of a predictable subject. That is why rupture becomes a central concept for theorizing acts that feature subjects who reveal themselves through actions with unpredictable and surprising outcomes but enjoin or actualize certain principles or spirits that pertain to injustice. Theorizing acts then means identifying events through which subjects reveal themselves as claimants against injustice and investigating the grounds (conditions of possibility) and consequences of their actions to see if these actions can come under the description of acts of citizenship. These actions are always situated in a specific time and place. The spaces where subjects acting together appear produce sites. Just as using the phrase 'acts produce subjects' is counterintuitive so too is the notion that 'acts produce sites'. But the actions of actors do indeed produce sites in the sense of making a scene. This is where theorizing acts perhaps borrows most from the dramaturgical or performance features of acts, where it is the performance of actions that makes scenes. Such scenes depend on bodies, which must collude, collide and make contact with each other and things that create a site. The intensity of any site reverberates beyond the scene that it has created and reaches beyond it. This reach indicates the scale of the event: how it reverberated and where it reached. The site and scale of an event, the actions that produced it, the subjects that are produced by it and the principle or spirit that it enjoins become matters of investigation and cannot be determined in advance. This book has attempted to make a contribution to investigating such acts. My hope is that it begins a spirit of the law of acting across frontiers and developing forms that recognize citizens without frontiers.

ACT 19. OF ENFRANCHISEMENT: IF THE WORLD COULD VOTE

The idea of voting across borders is an intriguing one. It captures an essential aspect of the concept of 'citizens without frontiers'. Traversing frontiers with an act is as old as citizenship but voting in another jurisdiction, if only symbolically, is an entirely different effect. It illustrates the resignification of an existing script or repertoire in a particularly poignant manner. For many around the world, both the 2000 and 2004 elections in the Unites States of America were disappointing if not traumatic. In 2000, it was widely believed that Al Gore would be a better president for the international community. Yet he lost what became an acrimonious election where debates over electoral votes against popular votes and dimpled versus pregnant chads took contestants all the way to the Supreme Court. Although Al Gore made light of his election loss later by introducing himself with the words 'I used to be the next president of the United States of America', it was more troubling for the rest of the world. Similarly, in 2004, many people around the world expected American citizens to vote George W. Bush out of office especially after the disastrous Iraq War and its fabricated justifications. Many around the world did not have to wait a decade to know that there was no case for war. It is really not hubris then to think that, as Mahbubahni thinks: 'The U.S. Presidential election may be the most undemocratic in the world. Only some 126 million Americans vote, yet the result is felt by 6.6 billion people.'[24] That raises the spectre: what if the world could vote in the US presidential elections?

That is exactly what motivated three young people in Iceland to create a website during the 2008 US presidential election and call it, well, 'if the world could vote'.[25] The website allows any one to vote in any election and on many other issues. To be sure, by valorizing voting as an act of 'world citizenship', the website runs the risk of overemphasizing the importance of voting as an act of citizenship (at a distance). Yet, the act of voting across or despite frontiers raises a fundamental question about the limiting presence of borders in political and social change. If the world could vote in the US presidential elections, apparently US politics and the government would look very different. A similar question for many states would yield a similar result.[26] '[I]t is assumed,' as Archibugi notes, 'that governments should be the only institutions to represent their own citizens.'[27] The US presidential election seems to be one example that fulfils this without question. Only American citizens can vote for an American president. Yet America's political decisions have long been recognized as having a profound impact on the rest of the world. As Mahbubahni continues 'indeed, in some ways it matters even more to non-Americans. The president is constrained domestically by many constitutional checks and balances, but this is far less true in foreign affairs.'[28]

In 2008, during the American presidential election, what non-American citizens would do if placed in the same voting situation arose as a question.[29] A website was created for internet users to vote on Barack Obama or John McCain as if they were American citizens.[30] Results were presented on a map and table showing percentages by country of origin.[31] Admittedly, as with many internet polls, the website had no statistical sampling or weighting or a verification system through which respondents could be traced to place of origin (assuming trust in IP addresses). Nevertheless, as a symbolic act, it shifts the idea of world citizens, as understood in largely cosmopolitan or global terms, to one which realizes what it could mean to enable people to act as though they are citizens traversing frontiers on issues that cannot be confined within nation-state borders.[32] In a sense, it radically democratizes voting by producing subjects whose acts traverse frontiers.

A more robust survey, called 'If the world could vote', was also conducted by Gallup's World Poll service, in partnership with *Foreign Policy*. It gauged the opinions of respondents in 73 countries during the US presidential election, with almost three-quarters of the world's population being represented.[33] Gallup asked two simple questions: 'Who would you personally rather see elected President of the United States?' and 'Do you think who's elected President of the United States makes a difference to your country or not?'[34] Construction of polls is always political in the sense of not only creating phenomena but also subject positions.[35] On the one hand, the poll creates a virtual citizenship to gauge the hypothetical question of 'Would the world elect Barack Obama or John McCain?'[36] On the other, it presumes the influence of US foreign policy by focusing on general indicators as to the possible biases and pitfalls of electing an American president. More interestingly, if voter decisions are influenced by the esteem in which others around the world (73 countries in this case) hold their leaders, this will have an effect on election results. Yet, the poll could also function as intelligence gathering on which regions of the world are engaged with American politics. Or it could function as a demand on the part of the citizens polled that they should have a right to have a say in the electoral process given their intertwined fate. Still, the performative force of the act of responding to this question seriously should not be underestimated as it unintentionally entitles constituents – those who think they have a right to have a say.

Anyway, the poll consequently showed that in most of the 73 countries surveyed, Barack Obama trumped John McCain.[37] Two exceptions were Georgia and the Philippines, where McCain gained a slight margin above Obama. Yet the picture becomes more complex once the 'Don't know/Refused' answer is taken into account. Gallup says

> 24% of citizens say they would personally rather see Obama elected president of the United States, compared with just 7% who say the same about McCain. At the same time, 69% of world citizens surveyed did not have an opinion.[38]

The so-called developed countries featured less in the 'Don't know/Refused' category and those experiencing higher levels of political repression on freedom of speech scored higher.[39] However, most African nations overwhelmingly favoured Obama, with proportionately less in the 'Don't Know/Refused'. Kenya showed the most support out of the entire sample with 89 per cent favouring Obama.

The second question revealed more about the intricate relationship between America and different countries. Thus, in Pakistan, where Obama's campaign message took a more forceful stance on intensifying the hunt for al-Qaeda, only 10 per cent stated that it would make a difference as to which candidate was elected.[40] However, 72 per cent did not know or refused the question. Gallup attributes this to 'a great disconnect between many of the world's poorest inhabitants and the politics of the United States'.[41] Yet in some cases, differentiation between candidates was explicitly seen as irrelevant to the problems facing a country. For example, Palestine stood out from its neighbours with 72 per cent of the opinion that the election result would not make any difference to the situation of the territories. This was 56 points higher than the world average on the same question.[42] Those that did care about the election results came mainly from countries with more durable trade, political and military links with the United States, such as South Korea, Ireland, Australia, United Kingdom, France and others.[43]

Arguably, we will never know if Gallup would have conducted this survey had those three young people from Iceland not created the website 'if the world could vote' in the first place. What this act against borders exposes is the paradox of global discourse on connectivity and its 'we, the connected' narrative. For people, acting as citizens by traversing frontiers remains as fraught with difficulties as ever.

ACT 20. OF MUSIC: BARENBOIM WITHOUT WORDS

Perhaps it is music that enables us to do things without words. Barenboim implicitly thinks so:

> our thoughts take shape in words; therefore, the words on the page must compete with the words in our minds. Music has a much larger world of associations in its disposal precisely because of its ambivalent nature; it is both inside and outside the world.[44]

When Daniel Barenboim co-founded West-Eastern Divan youth orchestra with Edward Said in 1999, their act was not overtly or intentionally political. After all, one might say, all an orchestra does is perform music. But an act is always more perforated than its performance. The West-Eastern Divan youth orchestra includes Egyptian, Iranian, Israeli, Jordanian, Lebanese, Palestinian and Syrian musicians. Yes, at the outset, it is difficult to interpret the orchestra as a political act though there is every reason to make that move. Barenboim himself points to the difficulties of 'ready-made' interpretations. He says

> the Divan is not a love story, and it is not a peace story. It has very flatteringly been described as a project for peace. It isn't. It's not going to bring peace, whether you play well or not so well. The Divan was conceived as a project against ignorance.

That sentiment itself requires reflection on how an act always exceeds the intentions of its subjects and how those subjects can come to describe repertoires from which they are enacted.[45] There is also something to be said about a professional classical music performer and conductor investing himself in a site of politics as contentious as the Israeli–Palestine conflict.

All said and done, is the way in which Barenboim used his creativity and inventiveness and traversed frontiers to enact himself as an autonomous political subject an act that comes closest to the core concept of this book: 'citizens without frontiers'? Said seems to disagree. Reflecting on Barenboim's act, Said attempts to put it in a broader context. He says

> All societies are made up of a majority of average citizens – people who follow along the major patterns – and a tiny number who by virtue of their talent and their independent inclinations are not at all average, and in many ways, are a challenge and even an affront to the usually docile majority.[46]

This is a curious formulation. Rather than setting the context as domination and emancipation and thus political subjectivity, it creates a generic image of average majority versus talented minority. For Said, 'The problems occur when the perspective of the docile majority tries to reduce, simplify, and codify the complex and un-routine people who are a tiny minority.' So it is not that there is always a political struggle between the dominant and the dominated but it is between a docile majority and 'un-routine' minority. Said continues 'This clash inevitably occurs – large numbers of human beings cannot easily tolerate someone who is noticeably different, more talented, more original, than they are – and inevitably causes rage and irrationality in the majority.'[47] Said misses the momentousness of Barenboim's political act by interpreting it as a gifted artist's heroic gesture against a majority. For Said, 'Barenboim is a gifted, extremely unusual figure who crossed too many lines and violated too many of the many taboos that bind Israeli society'. Although we can agree with Said that 'Few important achievements in matters of art or science are accomplished by living within the boundaries designed to regulate social and political life' and that '. . . music for the most part is transnational; it goes beyond the boundaries of a nation or a nationality and language', we need to interpret such crossing of boundaries in the context of political domination and emancipation. Yet, for Said, crossing boundaries means '. . . that reason, understanding, and intellectual analysis, and not the organization and encouragement of collective passions such as those that seem to impel fundamentalists, are the way to be a citizen'.[48] Said is adamant that

> politicians can say all the nonsense they wish and do what they want, and so can professional demagogues. But for intellectuals, artists, and free citizens, there must always be room for dissent, for alternative views, for ways and possibilities to challenge the tyranny of the majority and, at the same time and most important, to advance human enlightenment and liberty.[49]

This image of talented artists and free citizens against a docile (and presumably talentless) majority contradicts almost all of the acts we have discussed in this book. What Said neglects is to inform his analysis with a sociology of power. As Bourdieu demonstrated relentlessly, there are social and political reasons why certain talents are valued and certain talents remain undervalued. It is the formation of fields and markets that determines such values and social groups that give them their shape. To put it another way, the value of Barenboim as a musician is embedded in the historical formation of the music performance field. To recognize this does not diminish Barenboim's talents but gives a sociological framing through which to understand their deployment. In fact, Barenboim's act becomes all the more pertinent since it ruptures the logic of a field. He breaks his habitus as a heroic gesture not against a majority but simply against his own habitus itself and the field that gives its performative force. Perhaps Said can be forgiven because he is speaking about a gifted and talented musician and his act. But by turning this into a contrast between the political struggle of a docile majority and talented minority, Said misses the political poignancy of Barenboim's act.

This is perhaps what Barenboim did in Jerusalem on 7 July 2001 when he conducted the Berlin Staatskapelle orchestra's performance of Richard Wagner's 'Overture to Tristan und Isolde' as an encore. The anti-Semitism of Wagner the man is well known and the performance of his music by a conductor with Israeli citizenship is contentious enough. That it was performed in Jerusalem makes it an even more poignant moment. But what makes this act political is the fact that the Wagner overture was performed as an encore. There is so much that can be said about how this captured, if not captivated, an audience and made a case without words. What case was made? There are multiple ways of interpreting this act. The most evocative and paradoxical is that it simultaneously asserts that music is political and it affirms that it is not. By performing Wagner, Barenboim says let us hear this music without prejudice to the man who composed. It is as if to say music produces its subjects and not the other way around. By performing Wagner in Jerusalem, Barenboim also says we must break away from a habit that has become sedimented, boring and mimetic. Perhaps then the question is not even whether this act is political. Its most effective evocation is that while it disavows a conception of the political, it enacts another.

The act of performing music then illustrates some of the issues we discussed under citationality, iterability and repetition one the hand and creativity, inventiveness and autonomy on the other. Music expresses these issues with effective resonance. As quoted earlier, Barenboim highlights something profound: 'Music has a much larger world of associations in its disposal precisely because of its ambivalent nature; it is both inside and outside the world.' Consider, for example, musical forms at least in Western music. There are slowly evolving forms in music such as the sonata, trio, quartet, concerto and symphony. Each has its own history, its own citations, iterations and repetitions and these serve as forms through which the most creative, inventive and autonomous composers created music. Take, for example, Brahms. An animated *Guardian* editorial says 'Brahms's lifelong quest to express his strongest and most radical musical ideas within the strict disciplines of established forms gives his works huge creative charge'.[50] It continues 'The balance between tradition and innovation is an enduring conundrum not just in the arts but in religion, politics and social evolution.' More precisely, we can cast that sentence in relation to the main argument of this book: the tension between citationality and creativity, between iterability and inventiveness and between repetition and autonomy are not only the enduring troubles of social, political and religious life but also the very arts that we humans produce. Without such forms as the sonata and symphony that change very slowly but through citation, iteration and repetition, it would be impossible to create music with creativity, inventiveness and autonomy. Take, for example, Shostakovich's love of mischievous and playful citations of not only other composers but also his own music. Or, how Mahler performs classical forms in his symphonies and yet renders them through such creative and inventive expressions and arrangements that one forgets that it is a symphony. (It feels more like musical storytelling, a kind of existential dialogue.) Or, Beethoven's magnificent last three piano sonatas that are so classical and conventional in form and yet so radically transformative of its performers (both listeners and players alike) into wholly new experiences, and every time.

Are Climate Camp activists, Mariyam Manike, Sezai Ozan Zeybek and perhaps even LulzSec any less so in both creating new forms and resignifying existing repertoires (forms)? It seems as if the creative, inventive and autonomous acts that we cherish and encourage in aesthetic life are never given the licence and legitimacy in political lives. It is almost as if we fear creativity, inventiveness and autonomy and literally prison those qualities in a life that we call 'aesthetic'. That's tragic. Artists such as Barenboim and Banksy not only expose this tragedy but also show ways out of it by traversing frontiers. They rupture the way we expect to relate to music and music to relate to us by traversing their sites of enactment and scales of reach. It is this rupture that interrupts a comfortable relationship to music (or painting) and instead establishes an ambivalent tension. How could it be otherwise?

Notes

1   J. Stevens, *States without Nations: Citizenship for Mortals* (New York: Columbia University Press, 2009).

2   I. Salehyan, *Rebels without Borders: Transnational Insurgencies in World Politics* (Ithaca, NY: Cornell University Press, 2009).

3   I have in mind Foucault's chapter with the title 'The Great Confinement' in M. Foucault, *History of Madness* (London: Routledge, 2006).

4   All references to this text J. Bentham, 'Emancipate Your Colonies! Addressed to the National Convention of France,' in *The Works of Jeremy Bentham*, ed. J. Bowring (Edinburgh: William Tait, 1793). It can be found at http://goo.gl/9vNb3.

5   J. Bentham, 'Panopticon; or, the Inspection-House: Containing the Idea of a New Principle of Construction Applicable to Any Sort of Establishment, in Which Persons of Any Description Are to be Kept under Inspection; and in Particular to Penitentiary-Houses,' in *The Works of Jeremy Bentham*, ed. J. Bowring (Edinburgh: William Tait, 1793).

6   A Möbius strip can be made with a piece of paper and glue. If a person were to be able to walk along the length of this strip, he or she would return to its starting point having traversed every part of the strip (on both sides of the original paper) without ever crossing an edge.

7   There has been some discussion about the 'influence' of intellectuals on the movement. J. Dugdale. 2011. Occupy: The Intellectual High Ground. *The Guardian*, 27 October 2011 [cited 16 November 2011]. Source: http://goo.gl/e28sO. Dugdale says 'Naomi Klein, Jeffrey Sachs, Cornel West and Slavoj Žižek are among those who have spoken to the New York or Boston protesters. Naomi Wolf was arrested while backing a related demo. Noam Chomsky delivered a public lecture in Boston. Writers, including Salman Rushdie and Margaret Atwood, have signed the Occupy Writers online petition.' Other intellectuals whose works have been mentioned include Gene Sharpe, David Graeber and Guy Debord.

8   This is not the kind of openness that Žižek fears. S. Žižek. 2011. Occupy First. Demands Come Later. *The Guardian*, 26 October 2011 [cited 16 November 2011]. Source: http://goo.gl/446bC. He said 'while it is thrilling to enjoy the pleasures of the "horizontal organisation" of protesting crowds with egalitarian solidarity and open-ended free debates, we should also bear in mind what GK Chesterton wrote: "Merely having an open mind is nothing; the object of opening the mind, as of opening the mouth, is to shut it again on something solid." This holds also for politics in times of uncertainty: the open-ended debates will have to coalesce not only in some new master-signifiers, but also in concrete answers to the old Leninist question, "What is to be done?" '

9   A. Chakrabortty. 2011. Athens Protests: Syntagma Square on Frontline of European Austerity Protests. *The Guardian*, 19 June 2011 [cited 16 November 2011]. Source: http://goo.gl/6y9Fg

10   L. Browne. 2011. Israeli Activists Squat Empty Jerusalem Buildings to Protest over Costly Housing. *The Guardian*, 28 August 2011 [cited 16 November 2011]. Source: http://goo.gl/ivnYF

11 N. Schneider, 'From Occupy Wall Street to Occupy Everywhere,' *Nation* 293, 18 (2011).
12 M. Townsend. 2011. Veterans Join Occupy Protest as St Paul's Canon Shows Support. *The Guardian*, 12 November 2011 [cited 20 November 2011]. Source: http://goo.gl/Sresw
13 It is even more difficult to call these movements as being about 'real democracy' and interpret them as a crisis of political representation as Hardt and Negri have suggested. M. Hardt et al. 2011. The Fight for 'Real Democracy' at the Heart of Occupy Wall Street. Foreign Affairs, 11 October 2011 [cited 27 October 2011]. Source: http://goo.gl/nRhF1
14 R. Williams. 2011. Archbishop's Speech at Lord Mayor's Banquet. The Archbishop of Canterbury, 14 November 2011 [cited 16 November 2011]. Source: http://goo.gl/jMlFh
15 But here the Archbishop draws a sharp difference between the London riots of the same year and the encampment. 'But there's also the different kind of theatre we saw in some of our cities this last summer – a theatre of lawlessness and greed from one point of view, yes, but also a dramatic reminder that there are people in our society – more than is comfortable – who feel they have no stake in its 'good order' and feel little sense of obligation to sustain it.'
16 This is what David Hume says 'Did one generation of men go off the stage at once, and another succeed, as is the case with silkworms and butterflies, the new race, if they had sense enough to choose their government, which surely is never the case with men, might voluntarily, and by general consent, establish their own form of civil polity, without any regard to the laws or precedents, which prevailed among their ancestors[?]' D. Hume, *Essays: Moral, Political, and Literary*, ed. E. F. Miller (Indianapolis: Liberty Classics, 1985), Part II, Essay XII.
17 Arendt, 'No Longer and Not Yet,' 158.
18 Avaaz. 2011. What Is Avaaz? 2011 [cited 22 December 2011]. Source: http://goo.gl/ijZt
19 Ibid.
20 Ibid.
21 Avaaz. 2011. End the War on Drugs 2011 [cited 22 December 2011]. Source: http://goo.gl/5IMzK
22 Email received on 21 December 2011 from Avaaz with the subject 'we're winning'.
23 This point has been made in terms of 'slactivism' or 'clictivism'. See P. Kingsley. 2011. Avaaz: Activism or 'Slacktivism'? *The Guardian*, 20 July 2011 [cited 24 December 2011]. Source: http://goo.gl/LBcz6; M. White. 2011. Clicktivism Is Ruining Leftist Activism. *The Guardian*, 12 August 2011 [cited 24 December 2011]. Source: http://goo.gl/bBD6S
24 K. Mahbubani. 2008. If the World Could Vote. *The Daily Beast* (Newsweek), 5 January 2008 [cited 18 September 2011]. Source: http://goo.gl/F0QCW.
25 If the world could vote. 2008. Frequently Asked Questions 2008 [cited 23 September 2011]. Source: http://goo.gl/MoN3Y
26 Ibid.
27 D. Archibugi, 'From the United Nations to Cosmopolitan Democracy,' in *Cosmopolitan Democracy: An Agenda for a New World Order*, ed. D. Archibugi and D. Held (Cambridge: Polity Press, 2000), 139.

28   Mahbubani, If the World Could Vote [cited 18 September 2011]. Source: http://goo.gl/F0QCW

29   U. Beck, *World Risk Society* (Cambridge: Polity Press, 1999).

30   World Votes! 2008. Frequently Asked Questions. World Votes! 2008 [cited 18 September 2011]. Source: http://goo.gl/MoN3Y

31   World Votes! 2008. USA Presidential Election 2008. World Votes! 2008 [cited 18 September 2011]. Source: http://goo.gl/GPYHm

32   R. Falk, 'The Making of Global Citizenship,' in *Global Visions: Beyond the New World Order*, ed. J. Brecher et al. (Boston: South End Press, 1993).

33   Gallup. 2008. World Citizens Prefer Obama to Mccain by More Than 3-to-1. Gallup, 28 October 2008 [cited 18 September 2011]. Source: http://goo.gl/m7FwI

34   Gallup. 2008. Electoral Map of the World. Foreign Policy 2008 [cited 18 September 2011]. Source: http://goo.gl/cmAJB

35   T. Osborne and N. Rose, 'Do the Social Sciences Create Phenomena?: The Example of Public Opinion Research,' *British Journal of Sociology* 50 (1999).

36   R. Frankel. 2008. What if the World Could Vote? Foreign Policy, 23 October 2008 [cited 18 September 2011]. Source: http://goo.gl/P5jvo

37   Gallup, World Citizens Prefer Obama to McCain by More Than 3-to-1 [cited 18 September 2011]. Source: http://goo.gl/m7FwI

38   Ibid.

39   Ibid.

40   Council on Foreign Affairs. 2008. Barack Obama. Council on Foreign Affairs 2008 [cited 18 September 2011]. Source: http://goo.gl/wpkPr

41   Asia One News. 2008. Rest of World Prefers Obama. Asia One News, 22 October 2008 [cited 18 September 2011]. Source: http://goo.gl/kJV3b

42   Gallup, Electoral Map of the World [cited 18 September 2011]. Source: http://goo.gl/cmAJB

43   Gallup, World Citizens Prefer Obama to Mccain by More than 3-to-1 [cited 18 September 2011]. Source: http://goo.gl/m7FwI

44   D. Barenboim, *Everything Is Connected: The Power of Music*, ed. E. Cheah (London: Weidenfeld & Nicolson, 2008), 3.

45   'Barenboim leads a panel on Arab Spring at conclusion of 2011 West-Eastern Divan Orchestra Workshop.' http://goo.gl/F5gfE

46   E. W. Said, 'Barenboim and the Wagner Taboo,' in *Music at the Limits: Three Decades of Essays and Articles on Music* (London: Bloomsbury, 2008), 292.

47   Ibid., 292, 293.

48   Ibid., 294, 295.

49   Ibid., 296.

50   Editorial. 2011. In Praise of . . . Brahms: Brahms's Music Still Thrives Thanks to His Drive to Express the Most Radical Ideas within Strictly Established Disciplines. *The Guardian*, 18 August 2011 [cited 6 January 2011]. Source: http://goo.gl/Mnbvf.

BIBLIOGRAPHY

Advisory Opinion. 2004. Legal Consequences of the Construction of a Wall in the Occupied Palestinian Territory. International Court of Justice, 9 July 2004 [cited 21 March 2011]. Source: http://goo.gl/9CH85

Afary, Janet and Kevin Anderson. *Foucault and the Iranian Revolution: Gender and the Seductions of Islamism* (Chicago: University of Chicago Press, 2005).

Agamben, Giorgio. *Homo Sacer: Sovereign Power and Bare Life* (Stanford, CA: Stanford University Press, 1998).

— *Means without End: Notes on Politics* (Minneapolis, MN: University of Minnesota Press, 2000).

Aitkenhead, Decca. 2008. From Darfur with Love. *The Guardian*, 24 April 2008 [cited 16 September 2011]. Source: http://goo.gl/d1mkE

Alatout, Samer. 'Walls as Technologies of Government: The Double Construction of Geographies of Peace and Conflict in Israeli Politics, 2002–Present,' *Annals of the Association of American Geographers* 99, 5 (2009): 956–68.

Al Jazeera. 2010. Another Aid Ship on Way to Gaza. Al Jazeera, 5 June 2010 [cited 22 January 2011]. Source: http://goo.gl/uT9Tx

— 2011. Israel Plans Wall for Egypt Border. Al Jazeera, 11 January 2011 [cited 21 March 2011]. Source: http://goo.gl/CUq5v

— 2010. Israel to Release Turkish Activists. Al Jazeera, 4 June 2010 [cited 22 January 2011]. Source: http://goo.gl/tF8uv

— 2007. West Bank Wall Divides Neighbours. Al Jazeera, 27 November 2007 [cited 21 March 2011]. Source: http://goo.gl/bmPQN

Allen, John. 'Powerful Geographies: Spatial Shifts in the Architecture of Globalization,' in *The Sage Handbook of Power* (London: Sage, 2009), 157–74.

— 'Three Spaces of Power: Territory, Networks, Plus a Topological Twist in the Tale of Domination and Authority,' *Journal of Power* 2 (2009): 197–212.

Allen, John and Allan Cochrane. 'Assemblages of State Power: Topological Shifts in the Organization of Government and Politics,' *Antipode* 42 (2010): 1071–89.

Allen, Nick. 2011. Lulzsec Hacker Group Disbands. *The Telegraph*, 26 June 2011 [cited 26 June 2011]. Source: http://goo.gl/3Of8j

Alston, Philip. Report of the Special Rapporteur on Extrajudicial, Summary or Arbitrary Executions (United Nations, 2010).

Amin, Ash. 'Spatialities of Globalisation,' *Environment and Planning A* 34 (2002): 385–99.

— 'Towards a New Politics of Place,' *Geografiska Annaler. Series B, Human Geography* 86, 1 (2004): 33–44.

Amnesty International. 2011. Landmark ECHR Ruling Recognizes Right to Conscientious Objection. Amnesty International, 7 July 2011 [cited 25 September 2011]. Source: http://goo.gl/y5V9O

— *Out of the Margins: The Right to Conscientious Objection to Military Service in Europe* (London: Amnesty International, International Secretariat, 1997).

Anderson, Benedict R. *Imagined Communities: Reflections on the Origin and Spread of Nationalism* (London: Verso, 1983).

Archibugi, Daniele. 'From the United Nations to Cosmopolitan Democracy,' in *Cosmopolitan Democracy: An Agenda for a New World Order*, ed. Daniele Archibugi and David Held (Cambridge: Polity Press, 2000), 121–62.

Arendt, Hannah. 'Concern with Politics in Recent European Political Thought,' in *Essays in Understanding, 1930–1954: Formation, Exile, and Totalitarianism*, ed. Jerome Kohn (New York: Schocken Books, 2005), 428–47.

— *Crises of the Republic: Lying in Politics, Civil Disobedience, on Violence, Thoughts on Politics and Revolution* (New York: Harcourt Brace Jovanovich, 1972).

— *The Human Condition* (Chicago, IL: University of Chicago Press, 1958).

— 'Introduction *into* Politics,' in *The Promise of Politics*, ed. Jerome Kohn (New York: Schocken Books, 2005), 93–200.

— 'The Nation,' in *Essays in Understanding 1930–1954: Formation, Exile, and Totalitarianism* (New York: Schocken Books, 2005), 206–11.

— 'No Longer and Not Yet,' in *Essays in Understanding, 1930–1954: Formation, Exile, and Totalitarianism*, ed. Jerome Kohn (New York: Schocken Books, 2005), 158–62.

— *The Origins of Totalitarianism* (New York: Harcourt Brace Jovanovich, 1951).

— *The Origins of Totalitarianism*, new with added prefaces 1973 ed. (New York: Harcourt Publishers, 1951).

— 'What Is Freedom?' in *Between Past and Future: Six Exercises in Political Thought* (New York: Viking Press, 1961), 143–71.

Aron, Jacob. 'Digital Conflict Spills into Real Life,' *The New Scientist* 208, 2791 (2010): 1.

Arthur, Charles. 2011. Alleged Lulzsec Hacker Released on Bail. *The Guardian*, 1 August 2011 [cited 7 August 2011]. Source: http://goo.gl/zrKVR

— 2009. China's Internet Users Surpass Us Population. *The Guardian*, 16 July 2009 [cited 5 February 2011]. Source: http://goo.gl/jsYcA

Arthur, Charles and James Ball. 2011. Lulzsec Leader Denies Links to Extremist Groups. *The Guardian*, 29 July 2011 [cited 7 August 2011]. Source: http://goo.gl/JBfRQ

Asia One News. 2008. Rest of World Prefers Obama. Asia One News, 22 October 2008 [cited 18 September 2011]. Source: http://goo.gl/kJV3b

Assange, Julian. 'Of the People and for the People,' *New Statesman* 140, 5048 (2011): 20–2.

Attewill, Fred. 2007. Last Climate Activists Quit Heathrow Camp. *The Guardian*, 20 August 2007 [cited 12 July 2011]. Source: http://goo.gl/kaQJv

Attia, Ashraf M., Nergis Aziz, Barry Friedman and Mahdy F. Elhusseiny. 'Commentary: The Impact of Social Networking Tools on Political Change in Egypt's "Revolution 2.0",' *Electronic Commerce Research and Applications* 10, 4 (2011): 369–74.

Auden, W. H. 'The Unknown Citizen (1939),' in *Collected Poems of W.H. Auden*, ed. Edward Mendelson (New York: Vintage, 1979), 85–6.

— 'Thanksgiving for a Habitat (1958),' in *Collected Poems of W.H. Auden*, ed. Edward Mendelson (New York: Vintage, 1979), 252–78.

Austin, J. L. *How to Do Things with Words* (Oxford: Oxford University Press, 1962).

Avaaz. 2011. End the War on Drugs 2011 [cited 22 December 2011]. Source: http://goo.gl/5IMzK

— 2011. What Is Avaaz? 2011 [cited 22 December 2011]. Source: http://goo.gl/ijZt

Aziz, Shaista. 'How I Became a Terror Tourist,' in *Peace under Fire: Israel/Palestine and the International Solidarity Movement*, ed. Josie Sandercock (London: Verso, 2004).

Azzam, Maha. 2011. Opinion: How WikiLeaks Helped Fuel Tunisian Revolution. CNN, 18 January 2011 [cited 18 January 2011]. Source: http://goo.gl/xVFcV

B'Tselem. 2011. Separation Barrier. B'Tselem, 21 March 2011 [cited 21 March 2011]. Source: http://goo.gl/fDgPu

Badiou, Alain. *Metapolitics*, trans. Jason Barker (London: Verso, 2006).

Baker, Luke. 2007. Illegal Immigrants March for More Rights. Reuters, 7 May 2007 [cited 5 July 2011]. Source: http://goo.gl/ck68H

Bakhtin, Michael. *Toward a Philosophy of Act*, ed. Michael Holquist (Austin: University of Texas Press, 1993).

Balibar, Étienne. 'Historical Dilemmas of Democracy and Their Contemporary Relevance for Citizenship,' *Rethinking Marxism* 20 (2008): 522–38.

— 'Culture and Identity,' in *The Identity in Question*, ed. John Rajchman (New York: Routledge, 1995).

— '(De)Constructing the Human as Human Institution: A Reflection on the Coherence of Hannah Arendt's Practical Philosophy,' *Social Research* 74 (2007): 727–38.

— *Masses, Classes, Ideas: Studies on Politics and Philosophy before and after Marx*, trans. James Swenson (London: Routledge, 1994).

— 'Racism and Nationalism,' *in Race, Nation, Class: Ambiguous Identities*, ed. Immanuel Wallerstein and Étienne Balibar (London: Verso, 1991), 37–67.

Bamberg, Michael G. W. and Molly Andrews. *Considering Counter-Narratives: Narrating, Resisting, Making Sense* (Amsterdam: John Benjamins Pub. Co, 2004).

Banerjee, Paula. 'Frontiers and Borders: Spaces of Sharing, Spaces of Conflict,' in *Space, Territory and the State: New Readings in International Politics*, ed. Ranabir Samaddar (Hyderabad: Orient Longman, 2002), 27–42.

Barenboim, Daniel. *Everything Is Connected: The Power of Music*, ed. Elena Cheah (London: Weidenfeld & Nicolson, 2008).

Barkhoff, Jürgen and Helmut Eberhart. *Networking across Borders and Frontiers: Demarcation and Connectedness in European Culture and Society* (Frankfurt am Main: Peter Lang, 2009).

Barnes, Rebecca, Timothy Auburn and Susan Lea. 'Citizenship in Practice,' *British Journal of Social Psychology* 43 (2004): 187–206.

Barney, Darin. *Prometheus Wired: The Hope for Democracy in the Age of Network Technology* (Vancouver: University of British Columbia Press, 2001).

Başkent, Can, ed., *Vicdani Ret Açıklamalari Almanağı, 1989–2010 [Declarations of Conscientious Objections (Turkey): An Almanac, 1989–2010]* (Istanbul: Propaganda Yayınları, 2011).

Basu, Ranu. 'Negotiating Acts of Citizenship in an Era of Neoliberal Reform: The Game of School Closures,' *International Journal of Urban and Regional Research* 31, 1 (2007): 109–27.

BBC. 2011. Activist Shawna Forde Guilty of Migrants' Murder. BBC, 15 February 2011 [cited 20 February 2011]. Source: http://goo.gl/u46He

— 2005. Art Prankster Sprays Israeli Wall. BBC, 5 August 2005 [cited 30 May 2001]. Source: http://goo.gl/46VwP

— 2009. Canada's Governor Eats Seal Heart. BBC, 26 May 2009 [cited 24 February 2012]. Source: http://goo.gl/aIw8B

— 2010. Cyber Attack Forces Wikileaks to Change Web Address. BBC, 3 December 2010 [cited 18 January 2011]. Source: http://goo.gl/MzaYr

— 2011. Data of Sun Website Users Stolen. BBC, 2 August 2011 [cited 7 August 2011]. Source: http://goo.gl/bUhxy

— 2011. Egypt: 'We Are All Khaled Said'. BBC, 17 February 2011 [cited 30 July 2011]. Source: http://goo.gl/Zp9Zj

— 2011. Gay Couple 'Removed from Soho Pub for Kissing'. BBC, 14 April 2011 [cited 24 February 2012]. Source: http://goo.gl/XYHEi

— 2011. Gay Kiss Pub Protest at Soho's John Snow. BBC, 15 April 2011 [cited 24 February 2012]. Source: http://goo.gl/M6Ozz

— 2006. Google Censors Itself for China. BBC, 25 January 2006 [cited 5 February 2011]. Source: http://goo.gl/1mp9F

— 2007. Heathrow Protesters Set up Camp. BBC, 12 August 2007 [cited 12 July 2011]. Source: http://goo.gl/9tPnl

— 2011. LulzSec Hacking Group Announces End to Cyber Attacks: A Hacker Group that Has Attacked Several High-Profile Websites over the Last Two Months Has Announced that It Is Disbanding. BBC, 26 June 2011 [cited 24 February 2012]. Source: http://goo.gl/8X7Us

— 2011. Profile: Egypt's Wael Ghonim. BBC, 9 February 2011 [cited 30 July 2011]. Source: http://goo.gl/FrbiP

— 2008. Profile: Maumoon Gayoom of the Maldives. BBC, 29 October 2008 [cited 10 July 2011]. Source: http://goo.gl/Dtk0q

— 2010. Q&A: The Digital Economy Bill. BBC, 9 April 2010 [cited 10 August 2011]. Source: http://goo.gl/Aur2

— 2007. Rally Call for Migrant 'Amnesty'. BBC, 7 May 2007 [cited 5 July 2011]. Source: http://goo.gl/bFEpd

— 2011. Us and Israel Were Behind Stuxnet Claims Researcher. BBC, 4 March 2011 [cited 13 March 2011]. Source: http://goo.gl/RCZ5p

Beaumont, Peter. 2011. Médecins Sans Frontières Book Reveals Aid Agencies' Ugly Compromises. *The Guardian*, 20 November 2011 [cited 21 November 2011].

Beck, Ulrich. *World Risk Society* (Cambridge: Polity Press, 1999).

Bell, Vikki. *Culture and Performance: The Challenge of Ethics, Politics, and Feminist Theory* (Oxford: Berg, 2007).

Bennet, James. 1998. U.S. Cruise Missiles Strike Sudan and Afghan Targets Tied to Terrorist Network. *The New York Times*, 21 August 1998 [cited 29 May 2011]. Source: http://goo.gl/BOhxW

Bentham, Jeremy. 'Emancipate Your Colonies! Addressed to the National Convention of France,' in *The Works of Jeremy Bentham*, ed. John Bowring, 11 vols, vol. 4 (Edinburgh: William Tait, 1793).

— 'Panopticon; or, the Inspection-House: Containing the Idea of a New Principle of Construction Applicable to Any Sort of Establishment, in Which Persons of Any Description Are to be Kept under Inspection; and in Particular to Penitentiary-Houses,' in *The Works of Jeremy Bentham*, ed. John Bowring, 11 vols, vol. 4 (Edinburgh: William Tait, 1793).

Berényi, József. 2010. The Situation of Roma in Europe and Relevant Activities of the Council of Europe. Council of Europe, 26 February 2010 [cited 31 August 2011]. Source: http://goo.gl/NaNe4

Bergen, Peter and Katherine Tiedemann. 2010. The Hidden War. *Foreign Policy*, 21 December 2010 [cited 2 March 2011]. Source: http://goo.gl/QDFEY

Bhattacharyya, Anindya. 2007. Strangers into Citizens Rally: 'We Are All Citizens'. Socialist Worker Online, 8 May 2007 [cited 5 July 2011]. Source: http://goo.gl/hFFwf

Bigo, Didier. 'Pierre Bourdieu and International Relations: Power of Practices, Practices of Power,' *International Political Sociology* 5, 3 (2011): 225–58.

Birdwell, Jonathan. *Service International* (London: Demos, 2011).

Boffey, Daniel. 2011. Students Given Tips to Stop Gap Year Travel Being 'a New Colonialism'. Thinktank Demos Warns Poorly Planned Volunteering Stints in Developing Nations Can Do More Harm Than Good. *The Guardian*, 30 July 2011 [cited 24 February 2012]. Source: http://goo.gl/U0P2U

Bourdieu, Pierre. *Distinction: A Social Critique of the Judgement of Taste* (Cambridge, MA: Harvard University Press, 1987).

— *Language & Symbolic Power* (Cambridge, MA: Harvard University Press, 1993).

— *The Logic of Practice* (Stanford, CA: Stanford University Press, 1990).

Bowman, Glenn. 'Israel's Wall and the Logic of Encystation: Sovereign Exception or Wild Sovereignty?' *Focaal – European Journal of Anthropology* 50 (2007): 127–36.

Boyle, James. *The Public Domain: Enclosing the Commons of the Mind* (New Haven, CT: Yale University Press, 2008).

Brady, Tara. 2010. Borough Welcome for 20,000 Illegals. *Harrow Observer*, 3 February 2010 [cited 6 July 2011]. Source: http://goo.gl/DU8nG

Brenner, Joel F. 'Privacy and Security Why Isn't Cyberspace More Secure?' *Communications of the ACM* 53, 11 (2010): 33–5.

Brown, Wendy. *Walled States, Waning Sovereignty* (New York: Zone, 2010).

Browne, Luke. 2011. Israeli Activists Squat Empty Jerusalem Buildings to Protest over Costly Housing. *The Guardian*, 28 August 2011 [cited 16 November 2011]. Source: http://goo.gl/ivnYF

Brysk, Alison and Gershon Shafir. 'Globalization and the Citizenship Gap,' in *People Out of Place: Globalization, Human Rights, and the Citizenship Gap*, ed. Alison Brysk and Gershon Shafir (London: Routledge, 2004), 3–9.

Burnell, Paul. 2009. 'Torture' Chief's Two UK Homes. BBC, 24 March 2009 [cited 10 July 2011]. Source: http://goo.gl/6ZALi

Butler, Judith. 'Burning Acts: Injurious Speech,' *U. Chi. L. Sch. Roundtable* 3 (1996): 221.

— 'Performative Acts and Gender Constitution an Essay in Phenomenology and Feminist Theory,' *Theatre Journal* 40 (1988): 519–31.

— 'Sovereign Performatives in the Contemporary Scene of Utterance,' *Critical Inquiry* 23, 2 (1997): 350–77.

— *Subjects of Desire: Hegelian Reflections in Twentieth-Century France* (New York: Columbia University Press, 1999).

— *Undoing Gender* (London: Routledge, 2004).

Caputo, John D., ed., *Deconstruction in a Nutshell: A Conversation with Jacques Derrida*, Perspectives in Continental Philosophy, No. 1 (New York: Fordham University Press, 1996).

Carens, Joseph H. *Immigrants and the Right to Stay* (Cambridge, MA: MIT Press, 2010).

— 'Aliens and Citizens: The Case for Open Borders,' *Review of Politics* 49 (1987): 251–73.

Caserio, Robert L. 'Auden's New Citizenship,' *Raritan* 17, 2 (1997): 90–103.

Castells, Manuel. *The Rise of Network Society*, vol. 1, The Information Age: Economy, Society and Culture (Cambridge, MA: Blackwell, 1996).

Castles, Stephen and Alastair Davidson. *Citizenship and Migration: Globalization and the Politics of Belonging* (New York: Routledge, 2000).

Castles, Stephen and Mark J. Miller. *The Age of Migration: International Population Movements in the Modern World* (New York: Guilford, 1993).

Chakrabortty, Aditya. 2011. Athens Protests: Syntagma Square on Frontline of European Austerity Protests. *The Guardian*, 19 June 2011 [cited 16 November 2011]. Source: http://goo.gl/6y9Fg

Channel 4 News. 2011. Egypt: Behind the Online 'Hero' Who Galvanised Protests. Channel 4 News, 9 February 2011 [cited 30 July 2011]. Source: http://goo.gl/xRNJq

— 2011. Google Executive Optimistic About Egypt's Revolution. Channel 4 News, 17 May 2011 [cited 30 July 2011]. Source: http://goo.gl/1943R

Chomsky, Noam. *Rogue States: The Rule of Force in World Affairs* (London: Pluto, 2000).

— 2004. A Wall as a Weapon. *The New York Times*, 23 February 2004 [cited 20 February 2011]. Source: http://goo.gl/JMx27

Çınar, Özgür Heval and Coşkun Üsterci, eds, *Conscientious Objection: Resisting Militarized Society* (London: Zed, 2009).

Citizens UK. 2010. Citizens UK Is the Home of Community Organizing in Britain. Citizens UK 2010 [cited 6 July 2011]. Source: http://goo.gl/mnbt2

Climate Camp. 2011. About Us. Camp for Climate Action 2011 [cited 12 July 2011]. Source: http://goo.gl/TUPby

— 2009. Copenhagen 2009: A Call to Action. Climate Camp 2009 [cited 12 July 2011]. Source: http://goo.gl/IuSm8

— 2009. Workshops Programme. Climate Camp 2009 [cited 12 July 2011]. Source: http://goo.gl/hu0Y7

CNN. 2003. Israeli Bulldozer Kills American Protester. CNN, 25 March 2003 [cited 22 January 2011]. Source: http://goo.gl/PY9Ts

Cohen, Steven. *No One Is Illegal: Asylum and Immigration Control, Past and Present* (Stoke on Trent: Trentham Books, 2003).

Collins, John. 'Between Acceleration and Occupation: Palestine and the Struggle for Global Justice,' *Studies in Social Justice* 4, 2 (2010): 199–215.

Cooley, Alexander and Hendrik Spruyt. *Contracting States: Sovereign Transfers in International Relations* (Princeton, NJ: Princeton University Press, 2009).

Council of Europe. 2010. The Strasbourg Declaration on Roma. Council of Europe, 20 October 2010 [cited 31 August 2011]. Source: http://goo.gl/UXo0f

Council on Foreign Affairs. 2008. Barack Obama. Council on Foreign Affairs 2008 [cited 18 September 2011]. Source: http://goo.gl/wpkPr

Darfuri Refugees. 'Selected Testimonials from Darfuri Refugees in Chad' (Waging Peace, 2007).

Davey, Francis. 2009. The Digital Economy Bill – A First Critical Look. Open Rights Group, 1 December 2009 [cited 9 August 2011]. Source: http://goo.gl/CTkWu

Davis, Tracy C. *The Cambridge Companion to Performance Studies* (Cambridge: Cambridge University Press, 2008).

de Man, Adr-Pieter. *The Network Economy: Strategy, Structure and Management* (Cheltenham: Edward Elgar, 2004).

Debray, Régis. *Éloge Des Frontières* (Paris: Gallimard, 2010).

Deibert, Ronald J. 'Dark Guests and Great Firewalls: The Internet and Chinese Security Policy,' *Journal of Social Issues* 58, 1 (2002): 143–59.

Deibert, Ronald J. and Rafal Rohozinski. 'Under Cover of the Net: This Hidden Governance Mechanisms of Cyberspace,' in *Ungoverned Spaces: Alternatives to State Authority in an Era of Softened Sovereignty*, ed. Anne L. Clunan and Harold A. Trinkunas (Stanford, CA: Stanford Security Studies, 2010), 255–72.

Delanty, Gerard. *Citizenship in a Global Age: Society, Culture, Politics* (Philadelphia, PA: Open University Press, 2000).

Deleuze, Gilles. *Foucault* (University of Minnesota Press, 1988).

— 'Postscript on Control Societies,' in *Negotiations* (New York: Columbia University Press, 1990), 177–82.

Deleuze, Gilles and Felix Guattari. *What Is Philosophy?* (Columbia University Press, 1994).

Della Porta, Donatella. *Globalization from Below: Transnational Activists and Protest Networks* (Minneapolis: University of Minnesota Press, 2006).

Demchak, Chris C. and Peter Dombrowski. 'Rise of a Cybered Westphalian Age,' *Strategic Studies Quarterly* 5, 1 (2011): 32–61.

Derrida, Jacques. *The Beast & the Sovereign*, ed. Michel Lisse, Marie-Louise Mallet and Ginette Michaud, trans. Geoffrey Bennington, vol. 1, The Seminars of Jacques Derrida (Chicago: Chicago University Press, 2009).

— *Limited Inc*, trans. Gerald Graff (Evanston, IL: Northwestern University Press, 1988).

— *On Cosmopolitanism and Forgiveness* (London: Routledge, 2001).

— *Politics of Friendship* (London: Verso, 1997).

— *Specters of Marx: State of the Debt, the Work of Mourning and the New International* (London: Routledge, 1994).

— *Without Alibi*, ed. Peggy Kamuf (Stanford, CA: Stanford University Press, 2002).

Doctorow, Cory. 2012. The Internet Is the Best Place for Dissent to Start: Ethan Zuckerman's Compelling 'Cute Cats Theory' Has Changed My Mind about the Internet's Role in the Struggle for Global Justice. *The Guardian*, 3 January 2012 [cited 5 January 2012]. Source: http://goo.gl/OgOie

Doty, R. L. 'Do You Know If Your Borders Are Secure?' *International Political Sociology* 4, 1 (2010): 92–5.

Douzinas, Costas. *The End of Human Rights: Critical Legal Thought at the Turn of the Century* (Oxford: Hart, 2000).

Dugdale, John. 2011. Occupy: The Intellectual High Ground. *The Guardian*, 27 October 2011 [cited 16 November 2011]. Source: http://goo.gl/e28sO.

Dunn, Kevin C. 'There Is No Such Thing as the State: Discourse, Effect and Performativity,' *Forum for Development Studies* 37, 1 (2010): 79–92.

Editorial. 2011. In Praise of . . . Brahms: Brahms's Music Still Thrives Thanks to His Drive to Express the Most Radical Ideas within Strictly Established Disciplines. *The Guardian*, 18 August 2011 [cited 6 January 2011]. Source: http://goo.gl/Mnbvf.

Eke, Chinedu. 'Darfur: Coverage of a Genocide by Three Major Us Tv Networks on Their Evening News,' *International Journal of Media and Cultural Politics* 4, 3 (2008): 277–92.

Elden, Stuart. *Terror and Territory: The Spatial Extent of Sovereignty* (Minneapolis, MN: University of Minnesota Press, 2009).

Elgot, Jessica. 2011. Israel to Build Egypt Security Wall. *Jewish Chronicle*, 11 January 2011 [cited 21 March 2011]. Source: http://goo.gl/Th8K8

Evans, David T. *Sexual Citizenship: The Material Construction of Sexualities* (London: Routledge, 1993).

Falk, Richard. 'The Making of Global Citizenship,' in *Global Visions: Beyond the New World Order*, ed. Jeremy Brecher, John Brown Childs and Jill Cutler (Boston: South End Press, 1993).

Falliere, Nicolas, Liam O Murchu and Eric Chien. 'W32.Stuxnet Dossier' (Symantec, 2011).

Farsakh, Leila. *The Political Economy of Israeli Occupation: What Is Colonial About It?*, Working Paper Series (Boston: Department of Political Science, University of Massachusetts, 2006).

Farwell, James P. and Rafal Rohozinski. 'Stuxnet and the Future of Cyber War,' *Survival* 53, 1 (2011): 23–40.

Faure, Gaelle. 'The Truth about Occupation,' in *Peace under Fire: Israel/Palestine and the International Solidarity Movement*, ed. Josie Sandercock (London: Verso, 2004).

Felman, Shoshana. *The Scandal of the Speaking Body: Don Juan with J.L. Austin, or Seduction in Two Languages* (1980) (Stanford, CA: Stanford University Press, 2003).

Fernández, Laura Zorrilla. 2010. Regularisation: Practical and Humane. Strangers into Citizens 2010 [cited 6 July 2011]. Source: http://goo.gl/bohR4

Fildes, Jonathan. 2011. Stuxnet Virus Targets and Spread Revealed. BBC, 15 February 2011 [cited 6 March 2011]. Source: http://goo.gl/R7Mh1

Foucault, Michel. *The Birth of Biopolitics: Lectures at the Collége de France, 1978–79*, ed. Michel Senellart (Basingstoke: Palgrave Macmillan, 2008).

— *The Care of the Self*, vol. 3, History of Sexuality (New York: Pantheon, 1986).

— 'Confronting Governments: Human Rights,' in *Power*, ed. James D. Faubion, Essential Works of Foucault, 1954–1984 (New York: New Press, 2000), 474–5.

— *The Government of Self and Others* (Basingstoke: Palgrave Macmillan, 2010).

— *The Hermeneutics of the Subject: Lectures at the Collège De France 1981– 1982* (New York: Palgrave MacMillan, 2005).

— *History of Madness* (1961) (London: Routledge, 2006).

— *Language Counter-Memory Practice* (Ithaca, NY: Cornell University Press, 1977).

— *Security, Territory, Population: Lectures at the Collége de France, 1977–78*, ed. Michel Senellart and Arnold I. Davidson (Basingstoke: Palgrave Macmillan, 2007).

— *Society Must be Defended: Lectures at the Collège de France, 1975–76*, ed. Mauro Bertani and Alessandro Fontana, trans. David Macey (New York: Picador, 2003).

— 'Technologies of the Self,' in *Technologies of the Self: A Seminar with Michel Foucault*, ed. Luther H. Martin, Huck Gutman and Patrick H. Hutton (Amherst, MA: University of Massachusetts Press, 1988).

— *The Use of Pleasure*, trans. Robert Hurley, vol. 2, History of Sexuality (New York: Pantheon, 1985).

— 'Useless to Revolt?,' in *Power*, ed. James D. Faubion (New York: New Press, 2000), 449–53.

France, Louise. 2008. She Was a Girl from Small-Town America with Dreams of Being a Poet or a Dancer. So How, at Just 23, Did Rachel Corrie Become a Palestinian Martyr? [Web Page]. *The Guardian* 2008 [cited 23 January 2011]. Source: http://goo.gl/RXyN4

Frankel, Rebecca. 2008. What If the World Could Vote? Foreign Policy, 23 October 2008 [cited 18 September 2011]. Source: http://goo.gl/P5jvo

Gallagher, Ryan. 2011. Why Hacker Group LulzSec Went on the Attack. *The Guardian* 2011 [cited 14 July 2011]. Source: http://goo.gl/VRkrQ

Gallup. 2008. Electoral Map of the World. Foreign Policy 2008 [cited 18 September 2011]. Source: http://goo.gl/cmAJB

— 2008. World Citizens Prefer Obama to Mccain by More than 3-to-1. Gallup, 28 October 2008 [cited 18 September 2011]. Source: http://goo.gl/m7FwI

Galvin, John R. *The Minute Men: The First Fight: Myths & Realities of the American Revolution* (1976), 2nd edn rev. ed. (Dulles, VA: Brassey's Book, 1989).

Gardham, Duncan. 2011. 'Hackney Speech Woman' Revealed to be Local Jazz Singer. *The Telegraph* 2011 [cited 16 August 2011]. Source: http://goo.gl/ OyJeU

Gilchrist, Jim and Jerome R. Corsi. *Minutemen: The Battle to Secure America's Borders* (Los Angeles, CA: World Ahead Publishing, 2006).

Goffman, Erving. *The Presentation of Self in Everyday Life* (Garden City, NY: Doubleday, 1959).

— *Strategic Interaction*, vol. 1, Series in Conduct and Communication (Philadelphia, PA: University of Pennsylvania Press, 1969).

Gold, Tanya. 2011. Marching with the Slutwalkers. The Slutwalk Movement Has Divided Feminists. Should Women Try to Reclaim the Word? And Is

Undressing the Best Way to Protest against Rape? *The Guardian*, 7 June 2011 [cited 24 February 2012]. Source: http://goo.gl/zBFRh

Goldman, David. 2010. Congress Slams China and Microsoft, Praises Google. CNN Money, 24 March 2010 [cited 20 February 2011]. Source: http://goo.gl/5B1w

Goodman, Peter S. 2005. Yahoo Says It Gave China Internet Data. *Washington Post*, 11 September 2005 [cited 5 February 2011]. Source: http://goo.gl/DG4ey

Goodwin, Morag. 2004. The Romani Claim to Non-Territorial Nation Status: Recognition from an International Legal Perspective. European Roma Rights Centre, 27 May 2004 [cited 31 August 2011]. Source: http://goo.gl/JCtrs

Gouldner, Alvin Ward. *The Two Marxisms: Contradictions and Anomalies in the Development of Theory* (London: Macmillan, 1980).

Grant, Drew. 2011. Google+ Shuts Down Invites . . . for Now: Is the Latest Social Network Playing Hard to Get, or Just Worried About More Privacy Lawsuits? Salon, 30 June 2011 [cited 20 January 2012]. Source: http://goo.gl/b3Q02

Gray, Sadie. 2007. Climate Change Protesters Set up Heathrow Camp. The Independent, 13 August 2007 [cited 12 July 2011]. Source: http://goo.gl/zzsxi

Grimm, Joshua. 'Patrolling Whiteness: Framing the Minuteman Project on the Evening News,' in Annual Meeting of the International Communication Association (Montreal, Canada, 2008).

Guardian, The. 2005. Banksy at the West Bank Barrier. *The Guardian* 2005 [cited 30 May 2011]. Source: http://goo.gl/DoCiM

— 2011. Reading the Riots. *The Guardian* in Partnership with the London School of Economics. Supported by the Jospeh Rowntree Foundation and the Open Society Foundations 2011 [cited 6 January 2012]. Source: http://goo.gl/EqxH6.

Guéhenno, Jean-Marie. *The End of the Nation-State* (Minneapolis, MN: University of Minnesota Press, 1995).

Guild, E. *Security and Migration in the 21st Century* (Cambridge: Polity, 2009).

Hacking, Ian. *Historical Ontology* (Cambridge, MA: Harvard University Press, 2002).

— 'Kinds of People: Moving Targets,' *Proceedings of the British Academy* 151 (2007): 285–318.

— *Rewriting the Soul: Multiple Personality and the Sciences of Memory* (Princeton, NJ: Princeton University Press, 1995).

— *The Social Construction of What?* (Cambridge, MA: Harvard University Press, 2000).

Halliday, Josh, Charles Arthur and James Ball. 2011. LulzSec Hacking Suspect 'Topiary' Arrested. *The Guardian*, 27 July 2011 [cited 7 August 2011]. Source: http://goo.gl/ODkFw

Hansard. 13p Parl. Deb. H.C. 14 May 2008 (House of Commons, 2008).

— 439wh Parl. Deb. H.C. 20 Jun 2007 (House of Commons, 2007).

Harb, Zahera. 'Arab Revolutions and the Social Media Effect,' *M/C* 14, 2 (2011).

Hardt, Michael and Antonio Negri. *Empire* (Cambridge: Harvard University Press, 2000).

— 2011. The Fight for 'Real Democracy' at the Heart of Occupy Wall Street. *Foreign Affairs*, 11 October 2011 [cited 27 October 2011]. Source: http://goo.gl/nRhF1

— *Multitude: War and Democracy in the Age of Empire* (London: Penguin, 2005).

Harris, John. 2011. The Year of the Networked Revolution: From the Occupy Movement to the Middle East, Calls for Political and Personal Freedom Were Aided by Social Media. *The Guardian*, 13 December 2011 [cited 5 January 2012]. Source: http://goo.gl/0fOTs

Harrison, Frances. 2003. Maldives Capital Tense after Riot. BBC, 22 September 2003 [cited 9 July 2011]. Source: http://goo.gl/xqtZv

Harvey, David. *The Condition of Postmodernity: An Inquiry into the Origins of Cultural Change* (Cambridge: Butterworth, 1989).

Hayter, Teresa. 'Open Borders: The Case against Immigration Controls,' in *The Cultures of Economic Migration: International Perspectives*, ed. Suman Gupta and Tope Omoniyi (Aldershot: Ashgate, 2007).

Hickman, Martin and Nigel Morris. 2011. Battle of Heathrow: Opposition to Baa's Injunction Grows. *The Independent*, 27 July 2011 [cited 12 July 2011]. Source: http://goo.gl/MD8PD

Higginson, Stephen A. 'A Short History of the Right to Petition Government for the Redress of Grievances,' *The Yale Law Journal* 96, 1 (1986): 142–66.

Hinsley, F. H. *Sovereignty* (Cambridge: Cambridge University Press, 1986).

Hobsbawm, Eric and Terence Ranger, eds, *The Invention of Tradition* (Cambridge: Cambridge University Press, 1992).

Hodge, Becky. *Barefoot into Cyberspace: Adventures in Search of Techno-Utopia* (Commons Attribution-ShareAlike 2.0, 2011).

House of Lords. *Surveillance: Citizens and the State* (London: Authority of the House of Lords, 2009).

Huffpost Green. 2009. Canadian Governor General Eats Raw Seal Heart in Support of Hunters. *Huffington Post*, 26 May 2009 [cited 24 February 2012]. Source: http://goo.gl/Th8TS

Hume, David. *Essays: Moral, Political, and Literary*, ed. Eugene F. Miller (Indianapolis, IN: Liberty Classics, 1985).

Idhikeeli. 2007. Vigil Held to Remember Torture Victim and Stand up against Torture. Idhikeeli, 22 September 2007 [cited 9 July 2011]. Source: http://goo.gl/vszdZ

If the World Could Vote. 2008. Frequently Asked Questions 2008 [cited 23 September 2011]. Source: http://goo.gl/MoN3Y

International Romani Union. 2001. Declaration of a Roma Nation. International Romani Union, 1 Jan 2001 [cited 15 September 2011]. Source: http://goo.gl/qtPei

International Solidarity Movement. 2011. About ISM. International Solidarity Movement 2011 [cited 19 September 2011]. Source: http://goo.gl/r2ocw

— 2011. Media Activists Needed in Palestine. International Solidarity Movement, 7 July 2011 [cited 19 September 2011]. Source: http://goo.gl/EdlCb

Isin, Engin F. *Being Political: Genealogies of Citizenship* (Minneapolis, MN: University of Minnesota Press, 2002).

— 'Citizenship in Flux: The Figure of the Activist Citizen,' *Subjectivity*, 29 (2009): 367–88.

— 'Theorizing Acts of Citizenship,' in *Acts of Citizenship*, ed. Engin F. Isin and Greg M. Nielsen (London: Zed Books, 2008), 15–43.

Isin, Engin F. and Bryan S. Turner, eds, *Handbook of Citizenship Studies* (London: Sage, 2002).

Isin, Engin F. and Ebru Üstündağ. 'Wills, Deeds, Acts: Women's Civic Gift-Giving in Ottoman Istanbul,' *Gender, Place and Culture* 15, 5 (2008): 519–32.

Isin, Engin F. and Melissa Finn. 'Bombs, Bodies, Acts: The Banalization of Suicide,' in *War, Citizenship, Territory*, ed. Deborah Cowen and Emily Gilbert (London: Routledge, 2007).

Jerusalem Post. 2010. Navy Boards 'Rachel Corrie' Off Gaza. *Jerusalem Post*, 6 May 2010 [cited 23 January 2011]. Source: http://goo.gl/eGYlG

Jones, Sam. 2005. Spray Can Prankster Tackles Israel's Security Barrier. *The Guardian*, 5 August 2005 [cited 30 March 2011]. Source: http://goo.gl/6Rxj6

Joppke, Christian. *Citizenship and Immigration* (Cambridge: Polity Press, 2010).

Kalaydjieva, Luba, Bharti Morar, Raphaelle Chaix and Hua Tang. 'A Newly Discovered Founder Population: The Roma/Gypsies,' *BioEssays* 27, 10 (2005): 1084–94.

Kantorowicz, Ernst H. *The King's Two Bodies* (Princeton, NJ: Princeton University Press, 1957).

Keck, Margaret E. and Kathryn Sikkink. *Activists beyond Borders: Advocacy Networks in International Politics* (Ithaca, NY: Cornell University Press, 1998).

Kil, Sang H., C. Menjíívar and R. L. Doty. 'Securing Borders: Patriotism, Vigilantism and the Brutalization of the American Public,' *Immigration, Crime and Justice* 13 (2009): 297–312.

Kim, Yun-Hee. 2011. Update: Google to Continue to Invest in China; Sets Sights on SE Asia *Wall Street Journal* 2011 [cited 20 February 2011]. Source: http://goo.gl/xJzKu

Kingsley, Patrick. 2011. Avaaz: Activism or 'Slacktivism'? *The Guardian*, 20 July 2011 [cited 24 December 2011]. Source: http://goo.gl/LBcz6

Klímová-Alexander, Ilona. 'Transnational Romani and Indigenous Non-Territorial Self-Determination Claims,' *Ethnopolitics* 6, 3 (2007): 395–416.

Krapp, Peter. 'Terror and Play, or What Was Hacktivism?,' *Grey Room* 21, Fall (2005): 70–93.

Krause, E. A. *Death of the Guilds: Professions, States and the Advance of Capitalism, 1930 to the Present* (New Haven, CT: Yale University Press, 1999).

Krishnappa, Samyuktha. 2011. Google Man Wael Ghonim Emerges as the Face of Egypt Protests. *International Business Times*, 9 February 2011 [cited 30 July 2011]. Source: http://goo.gl/LsGYs

Kymlicka, Will. *Multicultural Citizenship: A Liberal Theory of Minority Rights*, Oxford Political Theory (Oxford: Clarendon Press, 1995).

LA Times. 2011. Google Exec Wael Ghonim in Egypt Says Long Live the Revolution 2.0, 11 February 2011 [cited 30 July 2011]. Source: http://goo.gl/e8kD0.

— 2011. Wael Ghonim, Google Exec, Says Egypt's Revolution Is 'Like Wikipedia'. *LA Times*, 14 February 2011 [cited 30 July 2011]. Source: http://goo.gl/pj3jA.

Laclau, Ernesto. *On Populist Reason* (London: Verso, 2005).

Latour, Bruno. *Reassembling the Social: An Introduction to Actor-Network-Theory* (Oxford: Oxford University Press, 2005).

Latta, Alex. 'Environmental Citizenship,' *Alternatives Journal* 33, 1 (2007): 18–19.

Law, John. *After Method: Mess in Social Science Research* (London: Routledge, 2004).

Law, John and Annemarie Mol. 'Situating Technoscience: An Inquiry into Spatialities,' *Environment and Planning D: Society and Space* 19 (2001): 609–21.

Lee, Mark. 2011. Baidu's Profit Rises after Making Gains on Google in Advertising in China. Bloomberg, 31 January 2011 [cited 20 February 2011]. Source: http://goo.gl/lDpFB

Liang, Bin and Hong Lu. 'Internet Development, Censorship, and Cyber Crimes in China,' *Journal of Contemporary Criminal Justice* 26, 1 (2010): 103–20.

Lie, John. *Modern Peoplehood* (Cambridge, MA: Harvard University Press, 2004).

Linklater, Andrew. 'Citizenship and Sovereignty in the Post-Westphalian State,' *European Journal of International Relations* 2, 1 (1996): 77–103.

— 'Cosmopolitan Citizenship,' *Citizenship Studies* 2, 1 (1998): 23–41.

Loxley, James. *Performativity* (London: Routledge, 2007).

Lucas, John. 'Auden's Politics: Power, Authority, and the Individual,' in *The Cambridge Companion to W.H. Auden*, ed. Stan Smith (Cambridge: Cambridge University Press, 2004), 152–64.

Lynn, Jonathan. 2011. WikiLeaks Founder Assange Slams Swiss Banker Arrest. Reuters, 23 January 2011 [cited 23 January 2011]. Source: http://goo.gl/zNQmi

Lyotard, Jean-Francois. 'The Other's Rights,' in *On Human Rights*, ed. Susan L. Hurley and Stephen Shute (New York, NY: Basic Books, 1993), 135–47.

MacAskill, Ewen. 2011. Stuxnet Cyberworm Heads Off Us Strike on Iran. *The Guardian*, 16 January 2011 [cited 13 March 2011]. Source: http://goo.gl/Unkfp.

Macdonald, Keith M. *The Sociology of the Professions* (London: Sage, 1995).

Madison, D. Soyini and Judith Hamera, eds, *The Sage Handbook of Performance Studies* (London: Sage, 2006).

Magone, Claire, Michael Neuman and Fabrice Weissman, eds, *Humanitarian Negotiations Revealed: The MSF Experience* (London: C. Hurst & Co Publishers, 2011).

Mahbubani, Kishore. 2008. If the World Could Vote. *The Daily Beast* (Newsweek), 5 January 2008 [cited 18 September 2011]. Source: http://goo.gl/F0QCW.

Makovsky, David. 'How to Build a Fence,' *Foreign Affairs* 83, 2 (2004): 20–38.

Manike, Mariyam. 2008. 'My Son's Murder Helped Bring Down a Dictatorship.' *Financial Times*, 13 December 2008 [cited 9 July 2011]. Source: http://goo.gl/bCWpS.

Marshall, T. H. *Citizenship and Social Class* (1992), ed. T. B. Bottomore, Pluto Perspectives (London: Pluto Press, 1949).

Martin, Michael. 2011. Police from Khaled Said's Egypt Still Terrorize Egyptian Activists. International Business News, 30 June 2011 [cited 30 July 2011]. Source: http://goo.gl/GZqXb

Marx, Karl and Friedrich Engels. *The Communist Manifesto: A Modern Edition* (London: Verso, 1998).

Matras, Yaron. *Romani: A Linguistic Introduction* (Cambridge: Cambridge University Press, 2002).

McGarry, Aidan. 'Ambiguous Nationalism? Explaining the Parliamentary Under-representation of Roma in Hungary and Romania,' *Romani Studies* 19, 2 (2009): 103–24.

McNevin, Anne. *Contesting Citizenship: Irregular Migrants and New Frontiers of the Political* (New York: Columbia University Press, 2011).

— 'Political Belonging in a Neoliberal Era: The Struggle of the Sans-Papiers,' *Citizenship Studies* 10, 2 (2006): 135–51.

Mejias, Ulises. 'The Twitter Revolution Must Die,' *International Journal of Learning and Media* 4, 2 (2011): 3–5.

Menn, Joseph. 2011. Anonymous Is the Best Known 'Hacktivist' Group, a Virtual Mob that Makes It Easy for People to Participate in Protests. *Financial Times* 2011 [cited 23 September 2011]. Source: http://on.ft.com/ncyxtE

Mercer, Carmen. 2010. About Us. MinutemanHQ.com 2010 [cited 29 January 2011]. Source: http://goo.gl/Kegx3

Miller, R. 'Is WikiLeaks "the Press"?' *Econtent* 34, 2 (2011): 15.

Millward, David and Bonnie Malkin. 2007. Heathrow Climate Protest Grows by the Hour. *The Telegraph*, 14 August 2007 [cited 12 July 2011]. Source: http://goo.gl/NRWC1.

Milone, Mark. 'Hacktivism: Securing the National Infrastructure,' *Knowledge, Technology & Policy* 16, 1 (2003): 75–103.

Minivan News. 2005. 15 Minutes with Evan Naseem's Mother Mariyam Manike. Minivan News, 13 March 2005 [cited 9 July 2011]. Source: http://goo.gl/8rmBU

— 2008. Torture in the Jails Is Not Finished: Mariyam Manike. Minivan News, 20 September 2008 [cited 9 July 2011]. Source: http://goo.gl/QcM5M

Mitchell, G. 'Why WikiLeaks Matters,' *Nation* 292, 5 (2011): 4–6.

Mitchell, William J. *Me++: The Cyborg Self and the Networked City* (Cambridge, MA: MIT Press, 2003).

Mol, Annemarie and John Law. 'Regions, Networks and Fluids: Anaemia and Social Topology,' *Social Studies of Science* 24 (1994): 641.

Monbiot, George. 2007. Beneath Heathrow's Pall of Misery, a New Political Movement Is Born. *The Guardian*, 21 August 2007 [cited 12 July 2011]. Source: http://goo.gl/BZPgN.

MSF. 2011. Charter. Médecins Sans Frontières (MSF) 2011 [cited Tuesday, 8 March 2011]. Source: http://goo.gl/15wAY.

Mulholland, Helene. 2007. Heathrow Protesters Clash with Riot Police. *The Guardian*, 19 August 2007 [cited 12 July 2011]. Source: http://goo.gl/b7ngQ.

Naish, Ahmed. 2009. Defence Ministry Taken to Court. Dhivehi Observer, 3 February 2009 [cited 9 July 2011]. Source: http://goo.gl/Wa1aJ.

Nash, Kate. 'Between Citizenship and Human Rights,' *Sociology* 43 (2009): 1067–84.

Newman, Janet. 'Regendering Governance,' in *Remaking Governance: Peoples, Politics and the Public Sphere*, ed. Janet Newman (Bristol: Policy Press, 2005), 81–100.

Ngai, Mae M. *Impossible Subjects: Illegal Aliens and the Making of Modern America*, Politics and Society in Twentieth-Century America (Princeton, NJ: Princeton University Press, 2004).

Nielsen, Greg M. *The Norms of Answerability: Social Theory between Bakhtin and Habermas* (Albany, NY: State University of New York Press, 2002).

Nietzsche, Friedrich Wilhelm. *The Anti-Christ, Ecce Homo, Twilight of the Idols, and Other Writings*, ed. Aaron Ridley and Judith Norman, trans. Judith Norman (Cambridge: Cambridge University Press, 2005).

— *On the Genealogy of Morality*, ed. Keith Ansell-Pearson, trans. Carol Diethe (Cambridge: Cambridge University Press, 1994).

No One Is Illegal. 2011. Fight for the Rights of Migrant Workers. No One Is Illegal 2011 [cited 19 September 2011]. Source: http://goo.gl/svytn

— 2011. No One Is Illegal. No One Is Illegal, 9 June 2011 [cited 19 September 2011]. Source: http://goo.gl/2x0Mh

— 2003. No One Is Illegal Manifesto. No One Is Illegal, 6 September 2003 [cited 19 September 2011]. Source: http://goo.gl/MliJw

— 2011. Solidarity with Dale Farm. No One is Illegal, 11 April 2011 [cited 19 September 2011]. Source: http://goo.gl/GoAjW

— 2011. UK Retailer Backs National Campaign to End Controls. No One Is Illegal, 19 May 2011 [cited 19 September 2011]. Source: http://goo.gl/llxjG

— 2011. What You Can Do. No One Is Illegal 2011 [cited 19 September 2011]. Source: http://goo.gl/zvyKH

— 2011. World Passport. No One Is Illegal, 2011 [cited 19 September 2011]. Source: http://goo.gl/aP95y

Nye, Catrin. 2011. The Art of the Pithy Hashtag. BBC, 4 August 2011 [cited 7 August 2011]. Source: http://goo.gl/nHccN

Nyers, Peter. 'The Accidental Citizen: Acts of Sovereignty and (Un) Making Citizenship,' *Economy and Society* 35, 1 (2006): 22–41.

— 'No One Is Illegal between City and Nation,' *Studies in Social Justice* 4, 2 (2010): 127–43.

Oliver. 2009. Analysis of Victories in Copenhagen. Climate Camp, 29 December 2009 [cited 12 July 2011]. Source: http://goo.gl/0dexG.

Omer, Atalia. ' "It's Nothing Personal": The Globalisation of Justice, the Transferability of Protest, and the Case of the Palestine Solidarity Movement,' *Studies in Ethnicity and Nationalism* 9, 3 (2009): 497–518.

Ong, Aihwa. *Flexible Citizenship: The Cultural Logics of Transnationality* (Durham, NC: Duke University Press, 1999).

Open Rights Group. 2011. About ORG. Open Rights Group 2011 [cited 10 August 2011]. Source: http://goo.gl/2jgfN

— 2010. Digital Economy Bill: Brief to Lords on Second Reading 2010 [cited 9 August 2011]. Source: http://goo.gl/xKlBS

— 2011. Hargreaves Review of Ip and Growth. Open Rights Group, 22 February 2011 [cited 9 August 2011]. Source: http://goo.gl/1JxIY

Orbinski, James. 1999. Oslo Nobel Lecture: Médecins Sans Frontières, 10 December 1999 [cited 3 June 2011]. Source: http://goo.gl/9XzR6

Osborne, Thomas and Nikolas Rose. 'Do the Social Sciences Create Phenomena?: The Example of Public Opinion Research,' *British Journal of Sociology* 50 (1999): 367–96.

Paris, Natalie. 2007. Heathrow Campers Glued to Transport Office. *The Telegraph*, 17 August 2007 [cited 12 July 2011]. Source: http://goo.gl/a3sgv

PBS. 2006. The Return of the Taliban: Nek Mohammed 2006 [cited 28 May 2011]. Source: http://goo.gl/3QHxz

Pilkington, ed. 2010. Emily Henochowicz: Artist to Pro-Palestinian Activist. *The Guardian*, 21 August 2010 [cited 30 May 2011].

— 2011. Slutwalking Gets Rolling after Cop's Loose Talk about Provocative Clothing. Lecture to Toronto Students Ignites Protests across Canada and US at Culture of Blaming Rape Victims. *The Guardian*, 6 May 2011 [cited 24 February 2012]. Source: http://goo.gl/3xZPp

— 2011. WikiLeaks's Alleged Source Bradley Manning Held in 'Punitive' Conditions. *The Guardian*, 5 February 2011 [cited 20 February 2011]. Source: http://goo.gl/1yvjf

Pitzke, Marc. 2010. Remote Warriors: How Drone Pilots Wage War. Spiegel Online, 3 December 2010 [cited 2 March 2011]. Source: http://goo.gl/ZQGyI

Poggi, Gianfranco. *The Development of the Modern State: A Sociological Introduction* (Stanford, CA: Stanford University Press, 1978).

— *The State: Its Nature, Development, and Prospects* (Cambridge: Polity Press, 1990).

Poovey, Mary. *Making a Social Body: British Cultural Formation, 1830–1864* (Chicago: University of Chicago Press, 1995).

Praust, Jordan J. 'Self-Defence Targetings of Non-State Actors and Permissibility of U.S Use of Drones in Pakistan,' *Journal of Transnational Law & Policy* 19, 2 (2010): 237–79.

Preston, Jennifer. 2011. Movement Began with Outrage and a Facebook Page that Gave It an Outlet. *The New York Times*, 5 February 2011 [cited 30 July 2011]. Source: http://goo.gl/9d7Q6

Prokhovnik, Raia. *Sovereignties: History, Theory and Practice* (Basingstoke: Palgrave Macmillan, 2007).

Ramey, Charles. 2004. Uav Battlelab Stands up at Indian Springs. U.S. Air Force, 23 June 2004 [cited 3 February 2011]. Source: http://goo.gl/yxfyA

Rancière, Jacques. *Disagreement: Politics and Philosophy* (1995), trans. Julie Rose (Minneapolis, MN: University of Minnesota Press, 1998).

— *Dissensus: On Politics and Aesthetics*, ed. Steve Corcoran, trans. Steve Corcoran (London: Continuum, 2010).

— *On the Shores of Politics* (1992), trans. Liz Heron (London: Verso, 1995).

Reinach, Adolf. 'The Apriori Foundations of the Civil Law,' *Aletheia: An International Journal of Philosophy* 3 (1983): 1–142.

Reitan, Ruth. *Global Activism* (London: Routledge, 2007).

Republic of Maldives. 2004. Investigative Findings on the Death of Hassan Evan Naseem. Presidential Commission, The President's Office, 27 January 2004 [cited 12 December 2011]. Source: http://goo.gl/GSLk7

Reuters. 2011. Factbox-Stateless Groups around the World. Reuters, 23 August 2011 [cited 31 August 2011]. Source: http://goo.gl/khQDY

Reydams, Luc, ed., *Global Activism Reader* (London: Continuum, 2011).

Reynolds, P. 2010. Israeli Convoy Raid: What Went Wrong?, 2 June 2010 [cited 22 January 2011]. Source: http://goo.gl/SpwaR

Ringold, Dena, Mitchell Alexander Orenstein and Erika Wilkens. *Roma in an Expanding Europe: Breaking the Poverty Cycle* (Washington, DC: World Bank Publications, 2005).

Rishmawi, George and Neta Golan. 'Helping to Bring Back Hope,' in *Peace under Fire: Israel/Palestine and the International Solidarity Movement*, ed. Josie Sandercock (London: Verso, 2004).

Roberts, Mary Louise. *Disruptive Acts: The New Woman in Fin-de-Siécle France* (Chicago: University of Chicago Press, 2002).

Robins, Steven. 'Mobilizing and Mediating Global Medicine and Health Citizenship: The Politics of Aids Knowledge Production in Rural South Africa,' in *Globalizing Citizens: New Dynamics of Inclusion and Exclusion*, ed. John Gaventa and Rajesh Tandon (London: Zed Books, 2010), 56–78.

Rogers, Simon. 2011. WikiLeaks Data Journalism: How We Handled the Data. *The Guardian*, 31 January 2011 [cited 24 February 2012]. Source: http://goo.gl/uiByc

Roland-Gosselin, Louise. 'Petition: Summary' (Waging Peace, 2008).

Rygiel, Kim. *Globalizing Citizenship* (Vancouver: UBC Press, 2010).

Said, Edward W. 2003. The Meaning of Rachel Corrie. ZNET, 26 June 2003 [cited 22 January 2011]. Source: http://goo.gl/i3obR

— 'Barenboim and the Wagner Taboo,' in *Music at the Limits: Three Decades of Essays and Articles on Music* (London: Bloomsbury, 2008), 290–8.

Salehyan, Idean. *Rebels without Borders: Transnational Insurgencies in World Politics* (Ithaca, NY: Cornell University Press, 2009).

Saletan, William. 2011. Drones Are Death Warrants: Can the U.S. Send Drones to Execute American Citizens Like Anwar Al-Awlaki without Trial? You Bet. *Slate*, 3 October 2011 [cited 14 February 2012]. Source: http://goo.gl/WBJXl.

Salter, Mark B. *Politics at the Airport* (Minneapolis, MN: University of Minnesota Press, 2008).

— *Rights of Passage: The Passport in International Relations* (Boulder, CO: Lynne Rienner Publishers, 2003).

Sampford, Charles. 'Professions without Borders: Global Ethics and the International Rule of Law,' in Public Lecture (Brisbane: Queensland University of Technology, 2009).

Sand, Shlomo. *The Invention of the Jewish People* (London: Verso, 2009).

Sassen, Saskia. *Losing Control?: Sovereignty in an Age of Globalization* (New York: Columbia University Press, 1996).

Sayad, Abdelmalek. *The Suffering of the Immigrant* (Cambridge: Polity Press, 2004).

Schaap, Andrew. 'Enacting the Right to Have Rights: Jacques Rancière's Critique of Hannah Arendt,' *European Journal of Political Theory* 10 (2010): 22–45.

Schattle, Hans. *The Practices of Global Citizenship* (Lanham, MD: Rowman & Littlefield Publishers, 2007).

Schechner, Richard. *Performance Studies: An Introduction* (London: Routledge, 2002).

— *Performance Theory* (1977), Rev. and expanded ed. (London: Routledge, 1988).

Schneider, Nathan. 'From Occupy Wall Street to Occupy Everywhere,' *Nation* 293, 18 (2011): 13–17.

Searle, John R. *Speech Acts: An Essay in the Philosophy of Language* (Cambridge: Cambridge University Press, 1970).

Seitz, Charmaine. 'Ism at the Crossroads: The Evolution of the International Solidarity Movement,' *Journal of Palestine Studies* 32, 4 (2003): 50–67.

Shacat, Jonathon. 2008. Radio Show Focuses on Immigration Douglas Dispatch, 26 July 2008 [cited 20 February 2011]. Source: http://goo.gl/xVLLT

Shamir, Shlomo, Aluf Benn and Yuval Yoaz. 2004. Israel Firmly Rejects ICJ Fence Ruling Haaretz, 11 July 2004 [cited 15 February 2011]. Source: http://goo.gl/qWUX3

Shane, Scott. 2011. Accused Soldier in Brig as WikiLeaks Link Is Sought. *The New York Times* 2011 [cited 22 January 2011]. Source: http://goo.gl/vmbJf

Shelley, Mary Wollstonecraft. *Frankenstein, or, the Modern Prometheus* (1818) (London: Thomas Davison, Whitefriars, 1823).

Sherwood, Harriet. 2010. Gaza Aid Flotilla to Set Sail for Confrontation with Israel. *The Guardian* 2010 [cited 22 January 2011]. Source: http://goo.gl/fcVnH

Shie, Tamara Renee. 'The Internet and Single-Party Rule in China,' in *Debating Political Reform in China: Rule of Law vs. Democratization*, ed. Suisheng Zhao (New York: M. E. Sharpe, 2006), 215–29.

Sifry, Micah L. 2011. Did Facebook Bring Down Mubarak? CNN, 11 February 2011 [cited 30 July 2011]. Source: http://goo.gl/1SHpH

Simeant, J. 'What Is Going Global? The Internationalization of French Ngos "without Borders",' *Review of International Political Economy* 12, 5 (2005): 851–83.

Skinner, Quentin. 'The Sovereign State: A Genealogy,' in *Sovereignty in Fragments: The Past, Present and Future of a Contested Concept*, ed. Hent Kalmo and Quentin Skinner (Cambridge: Cambridge University Press, 2010), 26–46.

Smit, Martina. 2007. Climate Camp Protestors Skirmish with Police. *The Telegraph*, 19 August 2007 [cited 12 July 2011]. Source: http://goo.gl/BrTYg

Smith, Barry and Armin Burkhardt. 'Towards a History of Speech Act Theory,' in *Speech Acts, Meaning, and Intentions: Critical Approaches to the Philosophy of John R. Searle,* ed. Armin Burkhardt (Berlin: W. de Gruyter, 1990), 29–61.

Smith, Kevin. 2007. 'Strangers into Citizens' – for the Regularisation of UK People without Status. IRR, 11 January 2007 [cited 5 July 2011]. Source: http://goo.gl/5FYLd.

Smith, Michael P. and Matt Bakker. *Citizenship across Borders: The Political Transnationalism of El Migrante* (Ithaca, NY: Cornell University Press, 2008).

Sobotka, Eva. 'They Have a Dream: The State of Roma Affairs in the Czech Republic,' *Central European Review* 3, 18 (2001).

Somers, Margaret R. *Genealogies of Citizenship: Markets, Statelessness, and the Right to Have Rights* (Cambridge: Cambridge University Press, 2008).

Somers, Margaret R. and C. N. J. Roberts. 'Toward a New Sociology of Rights: A Genealogy of "Buried Bodies" of Citizenship and Human Rights,' *Annual Review of Law and Social Science* 4 (2008): 385–425.

Spruyt, Hendrik. *The Sovereign State and Its Competitors: An Analysis of Systems Change* (Princeton, NJ: Princeton University Press, 1996).

Squire, Vicki. 'From Community Cohesion to Mobile Solidarities: The City of Sanctuary Network and the Strangers into Citizens,' *Political Studies* 59, 2 (2011): 290–307.

Star, Alexander, ed., *Open Secrets: WikiLeaks, War and American Diplomacy*, Introduction by Bill Keller (New York: New York Times, 2011).

Stevens, Jacqueline. *States without Nations: Citizenship for Mortals* (New York: Columbia University Press, 2009).

Strangers into Citizens. 2010. Brent Council Backs Strangers into Citizens. Strangers into Citizens, 8 February 2010 [cited 6 July 2011]. Source: http://goo.gl/bJNyF

— 2011. Why Regularisation? Strangers into Citizens 2011 [cited 6 July 2011]. Source: http://goo.gl/DuyJC

Strayer, Joseph R. *On the Medieval Origins of the Modern State* (Princeton, NJ: Princeton University Press, 1971).

Tabajdi, Csaba. 2002. Legal Situation of the Roma in Europe. Council of Europe, 19 April 2002 [cited 31 August 2011]. Source: http://goo.gl/KSMcQ

Takemura, Hitomi. *International Human Right to Conscientious Objection to Military Service and Individual Duties to Disobey Manifestly Illegal Orders* (Berlin: Springer, 2009).

Tambini, Damian. 'Civic Networking and Universal Rights to Connectivity: Bologna,' in *Cyberdemocracy: Technology, Cities, and Civic Networks*, ed. Roza Tsagarousianou, Damian Tambini and Cathy Bryan (London: Routledge, 1998), ix, 185.

Tarnovschi, Daniela. 'The Construction of a New Roma Ethnic Identity,' in *Interculturalism and Discrimination in Romania: Policies, Practices, Identities and Representations*, ed. François Rüegg, Rudolf Poledna and Călin Rus (Berlin: Lit Verlag, 2006), 105–34.

Tarrow, Sidney G. *The New Transnational Activism* (Cambridge: Cambridge University Press, 2005).

Tilly, Charles. *Coercion, Capital, and European States, AD 990–1992* (Oxford: Blackwell, 1992).

— *Contentious Performances* (Cambridge: Cambridge University Press, 2008).

— *Reflections on the History of European State-Making*, ed. Charles Tilly (Princeton, NJ: Princeton University Press, 1975).

Topping, Alexandra. 2011. 'Slutwalking' Phenomenon Comes to UK with Demonstrations in Four Cities. British Cities to Host Mass Anti-Rape Demonstrations as Part of Global Movement Sparked by Canadian Policeman's Remarks. *The Guardian*, 9 May 2011 [cited 24 February 2012]. Source: http://goo.gl/DnWjN

Torpey, John. *The Invention of the Passport: Surveillance, Citizenship and the State* (Cambridge: Cambridge University Press, 2000).

Townsend, Mark. 2011. Veterans Join Occupy Protest as St Paul's Canon Shows Support. *The Guardian*, 12 November 2011 [cited 20 November 2011]. Source: http://goo.gl/Sresw

Traynor, Ian. 2007. Russia Accused of Unleashing Cyberwar to Disable Estonia. *The Guardian*, 17 May 2007 [cited 6 March 2011]. Source: http://goo.gl/1kctK.

Tsaliki, Liza, Christos A. Frangonikolopoulos and Asteris Huliaras. *Transnational Celebrity Activism in Global Politics: Changing the World?* (Chicago, IL: Intellect Books, 2011).

Tucson Chapter Leader. 2007. Minutemen Shock and Awe in Green Valley, Az [web page]. The Minutemen Civil Defense Corps Border Operations Headquarters 2007 [cited 29 January 2011]. Source: http://goo.gl/Km9vs

Turner, Victor Witter. *The Anthropology of Performance* (New York: PAJ Publications, 1987).

UK. *Digital Economy Act.* 2010, c. 24.

UN. United Nations Framework Convention on Climate Change. 2009. The United Nations Climate Change Conference in Copenhagen, 7–19 December 2009. United Nations 2009 [cited 12 July 2011]. Source: http://goo.gl/PRSZh

UNISON. 2007. Supporting Migrant Workers. UNISON, 4 May 2007 [cited 6 July 2011].

UNOCHA. 2007. Three Years Later: The Humanitarian Impact of the Barrier since the International Court of Justice Opinion. United Nations Office for the Coordination of Humanitarian Affairs 2007 [cited 23 March 2011]. Source: http://goo.gl/IjKee

Vaughan-Nichols, Steven J. 2011. The Internet Goes Dark in Egypt. ZDNet, 27 January 2011 [cited 30 July 2011]. Source: http://goo.gl/5XmHz

Vermeersch, Peter. *The Romani Movement: Minority Politics and Ethnic Mobilization in Contemporary Central Europe* (Oxford: Berghahn Books, 2007).

Villa, Dana Richard. *Arendt and Heidegger: The Fate of the Political* (Princeton, NJ: Princeton University Press, 1996).

Waging Peace. 2008. 25 April 2008: Petition Containing the Voices of over 60,000 Darfuris Delivered to Downing Street. Waging Peace 2008 [cited 16 September 2011]. Source: http://goo.gl/fG1RM

Walker, R. B. J. *After the Globe, before the World* (London: Routledge, 2010).

Walsh, David. *The Modern Philosophical Revolution: The Luminosity of Existence* (Cambridge: Cambridge University Press, 2008).

Walton, Greg. 'China's Golden Shield: Corporations and the Development of Surveillance Technology in the People's Republic of China' (Toronto: International Centre for Human Rights and Democratic Development, 2001).

Ware, Vron. *Who Cares about Britishness: A Global View of the National Identity Debate* (London: Arcadia Books, 2007).

Warner, Dennis B. 'International Peacemakers Enter Bethlehem Church of Nativity,' in *Peace under Fire: Israel/Palestine and the International Solidarity Movement*, ed. Josie Sandercock (London: Verso, 2004).

Wasik, Bill. 2011. #Riot: Self-Organized, Hyper-Networked Revolts – Coming to a City near You. Wired, 16 December 2011 [cited 5 January 2012]. Source: http://goo.gl/lyoZ7

Watts, Susan. 2011. Newsnight Online 'Chat' with Lulz Security Hacking Group. BBC, 24 June 2011 [cited 7 August 2011]. Source: http://goo.gl/twj4g

We Are All Khaled Said. 2010. One Message in Many Languages Campaign. We Are All Khaled Said, 31 July 2010 [cited 30 July 2011]. Source: http://goo.gl/LocoZ

Weber, C. 'Citizenship, Security, Humanity,' *International Political Sociology* 4, 1 (2010): 80–5.

Weber, Max, Guenther Roth and Claus Wittich. *Economy and Society: An Outline of Interpretive Sociology* (1921), ed. Guenther Roth and Claus Wittich, trans. Ephraim Fischoff, 2 vols (Berkeley, CA: University of California Press, 1978).

White, Micah. 2011. Clicktivism Is Ruining Leftist Activism. *The Guardian*, 12 August 2011 [cited 24 December 2011]. Source: http://goo.gl/bBD6S

WikiLeaks. 2011. Submissions 2011 [cited 22 January 2011]. Source: http://goo.gl/9ZjC2

— 2011. What Is WikiLeaks? 2011 [cited 22 January 2011]. Source: http://goo.gl/lclLg

Williams, Alison J. 'Reconceptualising Spaces of the Air: Performing the Multiple Spatialities of UK Military Airspaces,' *Transactions of the Institute of British Geographers* 36, 2 (2011): 253–67.

— 'Hakumat Al Tayarrat: The Role of Air Power in the Enforcement of Iraq's Boundaries,' *Geopolitics* 12, 3 (2007): 505–28.

Williams, Christopher. 2011. Stuxnet: Cyber Attack on Iran 'Was Carried out by Western Powers and Israel'. *The Telegraph*, 21 January 2011 [cited 6 March 2011]. Source: http://goo.gl/Vprym

Williams, Rowan. 2011. Archbishop's Speech at Lord Mayor's Banquet. The Archbishop of Canterbury, 14 November 2011 [cited 16 November 2011]. Source: http://goo.gl/jMlFh

World Votes! 2008. Frequently Asked Questions. World Votes! 2008 [cited 18 September 2011]. Source: http://goo.gl/MoN3Y

— 2008. USA Presidential Election 2008. World Votes! 2008 [cited 18 September 2011]. Source: http://goo.gl/GPYHm

Yang, Guobin. 'The Internet and Emerging Civil Society in China,' in *Debating Political Reform in China: Rule of Law vs. Democratization*, ed. Suisheng Zhao (New York: M. E. Sharpe, 2006), 196–214.

Zee, Bibi van der. 2011. Climate Camp Disbanded. *The Guardian*, 2 March 2011 [cited 12 July 2011]. Source: http://goo.gl/OAMJ6

Žižek, Slavoj. 'Against Human Rights,' *New Left Review* 34 (2005): 115.

— 2011. Occupy First. Demands Come Later. *The Guardian*, 26 October 2011 [cited 16 November 2011]. Source: http://goo.gl/446bC

INDEX